ARTHUR CONAN DOYLE'S

BOOK OF THE BEYOND

ARTHUR CONAN DOYLE'S

BOOK OF
THE BEYOND

Second Edition

THE WHITE EAGLE PUBLISHING TRUST
NEW LANDS · LISS · HAMPSHIRE · ENGLAND

First published as THY KINGDOM COME, December 1933
THE RETURN OF ARTHUR CONAN DOYLE published 1956
(three further editions to 1980)
ARTHUR CONAN DOYLE'S BOOK OF THE BEYOND
first published 1994
Second edition, with corrections and additions, 2003

British Library Cataloguing-in-publication Data
A catalogue record for this book is available from
the British Library

ISBN 0-85487-147-0

*Set in 12 on 13pt Monotype Bembo by the publisher
and printed in Great Britain by*
CAMBRIDGE UNIVERSITY PRESS

CONTENTS

PART THREE: TWO WHITE EAGLE TEACHINGS

LIST OF ILLUSTRATIONS

HOW TO READ THIS BOOK

READERS who are already familiar with the outline of the messages received from a being who identified himself as Sir Arthur Conan Doyle can simply read this book straight through. Our understanding of the story, however, has broadened out and detail has been added over the years; so the new reader will do much better to begin with the original story at its commencement in chapter III, p. 63, and then return to the prefatory matter after reading the rest. Someone who simply wants one of the most comprehensive and most beautiful accounts of the afterlife ever conceived may even prefer to concentrate simply upon the messages themselves, which comprise the whole of Part Two of the book, beginning on p. 153.

PREFACE (1994)

AMID all the fame that has surrounded Sir Arthur Conan Doyle, largely attributable to his characters Sherlock Holmes and Dr Watson, the mission by which Sir Arthur set perhaps even more store during his lifetime, the proof of survival after death—a mission which, on his passing, drove him to communicate a greatly expanded vision of the life after death—tends to go unnoticed. Although this is regrettable, it is perhaps in part because it was simply *his attempt*, and attempts succeed one another and are outgrown, one by one. Today we are in any case less preoccupied with that search for proof, through spiritualistic means; although the extraordinary documentation of near-death experiences *does* preoccupy us.

In this book we have, not the account of a near-death experience, but of a post-death one. The reader can for him or herself make conclusions about their authenticity; as also about the identity of the speaker in the messages that together form that account. That this speaker was Sir Arthur is not, now, so important; at the time, the communication gave sufficient evidence to his family to convince them that all or part of the messages were his. More important *now* is the very picture drawn by Sir Arthur, a picture of enormous force and clarity: the vision extends from the grey November fogs that are so redolent of his own stories—the astral planes, a world like Dante's 'Inferno'—to a celestial world which is described with an equally Dantesque clarity, a paradise vision which is extraordinarily real. This is no mean accomplishment.

In keeping with the preoccupations of the time that they were given—some sixty years ago—the messages have something of the character of a dialogue with the orthodox Spiritualism of the day. The reader is unlikely to find that this obscures the vision as just described. For Sir Arthur had written during his lifetime about the afterlife as described in spirit messages of the time (notably in his books THE NEW REVELATION and THE VITAL MESSAGE): the messages he himself gave, those in this book, were quite deliberately and consciously an attempt to update and improve what had been set out in such books (which even a casual inspection will show to be vastly inferior). The messages were given in 1931 and 1932, and it is an indication of their appeal that they have been kept in print more or less ever since, though under three different titles including the present one. Their first publication was in December 1933, and the book that contained them and told their story was called THY KINGDOM COME. It was edited by Ivan Cooke, the husband of Grace Cooke, through whom Sir Arthur spoke. Later, it was thought better to reissue them in another form, and they duly appeared as THE RETURN OF ARTHUR CONAN DOYLE in 1956, Ivan Cooke having rewritten much of his editorial material for that publication. For the title, for research, and for many other editorial suggestions he was indebted to his son-in-law, my father Geoffrey Hayward.

In this new edition, as in THE RETURN OF ARTHUR CONAN DOYLE, the substance of the Conan Doyle messages is preserved intact. It is the telling of the surrounding story that has altered, and it may be helpful to examine why so much attention has been given to the story as well as to the messages.

There is a double importance to the material that this book contains, when seen from the perspective of 1994. First, there is the import of the message itself—the phrase 'the most accurate description of the life beyond ever given' which was applied to THY KINGDOM COME, I think by the occultist Shaw Desmond, has stuck. But the communicator of the messages, whom I am sure we are right to regard as Sir Arthur, spoke of a great work which was to come:

'I am under the direction of the Wise Ones. I am their servant, their instrument, and I have presently to organize this group for a future work in London. *This teaching, these messages are to be the foundation of that work.*'*

'That work' is without doubt the organization, the White Eagle Lodge, which was founded a very few years after the messages were given and which is still growing, internationally, today. Sir Arthur's work thus continues. It is partly because of the continuing growth of that organization (the beginning of which is so inextricably interwoven with the communication of the messages in this book) that the story needs constant updating: not so much to record its material growth as to reconnect in a new way with the original plan.

Our perception grows precisely when we are not tied to structures of belief that limit possibilities. Today's generation, both those familiar with the White Eagle Lodge and those who come to this book afresh, will look at the Conan Doyle messages with a new eye. May they have from them both the reassurance and the clarity that the messages have been bringing for the last sixty years, and also a revelation which will take them into new perceptions of truth.

The plan of the present book follows that of THE RETURN OF ARTHUR CONAN DOYLE, except in the following respects. The introductory chapter that follows this Preface takes the place of Ivan Cooke's first chapter. The information that appeared in the old section 'Retrospect', at the end of the book, which updated the story up to the 1975 edition, now forms chapter XII in a very slightly amended version. Otherwise, Ivan Cooke's chapters (II to XI) are altered only slightly (a few brief cuts have been made so that the story will remain relatively contemporary). Two White Eagle teachings have been added at the end of the book, for reasons given in the introductory chapter. The numbering of the chapters is otherwise the same, Parts One and Three being comprised of chapters with Roman numerals, and Part Two with Arabic-numeral chapters. Footnotes taken over from the previous editions have been noted as such; the rest are new to this edition.

A word must be added about the text of the messages. Almost all of them were recorded by the same hand, W. R. Bradbrook, Secretary of the Conan Doyle Memorial Committee. The original scripts are lost. A number of the messages were translated (see chapter I) into

---

*From the preface to the second edition of THE RETURN OF ARTHUR CONAN DOYLE, 1963, p. viii.

French and appeared in the *Bulletin des Polaires*. Comparison between the 1933 and 1956 versions has shown the former to contain the more reliable text. It is here reinstated, with only the minimal editing that continuity and sense demand when spoken messages are put into print. A few archaisms have been modernized. The editing has been done silently, but where we have actually needed to add a whole phrase for coherence or continuity, we have followed scholarly practice and put it in square brackets. On the other hand, the organization of the messages given in THE RETURN OF ARTHUR CONAN DOYLE is very considerably clearer than in the earlier book. The present volume, therefore, keeps to that arrangement while using the earlier text as its basis. It does not take the messages consecutively, but organizes them more or less by theme and to follow a line of logical development. To do this almost seamlessly was perhaps the great achievement of the 1956 volume, for which reason we have preserved that approach. For reference, the actual dates of the messages have been inserted in the margins of the present edition, with the place where known; most readers will be content to ignore these.

In contrast to White Eagle, Conan Doyle does not stress the way in which God is both Father and Mother. Similarly, following the general practice of the age in which the messages were given, he uses the masculine pronoun almost universally. We have left this unaltered, and believe that it is best simply to acknowledge this, and not alter the text.

In addition to thanks which have already been implied or stated, I should like to thank Pat Rodegast, the channel for Emmanuel, for her generous permission to quote the words on p. 44; the Librarian and President of the College of Psychic Studies for their help in locating a copy of *Light* in which ACD's words are printed; Mrs A. Hamilton for writing out the story of her husband Peter which is recounted on p. 40: a number of friends who have read through the introduction and offered advice, those who have made translations from the French to assist our understanding of the story (Mary Blair Smith, Philippa Adams and Margot Kemhadjian, and others now unknown); and our sub-editor and proofreader Ann Slocock, whose suggestions have been penetrating as well as useful. The publisher of the postcard on p. 12 is unknown; we use it in good faith.

I have also benefitted in the second edition from discussing material with the historian Dr Geoffrey Basil Smith.

Colum Hayward, 1994, 2003

PART ONE : THE STORY

In the vicinity of Bagnaia, Italy, April 1994.

A postcard of Lordat, sent by Minesta to her daughters
from the visit with the Polaires, 13th July 1931.

CHAPTER I

AN INTRODUCTION
AND REVIEW

by Colum Hayward

IN 1994 I visited Italy with my mother Ylana Hayward, herself the daughter of Grace Cooke, through whom the messages in this book were given. Before we left, a friend had said to me, 'Have you ever visited Bagnaia?' I was caught slightly off-guard. Bagnaia is the place in Italy described in chapter IV of this book, where a remarkable meeting took place *pp. 70–75* at the beginning of this century between a young man with little interest in spiritual things: 'firmly attached to the things of the world' (*solidement attaché aux choses de la vie*), and a hermit who was in many ways the complete opposite: some-one who had the outward appearance of a wild man, but with deep inner illumination, perhaps, even, a Master. The meeting was the moment of conception, or perhaps it would be better to say the moment of annunciation, for the Fraternité des Polaires, an occult group with noble aims for spiritual brotherhood between men and women worldwide, which operated from headquarters in Paris from 1926 until (so far as we know) the wartime Occupation. (It is from the Polaire *Bulletin* that the quotation in French is taken, above.) In 1934 an English branch of the Polaires was formed, which separated soon after from the French organization, and became the White Eagle Lodge in 1936. The story will be told in more detail shortly.

Bagnaia was a name well-known to me from the story of the

Polaires, but I realized it had never entered my consciousness where in Italy it was. To my friend I acknowledged a feeling that it was probably up in the mountains—I supposed the Alps—for no better reason than that I had some recollection of a hill in an account or a photograph; and with a lot else on my mind, I confess I was ready more or less to disregard the question.

We stayed in Florence, at the hospitality of the leader of the little White Eagle group there, Brenda Bencini, and her husband. It is our habit to go on at least one long car excursion with Brenda when we stay there: perhaps to Assisi, or some such place. On this occasion, however, Brenda came to us soon after our arrival to announce that a friend of hers had recently made a trip by coach to Bagnaia and neighbouring Viterbo, and had spoken of it with enormous enthusiasm—not for its associations but for the beauty of Viterbo's churches and for the gardens of the former papal villa at Bagnaia. Why did we not, in view of our shared connection with Bagnaia, all go there?

I was embarrassed to discover that Viterbo, to which Bagnaia is an outlying village, is north of Rome, not in the mountains at all; but there was certainly nothing to prevent our going.

The autostrada took us to Orvieto, and from there we drove cross-country on something of a back road to Viterbo. Soon the signposts and the road atlas failed to tally, and at about noon we found before us a low cliff on which stood a village. It could have been Bagnaia, but it equally well might not have been. There was a hairpin bend in the road before the village, and on the outside of this hairpin a small metalled track went off to the left. My mother and I turned to each other, and we knew we both felt that this was the road we wanted. I did a three-point turn in the road, and followed the track for a short distance to where a hill opened out before us. It was raining gently, and rather dark.

The road now went on round the hill to the left, but that way did not seem right. A variety of paths and small tracks made as if to ascend the hill, and they seemed more propitious. Ultimately, it was a track that went off to the right that felt to be just the one. We got out of the car and, heedless of the rain (it always rains for me on these occasions of spiritual significance!), we set off again.

What was the source of such strong intuition about the locality? The Polaire records are remarkably uninformative about Bagnaia. I do not know whether any Polaire went back there, to confirm the place; certainly, the account in the Polaire *Bulletin*, translated in the main story below, speaks only of the village, and of vines and pastures. It was clearly outside the village, though, that the bulk of the meetings took place. However, I realized that for my part I had a completely clear picture of what the place had looked like. I can see, still, an old black-and-white photograph, I think in a book, with a border round it in the style of the time—the 1930s, I suppose. In the photo, the hill is reasonably steep, the vegetation is not so much wood as thicket; there are brambles—not so common in Italy as in England—and there are whitish rocks. A cart-track goes up from bottom left of the photograph to top right; I think there is a division of the ways near the top.

Nowadays the track, which I recall light-coloured or even white in the photograph, has a black surface. I guess it has had a dressing of cinders, but I did not investigate closely. There is not much sign of a bifurcation in the track at the point I would expect it. Everything else, however, is correct. I know the colours are right (even though the photo is in black and white): the brambles are there, the angle of the hill is right; and the rocks are if anything even more pronounced than I expected. There are stunted oaks below, but most of the hill is either coppiced chestnut, or wilder thicket. The chestnut must have regenerated many times since 1908, the date of the meeting. Today the flowers are, incidentally, exquisite. At the top of the hill, there is a striking outcrop (that, and the cross which has been erected there, are outside my remembered photograph).

There was no doubt between my mother and myself that we were in the right place, yet she and I had not compared notes hitherto. She recalled it, I now know, from her meditations. For myself, it was certainly the photograph that identified it.

And yet there is no photograph. I racked my brains for where I
pp.
73–74 might have seen it. In the *Bulletin*; in ASIA MYSTERIOSA, the book
about the Polaire Oracle by Zam Bhotiva; or in his book about
the magic of singing, which I do not believe I have actually
seen; maybe in an article, somewhere, about the Polaires? On
my return to England, I checked the White Eagle Lodge
archives. Just as I had begun to expect, I found nothing.

The story is ultimately unimportant; it simply led us to this
place. There, the three of us felt we wanted to sit quietly and
absorb the atmosphere. By now it was around twelve noon, a
time when I try to 'send out the light'—that is, consciously to
project the highest and most beautiful of the atmosphere to be
found in that place and time in a healing way, out into the
world, for the bringing together of the nations. It was
surprisingly difficult to do, and I believe that once again both
my mother and I had much the same experience. When I
cannot 'send out the light' I believe I am trying too hard,
probably with my mind active, for the projection is truly of the
Christ light, and it seems to come from the heart, spontaneously, and not to be very responsive to the promptings of the
mind. So on this occasion I let go of my desire to help the
world, and at once I was aware of an experience quite the
opposite of the one I had been seeking. It was as though a great
searchlight of love was shining down on me. *Straight* down, as
far as I can recall, like the North Star overhead: and so powerful
that all my feeble efforts to send out light across the valley in
front of us were swept away in what felt like a great flood of
light coming from above and beyond us. Thus passed our visit
to Bagnaia.

Recently, I had an experience which reconnected with this
one, and by an extraordinary coincidence not only did my
mother once again share it, but Brenda was present too. It was
the closing service in London for the White Eagle Lodge's
summer 'term', the last day of July this year, and my aunt, Joan
Hodgson, was leading the short communion through meditation which along with the 'sending out the light' is the central
point of the White Eagle service. Again I had at first a little

difficulty in 'making the contact'; and then, suddenly, I was in a great light which seemed this time to come not so much as a spotlight but as a fountain, a great oval of light extending from way above, and I stood within it. I was surprised to find that I identified the consciousness I felt specifically with the hermit of Bagnaia (it was this that my mother so clearly experienced too). I don't know why I should have made this connection; but it was almost as though there was a special scent to the atmosphere in which I found myself; an atmosphere which although completely Christian in one sense (the communion, as celebrated in the Lodge meditation, uses the traditional Christian symbols) was also Hindu, and Buddhist, and all religions in one. If I felt an influence more specifically, it was that of what are tantalizingly described as 'the Masters of the Far East'. It was deeply loving.

It was in this awareness that I became conscious of something which had at least partially eluded me up to this point. It was the nature of the experience that the boy, the later founder of the Polaires, had when he met the hermit of Bagnaia. That man was all; he had seemed to come from nowhere, and he seemingly went nowhere (later, *Bulletins* suggested that he had set out on a long journey back to the Himalayas, and completed his earthly work in 1930). This mystery about him was one of the reasons the villagers feared him. He had about him, the boy said later, an aura, which the villagers in their worldliness misinterpreted. I am sure now, that he was a Master;* the scent of the vision is still with me as overriding evidence of that. His love was so great that it stretched between earth and heaven: hence the light in which we found ourselves. Only with hindsight have I linked it to the Pole Star, the star which of all stars in the heavens is most overhead.

The Polaires took their name not only from the Pole Star but also from the Polar myth, that of a continuing lineage of adepts deriving from a Hyperborean region that was habitable before

*In the Polaire account, the boy regarded him as an 'Illuminé', one who is illumined. The concept of an advanced being manifesting in a body for a specific purpose is less common in the Christian tradition, but frequent in the Buddhist one.

the earth shifted cataclysmically on its axis. But the Star is more important. It was undoubtedly as a result of instructions from their Oracle that they took the symbol of the six-pointed star that is on the cover of every one of their journals, but it is not recorded in detail. We are merely told that the Polaire Oracle had instructed that the star be used: *de signe de ralliement aux égarés, aux naufragés, à ceux qui sont dans la nuit* ('as a rallying sign to the wandering, the shipwrecked, and those who are in the night'). Elsewhere the small representation of the silver star the Polaires wore was described as a symbol of the greater star, *symbole de cette fraternité qui veut apporter un peu de soulagement aux âmes qui suffrent, qui veut unir les diverses pensées, les différentes fois, les différents peuples, et les guider vers un but de Lumière* ('symbol of the brotherhood which is trying to bring a little solace to suffering souls, which is trying to unite diverse opinions, different faiths, different peoples, and guide them towards a goal of Light') (*Bulletin,* 9th May 1930, pp. 3, 15).

That symbol, thus given to the founders of the Polaires by the Sages, is probably the greatest legacy the Polaires have left us. Here White Eagle describes what it means:

'The six-pointed star under which you work is the symbol of the perfectly balanced life, the symbol of the Christ-man and the Christ in man. It is the great symbol of man made perfect and it forms the foundation of matter as well as the expression of spirit.' (THE GENTLE BROTHER, p. 66)

It is to be noted (in the full story which follows) that the six-pointed star was effectively the cipher by which the authenticity of the medium, the Polaires and the Conan Doyle messages was demonstrated to each of the other parties.

p. 77 The six-pointed star is an ancient symbol, as the main text in part explains. As we look at it now, it is also very much a symbol, even a harbinger, of the Aquarian age, replacing the five-pointed star, which has a very different symbolism, in this respect.

*

The notes which follow may be of interest to readers who are already familiar with the Conan Doyle messages, since they give greater detail and colour to the whole story, and bring it up to date. Readers who have come to the messages for the first time may prefer to go straight to Ivan Cooke's telling of the story, which begins at Chapter II. What follows in the present chapter will not fully make sense unless the reader has an acquaintance with the main story, though for convenience I have cross-referenced it as far as possible: the page numbers in the margin indicate where this part of the story will be found elsewhere in this book.

For while it may seem that the story behind the Conan Doyle messages is given fairly exhaustively in the chapters which follow, the passage of time does permit the story to be clarified and set in context, and some brief additional notes here will make the point quite strongly that while the outcome was in the strict sense of the word wonderful, the events surrounding the messages were real birth-pangs, and that the achievement that was celebrated in those editions was not brought about without great personal pain and sacrifice. The story then becomes more human, and may be of rather greater encouragement to others who come after, and who also suffer great personal anguish in the achievement of their personal vision. Some of the amplification is taken from THY KINGDOM COME; the rest, from my own researches. This material includes surviving correspondence, and the very substantial notes my father made for THE RETURN OF ARTHUR CONAN DOYLE, some of which, unpublished at the time, are here used almost verbatim.

As is clearly stated, Minesta (that is, Grace Cooke: in the use of the name Minesta, the present edition follows the example of previous ones, even though the name both White Eagle and the Polaires normally used in addressing her at the time the messages were given was Brighteyes) had never met Sir Arthur *p. 68* when the latter died, so suddenly, on 7th July 1930. She had, however, met the novelist's daughter Mary and spent some days with her in June of that year, when both were invited to a cottage near Barmouth in Wales belonging to Mrs Mabel Beatty, a notable psychic.* White Eagle, speaking through

*See the photograph on p. 68

Minesta, predicted to Mary Conan Doyle and Mrs Beatty the wars and disasters of the 1930s, saying, however, that they were to be followed by a new age of the spirit. Miss Conan Doyle took a longhand transcript of the message to her father.

While it is the link to the Conan Doyle family through this meeting that is of the greatest outward significance, the acquaintance with Mabel Beatty is not to be underestimated in the story. Since 1926, White Eagle had been speaking through Minesta of a band of advanced souls and teachers known 'in the unseen' as the White Brotherhood. Even at the time of the opening of Kenton Spiritualist Church (formed in October 1928), a church with which Minesta was very closely associated, he intimated the desire of those in spirit by whose direction the church had come into being to make Kenton a church of the spirit, teaching not only survival but that higher and purer truth which should accompany and reinforce survivalistic teachings and proofs. White Eagle many times said that the aim of the Wise Ones was to found and establish groups on earth who would be faithful in service, for years of great extremity were drawing close, in which the spiritual forces would need the faith, service and cooperation of such groups if mankind were to be saved from self-destruction.

Although it would be unwise to identify this exhortation too closely with one group or another, Minesta's own participation in Mabel Beatty's Spiritualist circle at this time is some evidence that she shared the ideals of the group, and her later involvement with the Polaires is perhaps very usefully thrown into focus by this earlier commitment. Mabel Beatty had been advised by her own guides in spirit to begin her work in June 1928, and the outcome of the teaching received in her special circle was the book MAN MADE PERFECT, which was published in November 1929. She went on to publish THE TEMPLE OF THE BODY (1930) and THE NEW GOSPEL OF GOD'S LOVE (1931), all three books containing messages 'from the White Brotherhood'. Minesta attended a circle held in London by Mrs Beatty on 4th April 1930, at which White Eagle spoke; these circles continued approximately monthly into January 1931. Coincidentally to the present story, we may remember that it was in the first of these circles that White Eagle made the prediction rediscovered fifty years later and recounted in THE STORY OF THE WHITE EAGLE LODGE (p. 47), of the opening of the London White Eagle Lodge and the eventual building of the White Temple, described below.* *pp. 149–51*

It was as little as ten days after Sir Arthur Conan Doyle's passing that Minesta visited the novelist's widow at her Crowborough home and had her first spirit contact with him, *p. 82* which seems to have been useful and evidential to Lady Conan Doyle. A correspondence ensued and the strength of the friendship which developed is attested in the main text and can be seen clearly in later letters (they begin, 'Dearest Brighteyes'), some of which are quoted in this chapter, though the early ones have been mainly lost.

The story now unravels quite fast. On 7th October, White *p. 85* Eagle foretells (to the Cooke family) that contact would be made with a Society in France; and the following month, the Polaires learn through the Oracle that Sir Arthur would give his message concerning the afterlife through a medium (*Bulle-* *p. 79* *tins* of January–March 1931). During this time Minesta is still receiving communication from Sir Arthur, largely (it would seem) about mundane matters: of particular interest in the text is the description of her visit to Lady Conan Doyle at Bignell Wood, the novelist's second home in the New Forest, in *pp.* September, during which Sir Arthur gives precise instructions *83–84* about the composition of the Memorial Committee set up in his name.

Despite the evidential nature of these sittings in which Sir *p. 83* Arthur spoke, there seems to have been uncertainty in Minesta's own mind about the value of them; that is to say, she seems to have felt she was really only contacting Sir Arthur at the level immediately above the physical and that he might have more to say at a later date; and although she seems to have kept

---

*THE STORY OF THE WHITE EAGLE LODGE, White Eagle Publishing Trust, Liss, Hants., 1986. A further account of Mabel Beatty's circle is given in the volume of autobiography by Grace Cooke, THE SHINING PRESENCE (White Eagle Lodge, London, 1946), p. 21. Both books are now now out of print.

this to herself, that uncertainty may be seen to have a bearing on subsequent events. After all, she had already provided, by automatic writing, an extraordinarily detailed description of what the Spiritualists call the 'Summerland' world of after-death, and it had already been published, in 1929, as THE GOLDEN KEY.* Her own autobiographical volumes, published much later,† give much corroborating evidence that she had herself a sense of a deeper purpose opening up; the messages that White Eagle had given, through her, to Mrs Beatty's group, and others which she heard there, bear this out too. Certainly, when White Eagle himself spoke on 7th October, he gave a different sense of the progress of Sir Arthur's soul, stating clearly that the Conan Doyle Memorial

'...must be used, not for the furtherance of a personality but, as his life was spent, for the establishment of truth and justice. Thus will his name, after the death of his body, bring to the brothers the power they need to build on earth a temple of the spirit. So much seems to centre around a name, but that is but a means to an end. He, too, throws himself into this work with all joy and zest, because he has been shown the future—of an earth reborn, of truth set free.

p. 85   'And so the great White Brotherhood is at work.'
The message is given more fully in the main text, below.

At about the same time as this growth in Minesta's outlook was taking place, apparently at the prompting of spirit a Mrs Caird Miller was introduced to her. Mrs Miller was later to be present at most of the sittings described in this book and seems to have been a catalyst in the process by which the messages coming from Sir Arthur moved on from the circumstantial to the wide spiritual perspective of the scripts reproduced in this book. White Eagle called her 'Silver Star'. (These special names were dear to White Eagle even before his main ministry started. As already stated, he knew his medium as Minesta or more commonly at this time as Brighteyes; Ivan Cooke was known as Brother Faithful; while Lady Conan Doyle was often referred

*Republished in 1988 by Psychic Press, London.
†PLUMED SERPENT, London (Rider Books), 1942, and THE SHINING PRESENCE (see above, p. 21).

to as Heartsease and Sir Arthur was regularly Nobleheart.)

On 9th January 1931, at the last of Mabel Beatty's special circles, White Eagle announced (at the time, perhaps a trifle mysteriously) that 'the helper' was near and would make his presence known.

The story of the coming of the Polaire messenger is so well set out in Ivan Cooke's text that only a few notes may be added here. One thing to note, complementing Ivan Cooke's pp. 87–88 description given in the main story, is Minesta's own description of Zam Bhotiva, the messenger (in the text below he is regularly referred to as Monsieur Bhotiva, but Bhotiva was in fact an adopted name, as was his Persian first name, Zam). He was, first of all, 'one of the two most remarkable men I have ever met'. Secondly, 'as I came to know him better I found he had an understanding far in advance of most other mortals; he could be gentle as a child, sympathetic and kindly, and yet, on occasion, displayed an energy and resolution that made each word he spoke worthy of remembrance and careful weighing'. (THE SHINING PRESENCE, p. 25)

The second thing to note is that Lady Conan Doyle, herself the first recipient of the Polaires' overtures, responded with the caution of having Minesta psychometrize the letter Bhotiva had sent, in a sealed envelope, after she received it. Only then, when Minesta gave the answer that it was safe to proceed, that he was a helper, was M Bhotiva admitted to the circle. These, according to THY KINGDOM COME, were her actual words:

'Sea ... globe wandering ... Lady Doyle has no need to wonder about the writer of this letter. He is one who has been sent to her by us. She is quite safe in going forward. The writer of this letter is of good character, not very strong physically. Go to the circle tonight without fear. All will be well. You will be asked to take on some special work. We wish you to accept, although you at present know nothing about this—you must do it when you are asked.'

This message was posted the morning before the seance, which took place on 27th January 1931 at the Stead Library,* p. 80

*i.e., W. T. Stead's Borderland Library. See p. 68.

with Estelle Stead and Adrian, Denis and Jean Conan Doyle (the novelist's two sons and his widow), Ivan Cooke, and three friends present. Even after this, the true work did not proceed until still more proofs had been given which convinced both Minesta and Bhotiva that they were receiving their instructions from the same high source. A further note on the numerical tests employed is given in chapter XII.

pp.
137–
40

Lady Conan Doyle, despite being instrumental in the bringing together of Bhotiva and Minesta, always seems to have held back from full involvement in the work being undertaken. Even her letter of 3rd February that year to Zam Bhotiva, reproduced in the Polaire *Bulletin* at the time and subsequently in THE RETURN OF ARTHUR CONAN DOYLE, seems a little abstract, a little circumspect ('I am so glad that at the Seance [apparently the second one of the series, held in Wembley Park the previous day]... my husband came through and spoke to you unexpectedly about Les Polaires Brotherhood'). By 2nd April, Bhotiva was writing to Lady Conan Doyle responding a little testily to her desire for Spiritualist 'controls' upon the seances that were beginning to take place; the Polaires' view was that their own messages from the Oracle de Force Astrale were 'a means of control superior to any given by the best mediums in the world'. He stated, further, that the Polaire mission was 'the clearing from Spiritualism all that is foolish and not serious; and they are happy in the thought that their Brother Sir Arthur Conan Doyle is willing to help them in their mission'. Though Bhotiva ended with a cordial invitation to the Conan Doyle family to visit the Polaires in Paris, it is difficult to believe that the expressions in the letter were particularly grateful to Lady Conan Doyle, and she may even have taken it as a slight upon the work with which her husband had been so totally associated, that of evidential Spiritualism.

However, relations remained cordial; only six days later, Lady Conan Doyle was explaining to Ivan Cooke in a letter that M Bhotiva had, in a conversation with her son Denis, done a lot to clear up 'the little misunderstanding'. She also wrote that the message which had come through Minesta and was sent to her 'is very deep and full of some rather fine and new ideas and therefore valuable', though it is not absolutely clear whether this was a transcript of one of the Polaire/Conan Doyle sittings or a recent White Eagle message.

On 22nd May came the sitting so dramatically described in the main text, held at Mrs Miller's house (Shenley Park, near Bletchley), at which were present among others Lady Conan Doyle and both Zam Bhotiva and the Polaire 'Chief' (whose name comes down to us as 'R. Odin', and who should not be confused with the 'Mage', that is, the operator of the cipher and the one who had had the original contact with the hermit of Bagnaia). After this sitting Lady Conan Doyle and her family withdrew from the joint work. This may have been part of the plan all along, since at the same time Bhotiva wrote expressing his satisfaction at the outcome of his mission and intimating that the Polaire Brotherhood considered that the task laid upon them was now at an end, the remaining members of the circle being left to continue as they wished. However, her letter of 1st June to Minesta states that it encloses a copy of one to Mrs Miller regarding the 22nd May sitting—something which is now lost—and there is at least a hint in the tone of this statement that she was not entirely happy. That possibility is made all the more likely by a letter four days later to Zam Bhotiva from W. R. Bradbrook, who so faithfully transcribed all the messages of the sittings, apparently trying to act as something of a peacemaker. His letter is sufficiently interesting to quote at some length. He begins with a compliment to the Polaires, saying that everything he has heard of them from Mrs Miller and from Minesta leads him to believe in the goodness of their aims and objectives, and adds:

pp. 100–107

'That your prayers for the early manifestation of the Christ-spirit in Spiritualistic progress will be continued, I hope. I fear that both within and without Spiritualism the conception of Christ is largely a denominational rather than a universal one. Perhaps this is due in great measure to the fact that man does not yet nearly know himself and realize his seven-fold nature…. The sensitive spirituality which inspires the intellect intuitively and thereby enables it to use and control the emotions as a gifted artist uses colours on his palette, an organist the stops on his instrument, or as the flowers disperse their fragrance, is as yet rare…. Need I assure you that in my small way I shall do my best to make the way clear for Sir Arthur's work to be carried on [on] an octave higher, although recognizing that his unaffected honesty of purpose in pressing home to the minds of the most unsophisticated the essential objective truths and evidences for survival, achieved much that could not have been done by more subtle if finer methods….

'With regard to the Message, I recognized its accuracy from what I had already learned from the Other Side. His vocal intonation did not impress me so much…. I think Sir Arthur must have been helped a great deal and at times I think influenced…. Lady Conan Doyle is disappointed that the *personal* element was not more evident.'

I cannot tell for sure, but I think that in this letter there are one or even two keys to Lady Conan Doyle's unease about the communications, which I shall discuss in a moment. However, she did not resist them; a much later letter, written on 18th April 1933 and concerned by then with the publication of the messages in THY KINGDOM COME, confirms this:

'I am returning to you my husband's script, which you kindly lent us. I must apologize for keeping it so long, but since Mary had it, both my boys have read it through very carefully, as their father wished. They are both tremendously impressed with this script.'

On the other hand, it is clear that she deeply missed any evidential personal message among the communications; it is telling that even in this enthusiastic letter, she allowed the praise to come from her sons rather than herself. More importantly, however, I think Mr Bradbrook's letter gives a hint of some of the *philosophical* reasons not only why Lady Conan Doyle was suspicious of the Polaires, but also why Spiritualism as a movement, both at the time and subsequently, found it so difficult to accept the content of the Conan Doyle messages.

Partly, it is that conception of a *universal* Christ (one with which the Polaires and White Eagle both concurred), and partly, it is what Bradbrook refers to as 'an octave higher'—the sense of a universal, unfolding life of ever-increasing joy and wisdom, perfectly ruled by that Christ-spirit running through all life, incarnate and discarnate. This may not specifically have been what upset Lady Conan Doyle: but the tendency is for her letters to reveal a sensitivity towards what orthodox Spiritual-ists—her husband's friends and supporters, after all—might think, a sensitivity which seems to have prevented her more wholehearted commitment. In July 1931 Bradbrook wrote her another letter of comfort, which again seems to address her particular injuries; though personal in reference, his comments seem to me also to be relevant to the philosophical issue at stake:

'Dear lady, do not think for a single moment that advance in the spirit-realms makes love less human because it is more divine....

'I am fully convinced that a successful mastery of astral conditions, gives a more powerful influence and finer insight as well as a closer soul-contact with loved ones. This also carries with it the disillusionment that such fuller power must bring when contacting the true quality of many that appeared staunch.'

What the whole of the messages and all that has been written about them seem to demonstrate, is that the record of Sir Arthur was unique, or all-but unique, in being a record not of one who had recently passed over, but of one who had begun to ascend through the planes of consciousness and who was able to describe the brilliance of those worlds that lay beyond the Summerland so frequently described by the Spiritualists.

If in Lady Conan Doyle there was a reluctance to accept this difference between the soul newly passed over and the mature consciousness of one who had gone on further, it is perhaps understandable. She had naturally a greater attachment to the human personality of the communicator than any of the other sitters had; and it is to her great credit that despite her unease she steadfastly maintained her support for Minesta at a personal level. Thus on 15th June 1932 she wrote to Ivan Cooke: 'It is good to feel that there are such loyal and true souls like yourselves in the Movement.' She felt that in the vacuum following her husband's death there was a lot of sorting-out being done between true leaders and pretenders to leadership of the Spiritualist movement, and was grateful in precisely the way she described. The letter continues (the 'big Centre' must connect with her wishes for the use of the money donated in her husband's memory):

'Please thank dear White Eagle for his fine comforting message. It is nice to know that in the sifting which is going on, what a fine and dear group of people, including yourselves, are being collected together for the big Centre.'

What is most painful about this correspondence is that in the end the work of Minesta and her husband with Conan Doyle and the Polaires, and the hopes and aims of Lady Conan Doyle, were going in directions which were, frankly, quite opposite to one another—in spite of the loving respect each side bore the other. When it came to the messages being *published*, Lady Conan Doyle was adamant that the messages should not go out *under her husband's name*, although she was happy for it to be used in the context of the telling of the story as a whole (a somewhat difficult balance for an editor to hold, and perhaps a restriction a little difficult to understand when she so many times acknowledged the authenticity of the messages).

This was not, however, stubbornness. As she explained (28th June 1933), her deep understanding with her husband, presumably from conversations they had had while on earth, and perhaps backed up by statements coming from him to her via other mediums since his death, was not to accept them '*unless* he also communicated the same facts independently to me' (her italics). She once spoke of needing no less than three independent proofs. Yet Conan Doyle's own implied insistence, *within* the messages, was quite contrary to this. The reader is referred to the very precise message given through White Eagle about the use of his name in the Memorial, given in the main text and quoted briefly above. The matter in miniature is seen in the

pp. 22, 85

use of his photograph (to which, within certain restrictions, Lady Conan Doyle eventually assented; it is still there in this *p. 118* edition): in the text, Sir Arthur had asked that it be definitely included and, as Minesta or Ivan Cooke wrote to Lady Conan Doyle on 23rd July 1933, 'We feel ... it would be very disloyal of us to fail to abide by those instructions.'

It is now too late to know more than the letters tell us. Minesta and Ivan Cooke clearly felt that they had to go ahead keeping faith with instruction they felt they had from spirit. Lady Conan Doyle's letter of 9th December 1933, when she had seen the book (and the publisher's publicity for it, which exacerbated the matter still further), sets out her upset and her bewilderment. It is also clear, from the earlier letter quoted (28th June) and another of 7th August, that this was to be predicted. The depth of the direction from spirit that Minesta must have felt in order to enable her to go against Lady Conan Doyle's wishes in this matter—those of a personal friend, to boot—can never be known. Those feelings must have been costly and painful on all sides.

A little further indication of how sensitively she regarded her own role in the matter as a whole is given by the few letters that survive from and to M Bhotiva. On 21st November 1931,★ for instance, before the crisis had even begun to come to a head, Bhotiva was writing to her,

'My dear Brighteyes, Do not be downhearted, do not be worried. Everything is going on for the best. You will get the proofs sooner than you think and your work will be rewarded. Do not mind if the teaching does not confirm the present Spiritualist teaching. Never forget that Conan Doyle's teaching given through your mediumship is in perfect harmony with the ancient Hindu tradition, with the ancient Hindu wisdom....

'Nobody can stop the march of the six-pointed star. You are at work, we are at work, for humanity and not for individuals. So, I beg you, my dear sister, never mind about

★This letter is actually dated simply '21 of November' (in English) and may date from 1932 or 33, but I think that the 1931 date is the most likely.

personal feelings.'

But it was not only the deterioration of relations with Lady
Conan Doyle that had caused Minesta much heart-searching.
July 1931 was the month in which she had journeyed with a
number of the Polaires to Lordat in the Pyrenees to assist them
in their excavations for a supposed treasure to be found there.

p. 145 The occult forces were strong, she herself suffered a brief but
mysterious illness, and one of the Polaire group actually became
deranged and attacked another with a knife; and all in all, the
trip was sufficiently alarming to cause her to make a hurried will
on the 8th of that month, witnessed by Mrs Miller. Later she
wrote of that time, 'I used to call upon Christ with all the
strength of my soul. The thought of the cross of light and of
the Christ presence were ever with me through those hazardous
weeks.' The forces were strong for good as well as for apparent
ill, however, and she came back deeply enriched by the vision

pp. she had had of St John (which is described below). Yet in its
40–42, declared objective—that of finding a physical treasure, perhaps
146 even a manuscript, left by the Albigenses—the trip was a total
failure. It was years later that she began to realize its importance.

And there was more trouble to come. Bhotiva's initial
contact with Lady Conan Doyle and with Minesta in England
was made through the explicit direction of the Oracle de Force
Astrale. His instructions were very clearly set out, and as far as
we can tell, he began with the backing of the Fraternité as a
whole. The progress of the work was written up in the *Bulletin
des Polaires* throughout the early months of 1931. After the
momentous meeting on 22nd May, it may be recalled, his
official task was ended. The Polaires involved themselves in the
plans for the Lordat excavations, and Minesta and Brother
Faithful were invited to join the Polaires, and were initiated in
Paris on their way down to the Pyrenees, late in June or early
in July. That the spiritual power of the Polaires was helpful was
attested to by no less a person than Conan Doyle himself; as well
as those who attended the sittings in England, a group of six
Polaires in France had been projecting a thought-ray of power
and love every week. (Conan Doyle commented in retrospect:

'A power unknown came to my aid, giving me a vision of my *pp. 92–93* true state.' Minesta and Brother Faithful also attested to its power: see below.) It is clear, therefore, that the Conan Doyle venture evinced a lot of support.

The support, however, was not apparently universal, and although we can only piece the story together tentatively, the problem for the 'dissenting' Polaires seems to have been the very issue of the garb of Spiritualism which they felt was being projected onto their work. As early as March 1931, the Polaire Council felt it necessary in the *Bulletin* to issue a disclaimer, that they were not in any way seeking to impose spiritualistic beliefs on their members, but rather that they felt it was part of the Polaire work to bring light into the darkness. In August, they spoke of a possibility of the reunion of the original participants, including the Conan Doyle family and the Polaire representatives; but in October of that year, they felt obliged to issue another statement *que les Polaires* NE SONT PAS DES SPIRITES: 'that the Polaires are not spiritists'; and to insist that the representatives had attended the seances in London at the orders of their Chiefs, and that their very statutes included among their work that of bringing light to bear on Spiritualism. Despite assertions later that autumn that the Polaires, under the order of their Chiefs, would attend a further seance, in January 1932 a short article stated that the reports of the seances would henceforth be discontinued, the Polaire energies being directed towards their social plan of universal brotherhood in action; although a special issue of the *Bulletin*, outside the normal series, was promised. In the February *Bulletin* it was suddenly announced that Bhotiva was stripped of his duties, though he remained an active Polaire, with the direction that it remained only for him to terminate his mission to London (which had evidently been extended beyond 22nd May 1931).

On 9th March he again attended a sitting, and Lady Conan Doyle and her sons sat quietly at home in Sussex 'to "tune in" their thoughts and sympathies with ours' (THY KINGDOM COME, p. 210). Nothing, however, was reported in the *Bulletin* until September, when one of the oldest Polaires, Charles Aurey, accused his fellow Polaires of suppressing the truth and ostracizing the participants in the Conan Doyle experiment. In another article Bhotiva (if he is correctly identified from the initials after the article) responded insisting that the matter had not been badly dealt with, but rather, that it was best simply to leave the whole matter until a full résumé could be published, based on Ivan Cooke's forthcoming book. It was, he said, a matter of prudence and not of a suppression of the truth. There was only one further reference to the matter in the *Bulletins*: an open letter under the initials of several readers stating that they were deeply interested in the Conan Doyle revelations and were anxious to read the rest of his disclosures.★

In fact, we shall shortly discover that rather more debate seems to have been going on among the Polaires than this outwardly trivial controversy would suggest. But first, let me continue with the story as it affects the little group of Polaire brethren in England, from which group was later to emanate the White Eagle work as we know it today. First, it had been accepted from the beginning that the Conan Doyle messages were eventually to be published, so that their message could, in accordance with Conan Doyle's own wishes, transform the views about the life beyond held by many Spiritualists. THY KINGDOM COME was accepted by the publisher Wright and Brown and appeared in December 1933, in an edition of one thousand copies. Moreover, the English Polaires had kept faith with the aims of the Polaire Brotherhood and on 10th February 1934 received a message from the beyond saying that a Polaire Lodge would be formed in England. A later message indicated that although it would be attached to the Paris Polaire Brotherhood, its constitution would be adapted later, and that the role of the French Polaires was to make ready only. 'Your sign will be the Star; your spirit that of the Cross; your sympathies universal, without beginning and without end, as with the Circle' ... 'You will think of yourselves as the White Brotherhood, servants of the Great White Light.'

★By then, the *Bulletin* had become *Les Cahiers de la Fraternité Polaire*. At the time of writing, the issue which should contain a review of THY KINGDOM COME and any further details, is not available to us.

Application was made to the Polaire Brotherhood in Paris, and the fraternity deputed Zam Bhotiva (despite his earlier eclipse) to assist in the formation of the English group. From the start it was agreed that the English group would be 'absolutely independent ... its internal authority is absolute' (instruction from Bhotiva, 16th May 1934). Shortly after, Bhotiva came from Paris to initiate the English group, and the first 'Grand Chain of the Polaire Brotherhood in England' was held.

The work began well, but it very soon ran into difficulties. One of the Paris Polaires living in London was allowed, on Bhotiva's recommendation, to attend the English Brotherhood. There were personal difficulties which need not be entered into here, and she was finally asked to leave. There were accompanying resignations in England, Bhotiva's advice was sought, and his response was to put forward the one who had been asked to leave as the chief of the English Polaires, thus bringing the English group under the direct control of the Paris group. Inevitably, the suggestion was rejected. Early the following year, on White Eagle's advice, the English group severed all connection with the French. On 30th January 1935 White Eagle declared that the time was ripe for it to take the new name of the White Brotherhood, and to take for its symbols the six-pointed star and the cross within the circle.

During this time, despite the difficulties, no less than thirty initiations had taken place and an Edinburgh group of the Brotherhood had also been formed.

The reader today may well wonder why, in an organization proclaiming brotherhood between all people, the split which occurred between the English and the French groups should have occurred. The passage of time does not make it any easier to judge exactly what happened and why, and it is probably an oversimplification to say that the roots of the separation lay in a severe fracture which had taken place in the Polaire Brotherhood itself. However, it may be seen with hindsight that the break was as much part of the great plan of the brothers in spirit as anything else in this story.

As has already been suggested, the controversy surrounding

the Conan Doyle sittings was only the tip of an iceberg in terms of what seems, from the *Bulletins*, to have been a deep, and ultimately fatal, division within the fraternity. Not all of this, by any means, is germane to the present book and so we will consider it as briefly as the actual proceedings permit.

We begin with the announcement in February 1932 that Bhotiva would no longer take an active part in the work of the Polaires. Little has come down to us of what lay behind this, but the very brevity of the announcement, when Bhotiva was such a key figure within the group, is suggestive. However, Bhotiva's continued contributions to the *Bulletin* seem to imply that in fact some sort of reconciliation was soon achieved. In the following issue, there is mention of important letters being sent out to every Polaire: but the substance of an article in the May issue suggests that these may have related to a further revelation to be made to the Polaires from the beyond. The article was headed: *Celui qui Attend* ('He who waits') and the principle statement in it was that the year 1932 marked the end of an era; that 1933 was the beginning of a new age. *Après la Tempête viendra le Maître.... 'Celui qui Attend' sera donc parmi nous en 1933, ou en 1934 au plus tard. Si l'annonce de son arrivée indique que l'Année de Feu est proche, elle indique aussi que l'Aube des Temps Nouveaux va bientôt baigner de sa resplendissante lumière l'Humanité dolente* ('After the storm the Master will come.... "He who Waits" will therefore be among us in 1933, or in 1934 at the latest. If the announcement of his coming indicates that the Year of Fire is near, it indicates also that the dawn of the New Age is coming presently, to bathe suffering humanity in its dazzling light').

Similar statements about the year or years of fire are, of course, also to be found in the Conan Doyle messages themselves, and had been a part of what the Polaires put forward all along. A Special Number of the *Bulletin*, issued apparently in 1931, explains the identity of 'Celui qui Attend': he was the commander of the Polaires, the Knight of the Rosy Cross himself; the same note cites a message from the sages as early as 1925, announcing that 'the Master', though that day unknown and afar, would one day emerge as a great being and would serve among the brethren as their supreme authority. What is different about the statement of May 1932 is its particular urgency, the concentration on the immediate coming of the Master, and the giving of a more or less precise date for this.

At the same time as making these somewhat dramatic prophecies, the Polaires seemed to be clear that their work was passing from a metaphysical to a more active stage, to a social plan of brotherhood which the sacred land of France would give to the world. This is repeated in several *Bulletins*.

The May 1932 *Bulletin*, interestingly, stated that the most recent communication from the Oracle dated from about three months previously. After this, the Oracle is less and less mentioned. The impression is that communications became fewer and then, unaccountably, ceased during the year 1932.

In August 1932, a further division seemed to have occurred. A statement announced that the Council would, provisionally, be taking over direct responsibility for the *Bulletin*. An open letter from 'Mario Fille', the original and only operator of the Oracle, claiming to be written *en toute simplicité,* reminded his brothers and sisters of the three things that were necessary to be a Polaire: absolute certainty that after the approaching cataclysm would come a Christic age in which humanity would be united under the sign of the rose and the cross; the development within the individual of the spirit of sacrifice, judging no man and countering egotism in oneself; and holding an absolutely pure faith.★ Ultimately, the letter is a cry against atheism: how, he is saying, could anyone hope to understand and work for the Polaire Brotherhood who did not, from the heights to the depths of the human scale, believe all humanity sons and daughters of the same God? One can only speculate on the controversy which underlay this, except that Fille

★Early issues of the Polaire *Bulletin* are deeply impressive in conveying the group's ideals. Space precludes long quotation, but the reader is directed not only to the nine principles of the Brotherhood given in the *Bulletins,* but also to the issue of May 1930, which seems to have been used as a general prospectus. We note, for instance, this plea for disinterest: *'La Fraternité Polaire doit être au-dessus des opinions particulières.... Vous n'aurez point de richesse, point d'honneurs, point de gloire'*—an instruction received from the Oracle itself.

obviously felt that there were those within the fraternity who were not being true to its deepest ideals.

There is every indication that his heartfelt pleas went unheeded by all but the few. The *Bulletins* increasingly become vehicles for articles on a variety of occult subjects, and this process is symbolically confirmed when *Les Cahiers*—merely, 'the notebooks'—replace *Le Bulletin* in January 1933.

What was the way forward for the Polaires? With the grand social plan? As a forum for occult ideas? Or was it a question simply of awaiting the instructions of 'He who waits'? Or something truer to the original conception?

Perhaps some comment upon the particular prophecy over 'He who waits' is due. Few readers will want to claim that it came true. As I have already said, what was unusual about it was the precise date given, 1933 or 1934, and the description of a single 'year of fire' to announce it (by contrast White Eagle, who also speaks frequently of the 'years of fire', describes them as the whole period during which the age of Pisces gives way to the age of Aquarius; and speaks not of a new Master coming, but of a second coming of the Christ-spirit, reborn in men's hearts). Conan Doyle's own words in the messages are a little dissimilar from either, in that he too seemed to anticipate years of general catastrophe which would be succeeded by a new age of the spirit, but there is no sense at all that he confined his vision to so short a period of time. And, it has to be said, even his view of a new continent emerging is much more easily explained in symbolical terms than in literal ones. The Polaires of 1932 saw the coming Master as hyperborean; they also predicted conflict between the new teacher and the forces of darkness, with a hint that false masters could arise as well. But the Oracle also permitted them to call him *'aperta'*, the lost one. This is also a name given to Apollo, the Sun God. Veiled in this prophecy, beneath the time schedule which now seems absurd, there is still, perhaps, the incontrovertible and powerful archetypal memory of the eternal Return.

What next happened takes us further and further into the area of supposition. There is a certain amount of literature

pp.
192–
93

about the Polaires, but the interrelatedness of secret and occult societies in the Paris of the 1920s and 30s is so great that there is very little that can actually be relied upon. Some of the accounts were gathered together by the writer Arnaud d'Appremont into two articles in a modern French journal, *Le Monde Inconnu*, in September and October 1990. Notable features missing from these articles are any substantial acquaintance with the Polaire magazines themselves, and any knowledge of the continuing history in England. D'Appremont has Bhotiva separating himself from the group as early (perhaps) as 1931. The following paragraphs are notes and conjectures.

First, it does seem clear that the group lost its focus and at some time (earlier or later) both the original instigators either lost heart or were eclipsed. Our own attempts in the White Eagle Lodge, as inheritors of the tradition, to uncover the later history of the group in the mid-1950s came to an unsatisfactory end. The long-serving assistant in the publisher–bookshop in the Boulevard Haussmann in Paris which had issued ASIA MYSTERIOSA, Bhotiva's book which had set out the story of the Oracle, spoke of the author visiting the shop early in the 1950s and saying that all was at an end in France as far as the Polaires were concerned. This is not wholly true with regard to the Polaires outside of France: when the English group severed in 1935, it left a small 'rump' of English Polaires which maintained a link with the French group; this group appears to have met faithfully, into recent years at least.

Secondly, speculation is bound to exist regarding the onset of war in Paris, the German occupation, and how this affected the work. It may well be that there was almost no Polaire fraternity left by 1939 anyway: but certainly, attempts were made to stamp out whatever *was* left. ASIA MYSTERIOSA, for instance, was seized from the bookshops for destruction by the Bibliothèque Nationale. At the same time, just as they were on the one hand periodically accused of being covert Theosophists or Freemasons, so also were the Polaires accused on the other hand of right-wing and even fascist leanings (the story that holds the greatest currency here is probably the suggestion that

Maurice Magre, the respected chronicler of the Cathars, left the group because he did not like its politics). In the strongly polarized world of the 1930s, when few had an inkling of where right-wing politics might lead, when the waters of occultism were rich and murky and the pilots few, this taint is not wholly surprising. The concentration on the hyperborean Master does have its own risks, when taken into a political context; in his telling of the story in the present book Ivan Cooke rather beautifully shows it as a *myth* of great power, not a belief about history. What one can say with clarity, is that the French Polaires were by the outbreak of war far too compromised for the sort of role that the English Brotherhood was to take on during the war years, which I shall shortly describe. As White Eagle predicted in February 1934, it was not the Polaires who were to take the work forward: 'They make ready only,' he said. What remains, most touchingly, is the original vision and the simplicity with which it was held. Fille seems from the start to have taken on the role of 'Mage' almost in spite of himself. He left the cipher untouched at first, and in ASIA MYSTERIOSA Bhotiva explains how reluctant Fille was to involve himself in the arithmetic: 'It was very difficult for us to get really sustained and efficient work out of him ... he hates calculations ... such work bores him, all the more so in that his interest in the results he gets from it is only very relative' (*Il nous a été très difficile d'obtenir de lui un travail suivi et vraiment efficace ... il déteste calculer ... ce travail l'ennnuie d'autant plus que les résultats qu'il en obtient ne l'intéressent que d' une manière très relative*). Hardly a man with an overblown sense of mission, and nonetheless the sort of person, one might feel today, whom the Masters *would* choose, for his simplicity, to carry out the great plan.

Outside of these notes and memories, our sense of the Polaire brethren soon grows dim.

Polaire brothers, we salute you! Your work has not been lost. Many of you are with us again. The light shines into the darkness; and the torch will be carried on.

★

If a rather depressing note is struck by the account of human frailties we have just given, they can at least be set against the story of what grew out of this almost tragic loss of focus and ideals. Once through the painful birth period (which coincidentally involved the loss of the home, Burstow Manor in Surrey, that so many of White Eagle's followers believed was to be the centre of his work for the decades to come*), the child thrived. The White Eagle Lodge grew, not only in its membership but also in the inner, Brotherhood work which was the direct inheritor of the Polaire inspiration. By the outbreak of the second world war the dedicated group of those who had been initiated in England numbered as many as a hundred, while around the Brothers (Brothers and Sisters, we would now say) was, in the form of the White Eagle Lodge, a sizeable membership of subscribers to the teaching of the brotherhood in spirit, as given in the public services by White Eagle—and of course in the Conan Doyle messages, by then published. A book, THE WHITE BROTHERHOOD, telling the story of the Brotherhood's work and its role in the first of the years of fire was brought out a month after war was declared.† Here is a sample of the teaching in that book, which we give simply to indicate to the new reader the tenor of the Brotherhood work.

'There is great turmoil in the world. Do not participate in the destructive thoughts of those brethren unable to see with a clear vision. Be constructive in your thoughts. The forces of good are strong; but for the sake of the lesser brethren we need all the help we can get from you. So when you meet another always turn the conversation into channels of peace and goodwill, believing wholeheartedly in the omnipotence of God. Love will conquer all ill. This is your duty as brethren.' (p. 132)

The months up to the outbreak of war had already been a time of highly concentrated activity by the Brotherhood in the hope that if a sufficiently powerful concentration of light could be projected, war might actually be averted. That this was not to be did not diminish the work of the Brotherhood nor in any

*Described in THE RETURN OF ARTHUR CONAN DOYLE, pp. 84-85, and in THE STORY OF THE WHITE EAGLE LODGE, pp. 1–5.
†The White Eagle Lodge, London, 1939 (now out of print).

long-term sense daunt the brothers themselves. White Eagle gave very detailed guidance about the specific projection of the Light throughout the war years—to individual convoys of ships to protect them, to battlefields barely known to the brothers themselves, and to individuals over whom the invisible brotherhood watched.

One remarkable story from these times is that of a serving commander who was also a member of the Brotherhood. His company was completely surrounded on all sides by the enemy, with no chance of escape without great loss of life. He ordered the destruction of all papers, plans and suchlike, and went into a wood and prayed (doubtless with a concentration upon the Star). *Very* shortly afterwards, his wife recounts today, there was a tremendous thunderstorm, all firing ceased, the enemy retreated, and the company was allowed to escape.

These years were also a time during which some of the most profound of White Eagle's teaching continued to be given. The little book THE QUIET MIND, which was published many years later (1972) and has reached an audience far wider than any other volume of White Eagle's teaching, includes many sayings which occur in his messages to his Brotherhood in London during those early years. Moreover, despite all the difficulty surrounding it, there is to be taken into account the outcome of Minesta's visit to Lordat with the Polaires in 1931, which ultimately proved to be so important for her personally, and (just as important) the second visit she made in 1956. This visit too was a time of deep initiation for her and of blessing as well as a time of gaining of new direction for the work. Both these visits are described in chapter XII below (supported by the photographs on pp. 55–56); but to give us a better understanding of the power of what was touched at Lordat, here is the Lodge magazine for 1946, *Angelus*:

pp. 145-
47,
149-
50

> 'Not until some ten years had passed did even the medium herself begin to realize what had actually transpired at Lordat, and what purpose had underlain that expedition. For the treasure had proved itself to be wholly an intangible and spiritual treasure…. The treasure lay in that aura or influence

emanating from the holy brothers of the holy mount; from St John himself, if you will. Because she had become so wholly drawn into that aura or influence during the ten days or so spent at Lordat, because her soul had become wholly immersed in it, Brighteyes had indeed found the treasure as had been promised, and bore it with her when she left Lordat. In that sense, which after all is the true sense, the promise of the sages had been fulfilled.' (p. 240)

Minesta echoed this in her own description of the visit, in THE SHINING PRESENCE. The most tangible reward it gave her was the inspiration which (she felt) enabled her to receive from White Eagle the interpretation of St John's gospel which was later given to students in the Lodge, largely during the war years. These teachings are available in print as THE LIVING WORD OF ST JOHN, which originally appeared under the White Eagle Lodge imprint in 1949 and has been reissued by the White Eagle Publishing Trust in later editions of 1979 and 2000.

One final comment will help to make plain how deeply Minesta viewed her task, and what she viewed it to be. Though written for publication in 1946, this passage is remarkable in the way it refers back to what she and the Polaires knew they had to establish, at the cost of a great deal of orthodox Spiritualist teaching. She was comparing her experience at Lordat with an earlier manifestation at another Pyrenean shrine of a strangely similar name, Lourdes....

'It was not a physical spring of water which materialized on this occasion but a spiritual outpouring of the truth of divine living; the revelation of a vision which pointed the way of aspiration, sincerity and purity of living which would, in time, re-establish on this earth many centres of the true White Brotherhood. Surely this is the way the spirit of Christ works! Not through grand buildings and powerful organizations which tend to deny the spirit and concentrate upon the physical, but rather through the simple pure way of brotherhood and service to one another.

'Is not the way of true brotherhood the inner meaning of Christ's teaching which has been misinterpreted by the church in the doctrine of the vicarious atonement? When the soul passes through the ceremony of initiation into the temple of universal brotherhood it realizes the inner meaning of "atonement" for it finds itself irrevocably attached to its brothers and companions in spirit—to such a degree that it suffers with the suffering of its brothers and rejoices in its brothers' happiness. In this sense it is the Christ light in the heart which takes or absorbs into its own heart the sins or the sufferings of mankind. This can only be described as vicarious suffering, but instead of the word "atonement" being used, I believe it should be "at-one-ment" or perfect brotherhood of the spirit....

'It is not the man, the Master Jesus, whom the Christian world worships as the saviour and vicarious redeemer of the world; it is the teaching of the Christ-spirit or the love and brotherhood, the divine light in the heart of every man, which is the saviour of mankind. It is this little spark of divine life which the White Brotherhood endeavours to fan into a glowing flame so that it can absorb into itself and feel what its brother feels. This light, this truth *is* the vicarious at-one-ment—the essence of the teaching of the White Brotherhood.' (THE SHINING PRESENCE, pp. 35–36)

★

In a real sense the history of the White Eagle Lodge is part and parcel of the Conan Doyle messages, and that is one reason why it has been felt useful to rehearse the story so fully here. Yet I hope that the preceding pages also provide the reader with an opportunity to see the messages themselves in context. It may further be useful to add some notes about the messages themselves, perhaps clarifying them and despite their originally being linked to a particular time and place, pointing up their greater relevance.

In earlier editions, by way of example, the identity of the communicator was in itself important, as it gave greater proof of personal survival. In the present day, channelled teaching is much more widely accepted and it is far easier to concentrate on the quality of that teaching without the physical identity of the communicator being the important factor. In this spirit, though we have used the title 'ARTHUR CONAN DOYLE'S BOOK OF THE BEYOND', neither this, nor the controversy over the use of his name, seems very important any longer (it simply provides a link, for identification's sake, with the earlier editions). We shall henceforth refer to the communicator as ACD.

White Eagle himself has always somewhat resisted excessive concentration on the physical incarnation from which his name 'White Eagle' is drawn—if indeed the name is linked to a particular incarnation at all. Ivan Cooke speaks quite categorically of White Eagle dwelling in a physical body in the mountains of the East today. Although White Eagle does himself indicate this from time to time, I think it is perhaps easier for the modern mind to view this statement in a context similar to the way in which we perhaps regard the soul who took on the identity of the hermit of Bagnaia, so that the truths which were to come to the West could be transmitted, taking on a body when necessary, but not in any way tied to a physical incarnation. My own view of how White Eagle would prefer us to regard him (and it *is* a personal view), is closer to a passage in the introduction to a relatively recent White Eagle publication, Jenny Dent's A QUIET MIND COMPANION:

'Although we think of White Eagle as a distinct personality, he tends to imply that he would prefer to lay his personality on one side and remind us that he is the spokesman for a group, often referred to as the White Brotherhood. Our desire to define personalities is very human, very earthly. Maybe as you read you will begin to get a sense of what happens when the distinctions and labels of personality are softened. White Eagle is still 'dear old White Eagle', but he is also a loving emanation, [and his teaching is] a ray of the star which carries a greater sense of the love at the heart of things than any physical personality could.'   *p. 101*

This is rather confirmed by his own words in this book, when, though owning his *personal* being, he says that 'the Great

White Spirit shines through his personality'. I am reminded
further of the total identification which one can have with the
deep spirit of things when one who has touched the true heart
of love is speaking. Once I was at an evening meeting at which
the teacher Emmanuel spoke, and he was asked to explain his
identity in a way that would satisfy the earthly understanding.
To the questioner and those present, he responded with great
love and respect that he could not, in terms which would satisfy
the earthly mind, define his identity (the implication I suppose
being that the soul in its fulness cannot actually be limited in
that way). 'I am consciousness beyond human form, addressing
you through human form, so you can hear me.' But more
deeply, he said, the answer to the question is literally *'I am you'*:
i.e., when we really touch the teacher in his fulness, the answer
that comes back is the answer from the Universal, inside of
ourselves. We hear our own truth. The term 'the Universal'
which I have used here is one which will soon be familiar to
the reader of the ACD messages. ACD even refers to 'the full
gospel of Universalism'—not some strange 'ism' or earthly
doctrine but precisely what the full meaning of the word
expresses. In other contexts, we might call it 'the Oneness'.

ACD's messages will very soon remind us again that all truth
is simply not containable in the human mind. One such
example is when he speaks of reincarnation, and says that both
the case for reincarnation and the case against it are equally true.
The ordinary earthly mind cannot follow this paradox. He goes
on to say that at a certain level such impossibilities do actually
become possible. I will not try to explain this (even if I could)
but it is perhaps a clue to overcoming this difficulty that the
earthly mind really does have to be put on one side, so that the
truth remains undefined and therefore possible to be heard.

This separation between what the earthly mind can conceive, and what the unlimited mind can touch, is very plainly
to be seen in the teaching the messages contain about life after
death. Here it may be particularly helpful to compare White
Eagle's own teaching on what happens immediately after death,
an example of which is given at the end of this new edition of

the messages, in this light. We have to remember that ACD, when he gave the teaching reproduced in the book, was himself at times still very closely connected to his earthly incarnation. Just as the human mind demands an identification, a personality, to attach to the messages, so, for that newly-released soul there is quite an earthly attachment to strongly-delineated planes of consciousness. In THE RETURN OF ARTHUR CONAN DOYLE and THY KINGDOM COME, an artist's drawing prompted by ACD's description set them out in colour and in ascending order.

I have set this out simply as a table this time, overleaf, in the belief that too great a stress on systematization can be misleading. In the first place, the correlation between ACD's account of these planes and the diagram was only ever ninety-five per cent accurate, because of some lack of clarity in the text. Other teachers, such as The Tibetan (Alice Bailey's guide), have a very slightly different account, too. But in the second place, it seems to me that the possibility for this strongly linear sense of unfolding human consciousness being conceivable by earthly understanding is actually contradicted by White Eagle's teaching, and indeed in certain places by ACD himself. My understanding is that perhaps the human mind before death and very soon after still has an attachment to the distinctly human view that consciousness develops in a strict historical way, one plane of consciousness after another, as it were. However, the focus on the planes of consciousness is certainly not to be ignored. The regular meditator, for instance, may become very aware of them and through practice learn to raise his or her consciousness up through the planes, the ability to identify them being a positive help in the meditation.

In THE RETURN OF ARTHUR CONAN DOYLE, a footnote opposite the drawing explained that the diagram 'can give no idea of the interrelation of the spheres as they exist in human consciousness—which is the reason why man lives in more worlds than one'. White Eagle, who relatively speaking is freer than ACD of the limitations of the earthly mind, throughout his teaching seems even more to stress that the different planes

C E L E S T I A L — COSMIC OR UNIVERSAL SPHERE OF AT-ONE-MENT — C E L E S T I A L

THIRD CELESTIAL PLANE ('NIRVANA')

SECOND CELESTIAL PLANE

FIRST CELESTIAL PLANE

——————————— (REBIRTH) ———————————

THIRD MENTAL PLANE
(Waiting halls of meditation)

M E N T A L — SECOND MENTAL PLANE
(Intuitional realization; inspirational or thought-creation) — M E N T A L

FIRST MENTAL PLANE
(Intellectual realization—'the halls of wisdom')

——————————— (THE SECOND DEATH) ———————————

THE 'SUMMERLAND'
A place of rest and self-realization which spurs a soul again to the upward climb

A S T R A L — TWO PLANES OF DESIRE
(Not necessarily evil)
Earth tastes and longings are still felt. Here the average man awakes after death — A S T R A L

LOWER ASTRAL PLANE
(Greedy, self-centred. Self. Miserly, unloving)

EARTH PLANE
(The denser astral plane)
(Lusts, fierce bodily desires, hates, resentment, 'Hell')

of consciousness are levels that can be reached at any time, given the necessary choice and effort of will, through the technique of meditation—or for that matter which we can sink into through distraction and depression. All life is one, he says, and we operate in a sense on all planes at once, only our consciousness being limited in its perception, so that we are aware of the earth plane and shut out knowledge of the others.

Maybe the White Eagle teachings at the end of the book will very simply show the beauty of the ever-present link between the world of earthly perception and the equally real and equally present world we so frequently deny:

'When a soul leaves the physical body it is in reality passing *p. 244* inward to an inner state of being. Think of the physical life as an outward life, in which you are immersed in matter of a coarse condition. Away from your body your world will be of a finer and more malleable matter, matter more easily responsive to thought and emotion. Such matter is moulded by the soul, so whatever the soul is, whatever its habitual thoughts and life, it will externalize itself in this inner world.'

While I do genuinely hope that the inclusion of the two White Eagle teachings at the end of this book will take the reader on into a further awareness and a deeper freedom from earthliness, it would certainly not be fair to ACD to imply that the sense in which the distinctions between the different layers of consciousness are ultimately broken down, and in which we perceive life as one, was unknown to him. On a number of occasions he himself seems to imply a level of communication far more subtle and far more beautiful than the cut-and-dried this-world/that-world level. For instance:

'I repeat in this new life intercourse between the two worlds *pp.* proves not nearly so simple as I had been led to think, but *159–* communion can be a finer truth and more glorious reality *60* than is yet understood. Communication must come to mean a true communion of spirit....

'When such reality [of spiritual contact] becomes part and parcel of the soul life, all fear of death, sickness, and poverty will be wiped away.'

The reader of the messages may actually perceive that there are times when the full consciousness of ACD—the 'Nobleheart' consciousness, let us call it (using the name White Eagle gave him)—seems to break through, and other times when he seems more to shrink into limited consciousness. At the beginning of chapter 2, for instance, he describes the limitation he felt immediately after his reawakening:

p. 167

'After I left my earth body I could not free myself for a considerable period, yet it is impossible to describe exactly the 'geography' of my condition. I felt strangely linked with the place of my birth and early years. I could not escape either to return or to advance to that heavenly plane which I knew existed and was quite near. Truly I was tied....'

Then (as we have already seen) something led him on:

p. 168

'I seemed to be picked up, as it were, in a ray of light. A power unknown came to my aid, giving me a vision of my true state, and I subsequently learned that this ray of light was a projection of love and power from the Polaires Brotherhood.'

By the time he is communicating he is able to compare recent experience with the indescribable beauty which seems to lie ahead of him. One gets an impression then of his soul actually moving between the planes, knowing one by glimpsing it and then returning to a plane closer to the earth to be able to describe it:

p. 169

'After passing through the "death" of the astral body, when the man discards his astral vehicle and enters the heavenly life, we there find a condition of at-one-ment—attunement—a condition wherein the soul is conscious only of the one vibratory note of love and service.'

This is from true knowledge, surely; and yet that consciousness seems to go again when he is, for instance, describing the 'mists' that surround the astral planes. He seems both to retain

pp. 171, 169

some sense of linear time and to lose it. Compare, for instance, 'passing from earth in normal course of development, men reach this sphere of life in about thirty years' with the earlier assertion, 'time is nothing over here'.

Since we have had cause to consider the Polaires' role in the 'release' of the soul of Sir Arthur, it may be useful to anticipate the question as to why did so wise and great a soul require this help, why did he not immediately find his way into the realms of clarity and light? Apart from the information ACD himself gives about this, two things are perhaps worth mentioning. The first is that the very scope of Sir Arthur's life (described in chapter II), even the very energy with which he invested it, seems to imply an incarnated soul deeply attached *by choice to* this world. It is rather like the busy mind which does not let us get to sleep. Nothing critical is intended in the saying of this, for Sir Arthur fulfilled precisely the work that he had to do, without a doubt; but purely in the interests of explanation, it is perhaps unsurprising that the memories of the earth life held him for a while after death. It is interesting to compare ACD and the life which he himself depicted in a drawing as a horse 'drawing the formidable load of his lifetime's achievement' (to *p. 59* quote Ivan Cooke's account) with the life of the Bagnaia hermit, Father Julian, who seems by contrast to have slid with total ease into and out of incarnation.

The reader who is puzzled may possibly be enlightened by one of the Polaire accounts in which is summarized a teaching which is said to have come through Minesta, precisely describing what the liberation 'from the red and blue-violet rays' was all about. I say 'said to have come' simply because we have no English original, and White Eagle's name is nowhere mentioned.* This account may also be of interest to astrological students and may usefully be read alongside the account of ACD's astrological chart in the book THE STARS AND THE CHAKRAS by Joan Hodgson.†

'The higher ego,§ that is to say the spark which is the make-

*As a further point, in chapters VI and VII of this book, White Eagle variously describes the rays as 'red and violet' and 'red and blue'. This précis— and we do not know who translated it—nicely resolves that conflict.

†The White Eagle Publishing Trust, 1990. See especially pp. 173-74.

§In the sense in which it is used here, the term 'higher ego' seems exactly to coincide with what we more usually today call the higher self. 'Ego' is a frequent term in the main text, and it almost never seems to coincide with the use of the word in psychology, but rather to mean the deep individuality, normally in its higher function, as here.

up of the spiritual body of man, incarnates partially in the physical body at a moment of the birth of the human being. This incarnated part remains linked to the discarnate part by an indissoluble link.

'Thanks to the play of earth vibrations and astral ones, the higher ego is incarnated in a more or less large "quantity" into a physical body. Consequently we can say that the incarnation of the higher ego is ruled by the quality and force of astral and earthly vibrations which dominate at the precise moment of birth. These vibrations are called "rays" and are designated according to their quality by different names or colours.

'At the moment of the birth of man, a more or less large "quantity" of his higher ego will be incarnated in him, following the power of the dominant rays at the hour, day and geographical position where he sees light. And these rays, like immense tentacles, will take hold of the ego and partly imprison it in the physical body of the newly born.'
The account then relates this to the case of Sir Arthur Conan Doyle (some of the words obviously being the Polaires' own).

'Born under peculiar circumstances, at a moment when the earth emanated red rays, and space emanated blue-violet rays of extraordinary power, Arthur Conan Doyle incarnated—in his physical body—the whole of his higher ego.

'Today the same red and blue-violet rays still hold prisoner the "Great Soul" of this just man, arrested in the gulf of death by the same rays which ruled at his birth....

'Now, following the instructions we have received, confirmed by the message of Mrs Cooke, this net of red and blue-violet rays which imprison the "spirit" of Conan Doyle can be cut under special conditions. It is necessary that a projection of blue-violet rays should be thrown into space at a moment when the earth again emanates red rays, so that this projection, this transfusion of forces, should help the chained one to free himself. But for this transfusion of forces to take place, it has been necessary to find a medium—a channel—whose vibrations must synchronize with those of the "spirit" of Conan Doyle, so as to establish a link between the physical plane and the plane of the discarnate. It also has been necessary to find human beings who possess the necessary vibrations, the blue-violet rays. Now, Mrs Cooke seems to be the perfect channel for this transfusion of force, and people who are present at the London seances also seem to satisfy the necessary colour conditions. Besides, these seances have not had up to the present any other aim, to our knowledge, than to prepare, to refine, to synchronize the link between the different vibratory elements so that at a moment when the earth—at a moment indicated—emanates once more red rays, the crossing of rays indicated by the communications from the Sages should be effectuated for the freeing of the "Great Soul" of Conan Doyle. And this Great Soul will then give to the world the proof of his marvellous mission and the proof of the continuation of life on the other side.'

The reader will make what he or she wants of this. One further thing that emerges from it, however, is the importance of the vibrations of every one of the individuals who were brought together to do the special work that enabled ACD to speak. Twice in the main text of Part Two, ACD indicates in an aside to Ivan Cooke how closely the two of them, who shared a birthday, were able to work together. *pp. 211, 220*

If there is one part of the message that stands out particularly for me personally, it is the categorical statement which ACD makes as his primary discovery on waking in his new life: *personal responsibility and the redeeming power of love*. The words are conventional, almost: the thought is, to me, radical in the highest degree. It anticipates what White Eagle says about the origin of all things being in *thought*; that it is thought, before action, which produces karma—but it also gives a very fine articulation of the principle that people are absolutely in charge of their lives (indeed of all their lives), within the protection of the divine love. There is, he says, no separation—and that means no distinction—from God. *p. 105*

Incidentally, this is one of the places where there is in my own mind a little uncertainty about the actual words of the message. Where it comes in our present text, taken from THY KINGDOM COME, the passage reads:

p. 105 'He continued, "Yes ... yes ... yes. The redeeming power of love! I must conclude my message with this. Love! Not personal ... impersonal. Love for all men. I see the great need ... the Master."'

This message was largely reprinted in the Polaire *Bulletin* of June 1931, a fortnight later. There, the translation follows the paragraph above reasonably clearly until the end:

> *Et je dois conclure mon message en vous parlant de cet Amour, non pas compris sous une forme personelle et individuelle, mais sous la forme large de l'Amour impersonnel, de l'amour pour tous les hommes.*
>
> '*L'Amour: la Grande Nécessité!*
> '*L'Amour: Le Maître!*'

Most of this is close enough to our text not to require retranslation, but the last lines carry a different sense from the English. They would translate:

'Love, the great need!... Love: the Master!'

In other words, where our text implies that the great need is for the Master, the French text implies that the great need is for Love. Whatever were the words White Eagle actually spoke, I am inclined to believe that the sense ACD intended to convey is as in the French version: it is in any case beautifully close to White Eagle's own teaching.

★

We hope that in this new edition, Conan Doyle's words will have a freshness about them that will touch the reader, as it has us in editing them. In the Preface I mentioned the almost Dantesque scope of the vision. There *are* times when the 'inferno' part of the scheme, the account of the astral planes, feels a trifle gloomy, and it is perhaps fair to remind the reader that all Conan Doyle is saying is that the earth plane itself can be very like this—if that is the level of consciousness *on which we are allowing ourselves to operate.* The same may, perhaps, be true

p. 192 of the catastrophes predicted in chapter 6. And of course we do not have to limit ourselves to that consciousness. We can live *now*, in ACD's terms, at a higher level. But what is exceptional about the Conan Doyle messages is that they also give us a vision of the celestial worlds (where we could be functioning now), that is far too powerful to be forgotten. And, as he says, *'all the spheres of spirit life are, or can be, reached by* *p. 177* *incarnate man'*:

> 'From the celestial we pass to what has been referred to as *p. 176* the Christ sphere (but which I would prefer to call the "cosmic or universal spheres"). In this condition of life dwell those beings who, freed from rebirth to a physical plane of existence, are now concerned not only with the earth but with the cosmic life of the universe. From this plane go forth creative Masters, responsible for the life of the soul on other planets and in other spiritual spheres of existence.
>
> 'Thousands of years must elapse, of course, before the ego attains to full expression and development, and only after gaining all knowledge possible through physical existence does it pass onward, beyond the halls of waiting, onward beyond even the celestial, into a still higher plane. What term can prove adequate?—*The Christ sphere!*—the At-one-ment with Christ! The rapture of a perfect love, a perfected fulfilment.'

Ultimately, words do fail us. It is to be hoped that every reader who approaches the Conan Doyle messages hears the truth 'behind' them, beyond the literal sense, and that the messages will then reinforce the contact the reader has with his or her own truths within.

The reader may then feel that ACD's glorious vision is not so remote for him or her. I suggest it is indeed not , and I know that it may also be a challenge when ACD reminds us that we *p. 234* can find God through joy, and not only through suffering. If it is a challenge to reach this consciousness, I cannot think of a more beautiful one.

NOTES TO THE EDITION OF 2003

This second edition of ARTHUR CONAN DOYLE'S BOOK OF THE
BEYOND amends quite a number of small details in the preliminary
material, but the main story stands as it was first written. Since
1994, however, it has been possible to consider whether in any
way the emphasis needs correcting. If any correction does need
making, I feel that it should be in regard to the account I myself
gave of the Polaires. Re-reading such material as survives about
them, I feel that it would be fairer to them and to history to
make a clearer distinction than I did in 1994 between the early
Polaires—from their inception up to the time they came back
from Lordat in 1931, let us say—and the later group; and to pay
a greater tribute to the simplicity, purity and idealism of their
work in this earlier period. The statement on p. 37 that the
group lost its focus is one I have left unaltered, but I think it
understates the transformation that had occurred.

Why? First, because two unpublished accounts of these
years, both I believe written by Ivan Cooke, stress in a way I
had not previously noticed that there was a real gap between
the time that he and Grace Cooke were working with them
and Lady Conan Doyle on the transmissions from Sir Arthur
at the beginning (1931–2), and the later period (1934–5) when
under White Eagle's instructions contact was re-made with
them, with the explicit intention of forming a Polaire Brotherhood in England. Secondly, a great deal had happened within
the Polaires during this period about which we are hazy, but
nonetheless certain facts stand out. The Oracle had ceased
operating, either because of something within its own pro-
gramming, or because its operator simply chose no longer to
give his co-operation. The Lordat trip had ended in disarray;
Minesta virtually ceased contact with the Polaires afterwards.
In 1932 there had been tremendous prominence given to the

belief of the imminent appearance of 'He who waits', to a degree not seen in the early period. A group of French Polaires had objected vehemently to the work with Conan Doyle. Zam Bhotiva had been stripped of his offices, and then reinstated; yet when the application from England to create an English Brotherhood was received, Bhotiva was nonetheless called back from wherever he was to give the necessary instruction and pass on the rituals. This not only makes a strong statement about the level of Bhotiva's links with the group at that time, it also could suggest that there remained no-one else among them with the necessary knowledge. If so, the whole concept of a Polaire *Brotherhood* may have changed by then.

We know that another leader, R. W. Blanchard, took over in 1934, but it sounds as though changes had already taken place before that, and the change from the *Bulletin* to the *Cahiers* in January 1933 may also be symbolic of the changes. It seems that many of the original group, actually referred to at the time as 'La Racine' ('the Root'), began to leave soon after the Lordat trip. I am not even any longer certain that the 'Mario Fille' who wrote demanding the Star symbol back from England after the White Eagle brethren severed themselves from the Polaires was the same Mario as had been the operator, or one of the operators, of the Oracle. This distinction has never been suggested before, and the onus would certainly be on me to prove it if I really wished to assert the claim.

What happened to the Polaires is not wholly relevant here, but I am contributing an article to the White Eagle magazine *Stella Polaris* at roughly at the same time as I write these words, so the interested reader should find that in the April–May and June–July issues of 2003 there is further material. But to make a clear separation between the Polaires in their first years and the group who carried on after 1932–3 enables us to be much warmer in our endorsement of the early group. Grace Cooke herself called Bhotiva 'one of the two most remarkable men I have ever met'. The author (almost certainly Ivan Cooke) of an anonymous account of the English Brotherhood beautifully written out in copperplate in 1938, wrote 'There can be no question of the purity of motive, service and sacrifice given in those early days'. He paid tribute to the dedication of the Polaire Mage and of Bhotiva who had followed the instructions given by the Oracle absolutely without wavering, in the formation of the first Brotherhood. Again and again the message had been repeated about what they had to do, and in a strange capital, Paris (they both came from Italy), with very little money, they had obediently formed it. 'The Polaire Brotherhood at its prime formed a body of men and women strongly linked to a great Source of spiritual power, and with each Brother attuned or linked to the other, by a method unpractised since early Egypt,' says the same source. As to the veracity of the Oracle and the Sages in the East who communicated through it, here is Ivan Cooke in 1971, looking back with forty years of hindsight: 'Lengthy experience has since convinced us both of its truth and accuracy, and given us considerable respect for any messages coming from the Sages'. 'Its messages to our knowledge were always true, to the point, terse and vivid.' This same Oracle had, of course, initiated the work with Arthur Conan Doyle's spirit.

The other thing I should like to re-emphasise after all these years, is how clearly the attachment to the symbol of the Six-pointed Star stands out in the work of the early Polaires. The Star formed the central feature of the cover of every Polaire Bulletin; it was used in the initiation of brethren; and it was the symbol which White Eagle gave to the continuing English Brotherhood at its inception in 1934: 'Your sign will be the Star. Your spirit that of the Cross. Your sympathies universal, without beginning and without end, as with the Circle.' Many, one might almost say all, of White Eagle's teachings to the Brotherhood refer to the power of Star, both as a guiding light and also as a focus for the power to be directed to help humanity through the coming 'Years of Fire'. The words just quoted are a fitting dedication at the beginning of a work which began with the events of this book, and continues to grow—at the very heart of humanity's quest for peace, justice and truth.

Colum Hayward, March 2003

CHAPTER II

THE BOY WHO BECAME
WORLD-FAMOUS

by Ivan Cooke

EVERY river has its tributary streams which discharge into its waters, and one or more of these can be claimed as the actual source of the river.★

This can also happen with a story, when several lesser stories just meander separately and then merge into the main stream. Thus, the present story might begin with the strange tale of the hermit of Bagnaia in 1908; or with the later career of Sir Arthur Conan Doyle; or the early work of the well-known medium, authoress and seer, Mrs Grace Cooke. The lives of all three are inseparably interwoven in this story. But we naturally turn to that of the main protagonist in this book, Sir Arthur Conan Doyle—doctor, novelist, playwright, creator of 'Brigadier Gerard' and 'Sherlock Holmes', military historian, patriot, traveller, sportsman, supporter of humane causes, finally leader of the Spiritualist movement and lecturer throughout the English-speaking world. His varied life, his immense activity, and extraordinary personality have been the subject of three biographies since his passing in 1930;† even so, it may be that

---

★All the rest of Part One, as far as p. 147, is by Ivan Cooke.

†Evidently true in 1956, and the number is now far more; but Conan Doyle's life is less studied now than at the time this was written. In general, Ivan Cooke's words about rather little being known of Conan Doyle's leadership of Spiritualism is now almost poignantly true, and his biographers have not necessarily been his best friends in this regard.

in these days the public have almost forgotten his variety and accomplishment—save only the fact that his stories themselves lie at the origin of the modern vogue for the detective story!

As a boy the present writer looked forward each month to the arrival of a monthly magazine bearing on its cover a picture of the Strand, London, with a hansom cab in the foreground, and a long vista of other horse-drawn vehicles. At the end of the Strand Magazine were entrancing fairy stories by E. Nesbit, sometimes about a creature such as was never seen on land or sea called a 'Psammead'. Also there appeared stories by one Arthur Conan Doyle, concerning the adventures of Sherlock Holmes, ostensibly related by a Doctor Watson. Little did he realize that here before his very eyes were all but the first and certainly the very best of all detective stories, not to be equalled, far less surpassed by others in the subsequent spate of detective stories which they spawned. Nor did the actual name Arthur Conan Doyle mean much to him until in later years he read his STARK MUNRO LETTERS, a book which is more or less autobiographical. Its author seemed so British in his uncompromising love of truth, sincerity, and enthusiasm for sport and action and love of country. Also he had the knack of catching and holding his reader's interest with the first sentence of a story, of bringing a character to life in a sentence or two.

Not until years afterwards did it become plain that this vividness occurred because the writer was himself living in his characters, that he was born to his trade, and that his books were veritable expressions of himself. Also they were eminently readable because of their technical skill. Conan Doyle himself once said that his writing was at its best but plain English. But how plain an English was this, how forceful and sincere a style! It is not surprising that stories such as 'Silver Blaze' and the 'Brigadier Gerard' series came to be hailed as literary masterpieces of their time.

Arthur Conan Doyle was born in Edinburgh on 22nd May 1859. He died on 7th July 1930. During his seventy-one years of vigorous life he wrote about forty full-length books, several plays, a history of the South African war, and another of the first world war in six volumes (two major works, the writing of which might occupy a lesser writer for years), together with almost innumerable short stories of a quality which never flagged. His athletic achievements were no less notable. He excelled at boxing, played cricket for the M.C.C. at Lords, was a pioneer motorist, an expert at billiards, and the introducer of Norwegian skiing into Switzerland. It seems that whereas the ordinary man lives only a life half-alive, this man lived throughout his days with a full hundred-per-cent vigour and enthusiasm. Even during his last illness Sir Arthur occupied himself by drawing a pencil sketch which he called 'The Old Horse'—depicting himself as the old horse drawing the formidable load of his lifetime's achievement along a road where outstanding incidents of his career took the place of milestones. These included his school and university days, his adventures in a whaler, his medical practice, his mountaineering adventures, lecturing tours in America, activities during the Boer war, electioneering, and world tours as a propagandist for Spiritualism. Piled to a colossal height on the wagon were hosts of his books, short stories, plays, and so on, together with a series of five hundred lectures, the whole topped up by an array of golf clubs, boxing gloves, a cricket bat, billiard cues, skis, and other instruments symbolic of his love of sport.

The picture was an epitome of his life, about which, as we have said, no less than three biographies have appeared since his death. Yet the burden the old horse draws largely omits the activity into which he poured his utmost energy, health, and finances, and which finally curtailed his life. This mission led him to deny almost everything that he had attained—wealth, ease, comfort, home life, recognition and fame, even a peerage which was offered him—for the sake of an unpopular conviction which demanded all that he had left to give to life. We learn from his books that he had been interested in psychical research for many years. He had investigated several haunted houses and some poltergeist cases, and had met with startling experiences. Starting from a position of comparative materialism he had become receptive and continued to investigate psychic phenomena in the leisure hours of a very busy life.

'But the [first world] War came, and when the War came it brought earnestness into all our souls and made us look more closely at our own beliefs and reassess their values. In the presence of an agonized world, hearing every day of the deaths of the flower of our race in the first promise of their unfulfilled youth, seeing around one the wives and mothers who had no clear conception whither their loved one had gone to, I suddenly seemed to see that this subject with which I had so long dallied was not merely the study of a force outside the rules of science, but that it was really something tremendous, a breaking down of the walls between two worlds, a direct undeniable message from beyond, a call of hope and guidance for the human race at the time of its deepest affliction.'*

In this passage were expressed the writer's fearless confession of faith, and his conviction that here was the most important of all subjects open for man to study. Later came the additional conviction that here was something in the nature of a basic revelation. If death ended all for every person, then a person had lived for no purpose, since all his ideals, his hopes, achievements, affections, longings and the deep call of his heart for God all ended in extinction. So it must be with the host who had sacrificed their lives in Flanders. For if the individual man lived in vain then Christ also had lived and died in vain, for man had no soul to save. So also with the other world teachers; equally vain were the various faiths or religions they had inspired. St Paul's cry, *O grave, where is thy victory? O death, where is thy sting?* was meaningless. Without survival all that remains for man is to practise some system of morality (such as that of Confucius); and systems of morality are cold comfort for the loss of a million men during a war—a war which in itself constituted the breakdown of international morality.

These were the realizations that spurred Arthur Conan Doyle onward. He was then the highest paid of short-story writers—at the rate of ten shillings a word; but now his income

---

*THE NEW REVELATION (London, Hodder & Stoughton, 1918), pp. 48–49.

must go, except for an occasional short story; no more books must be written save on psychic matters, with survival as their theme. Boldly, trenchantly, he affirmed his new faith. 'Conan Doyle!'—went up the public cry of amazement—'He, of all men, to believe in this sort of thing!'

It mattered little what people said. Everything had to go. This was his calling, his crusade. Then began those tours (accompanied by his family) when the glad tidings had to be told across the world. For eleven years he drove himself, on exhausting lecture tours through Australia, South Africa, America and Britain, never sparing himself, and latterly heedless of warnings by his doctors. No man in his sixties could stand the strain. One of the last acts of his life was to struggle up to London to head a deputation to the Home Secretary about the centuries-old law under which Spiritualist mediums were prosecuted. Then came the end. Within a few days, the warrior was spent; his sword of the spirit was laid down at last.

His remains were laid in the garden of his home near Crowborough, near the hut where most of his stories were written.* It is said that the gathering was more like a quiet garden party than a funeral, for summer dresses were worn, and few people were in mourning. A huge crowd attended, and a host of telegrams poured in. A special train brought flowers. It seemed that his friends were world-wide. Thus was his body laid to rest. The flowers that had been sent covered the whole field. On the headstone was later inscribed his name, the date of his birth and four words:

'Steel true, blade straight.'

Mr John Dickson Carr's book, THE LIFE OF SIR ARTHUR CONAN DOYLE,† ends with these words, 'Let no man write his epitaph. He is not dead.'

It is true. Both his name and reputation have survived. In almost every bookshop will be found 'omnibus' volumes of his short stories, mostly the *Sherlock Holmes* series, and his books are frequently serialized over the air. Only books such as THE WHITE

---

*They were later moved to Minstead Church in the New Forest, Hampshire.

†London (John Murray), 1949.

COMPANY and SIR NIGEL and those about Spiritualism have fallen into the background, and these were dearest of all to their writer. Those books of his which have entertainment value look like continuing for years to come; his deeper and more thoughtful books—not these. 'He is not dead.' He lives on in these pages. Here is his final message.

CHAPTER III

MINESTA

THE LATE 1800s were the days of large families. To one of these a little girl was born, who came as the ninth child with a gap of five years between herself and the child before her. Her mother died when she was only seven years of age, and the intrusion of death in so poignant a form at so tender an age left memories, which she has never wholly forgotten, of her own loss through death. Having felt the sting of bereavement so early, her sympathy with others in similar circumstances has always been keen, and her desire to help and comfort them strengthened.

It appears that during her long illness the mother discussed with her husband the possibility of human survival after death, and the wife promised to communicate with him, if this were possible, after her passing. This for two staunch nonconformists living in Victorian days shows a certain enlightenment.

Some time after his wife had passed on, the husband was taken by a friend to the home of a noted medium, Mrs Annie Boddington. The two men sat at the back of the room, listening to the address, after which the medium gave 'clairvoyance', or 'spirit messages', to various persons in her audience. None came to the bereaved husband; but as he was unobtrusively leaving, the medium asked if the gentleman then going out would wait. He did so, and afterwards she came to him saying she had seen clairvoyantly that he had recently lost his wife, and that her spirit, waiting in the room to speak to him, had stood aside until the other people had gone—a form of timidity characteristic of her. Then the medium began to speak, as from the wife, giving the husband a message to each of her children by name, and showing by further evidence that she was conversant with all that had been happening in the home since her passing. What was so strangely convincing, however, was that while she was giving these messages the medium's hands were carefully arranging and rearranging the handkerchief in the husband's outside breast pocket; for this had always been a habit of the wife's.

Can it be wondered that the husband returned home walking on air, with never a doubt that his wife had fulfilled her promise, and that he had spoken to her? His certainty was shared by all his children, then mostly in their late teens. Forthwith the whole family became Spiritualists, and the father an ardent advocate and worker in the movement. In course of time he was speaking at one or other of the Spiritualist churches or halls every week. Those were the days when to affirm oneself a Spiritualist required courage. A Spiritualist might be abused in the street, or even have missiles flung at him; while church services were frequently interrupted by stones coming through the windows or by bricks thrown onto the roof. Spiritualist mediums, moreover, were continually being prosecuted under an Act for the 'suppression of witches' dating back to the middle ages.

Of course, the little girl, Grace, also became a Spiritualist. At an early age she attended the movement's Lyceum or Sunday school, since when she has never wavered in her certainty of survival and reunion.

This certainty, however, has not been based on messages received through other mediums, although she is familiar with this procedure, regarding it as natural and normal. Some are born to music, drama, painting or song, with gifts or faculties which are inherent and must be given expression if they are not to languish or die. Grace had perhaps the rarest faculty of all; for she was a natural born psychic, with gifts of clairvoyance, of second sight or prediction, of spiritual sensitiveness, and of power to diagnose and heal sickness, which needed no developing, for they were spontaneous.

These gifts were encouraged, of course, by her family's and her own familiarity with Spiritualism. They might easily have been crushed had she been born into some harder-headed materialistic family. But their use to her was as natural as breathing, and they manifested spontaneously. She was no more than thirteen when she gave a description and message to a woman (whom she had met for the first time) from someone who had died. She remembers telling the amazed woman that she was about to cross the seas to a distant land, where she would live in a house surrounded by a broad verandah on three sides. Afterwards little Grace was told that she had described some dearly-loved relative of the woman who had died, and given her a message she would never forget, especially as she was just about to return to her home in South Africa. One can imagine how impressive this communication must have been coming through a child who was a stranger.

After her mother's death Grace's life was none of the easiest. Her brothers and sisters were out in the world by now; her father had married again, not very happily. She was left alone for long hours in a big house in a somewhat lonely part of south London; and being an intensely sensitive child she was often frightened. But at such times a visitor whom she called the 'old man' would occasionally come and talk to her and comfort her. She remembers that he did not look like an ordinary person but rather as if he carried some sort of light inside him: it shone out so that he seemed illumined. After he had been with her she would fall asleep and dream happily; and so natural did the visitant seem to the child that it was not until later that she realized that he was not actually of this world.

Thus, though she lacked human society and made few friends of her own age, another order of existence offered her companionship. She grew to love that other world and her desire to serve its interests became a dominant factor in her life. So it was that in her late teens she appeared on the Spiritualist platform to give an address and clairvoyance; and as the simplicity and youth of the exponent created something of a sensation she was asked, in the years that followed, to speak at other centres. Eventually a week rarely passed without several of these engagements.

This was hard work, for it involved journeys about and across London, and also to provincial towns or cities such as Birmingham, Edinburgh or Glasgow. In fact, most of such engagements meant a wearisome Sunday journey, the giving of an address and clairvoyance, an even more wearisome return home, with little more in the way of material recompense than enough to cover expenses. This called for devotion to a self-imposed duty over a number of years. It was worthwhile, for the effort developed qualities of courage and steadfastness which were to fit her for the work that lay in the future, and brought her even nearer in spirit to her teacher and guide.

It has been suggested that the visitor who used to comfort the child Grace when she was alone and frightened was not of this world. He was, indeed, the child's guide or mentor, functioning from the unseen realms, and given this charge from her birth. His name, she learnt later, was White Eagle.

During all the many years the writer has known White Eagle, he has been extraordinarily reticent about himself, his past and his present mission. He says that he is just a friend to all, an old man who drops in because he likes to help people in their troubles. Maybe he is wiser than some of us because he stands a little higher and can see a little further, and thus knows what is going to happen.

White Eagle's contact with his medium is always by a process of projection. He lives, we have learned, in the mountains of the East, and he can project either himself or his influence half across the world to her, by functioning, like other initiates, in the ethereal body.★ So while he lives in a physical body, as do other initiates, he is able (as are they) to function in the ethereal world which pervades this physical globe, of which the latter is the replica. In that ethereal world (the real living world, in which our world of the senses is cradled) there is neither time nor space as we know it. Therefore he need not *actually* journey

★See introductory chapter, above, pp 43–44.

half across the sense-world, the physical, to get anywhere. At once he can be at any one place, or contact any one person, or answer someone's call for help. Only with the resumption of the physical or sense body does the sage resume or take on himself our mortal limitations and our burden. Not even then to the same degree as man. The sage's body is perfected, is no longer subjected to weariness, sickness or death as we know these things.

It is a habit of White Eagle's to bestow a new name on his friends, and one which usually seems to fit them better than the name with which they were christened. Sometimes it is the name of a biblical character, such as Peter, Matthew or Luke, or a name from THE PILGRIM'S PROGRESS. Sometimes it will denote some dominant trait in the personality or stimulate some quality which the personality needs. These 'soul' or 'character' names carry with them, moreover, an inkling of what is to be expected from the person concerned. A Peter, a Luke, or a John will display qualities, shortcomings or virtues, similar to those of their prototypes in the Gospels. Indeed it often happens that the new name will presently supersede the old one, and a man becomes known by it among his friends.

The name which White Eagle bestowed on his medium is 'Minesta', which means 'mother'; we shall see later how apt this name has been. From now on it will be convenient to refer to the medium, otherwise Mrs Grace Cooke, by the name of Minesta.

Minesta had been conducting services and giving clairvoyance each Sunday, and often on weekdays for about twenty years on behalf of Spiritualism. During these years her powers of clairvoyance and vision must have carried conviction to some thousands of people. Thus, the influence of her work had gone far and wide.

To contact and to serve the higher intelligence a medium must be a person of unusual and purposefully cultivated sensibility, and with qualities of character—of mind, motive and feeling—without which his or her gifts could never function. This is why so long a period of hard work and

*Minesta in Wales in June
1930, a month prior to Sir
Arthur Conan Doyle's
death.*

endurance was necessary to toughen and at the same time refine
her character even while at the same time her sensitivity was
increasing by reason of her work.

At the end of these years of what may be called preparation
Minesta had reached middle life, and was married with two
children and a home to look after. By then, however, the nature
of her work had changed somewhat in consequence of a
meeting with Miss Estelle Stead, daughter of the famous
journalist, W. T. Stead (who drowned in the *Titanic* in 1912),
and leader of the 'Stead Borderland Library', regarded as one
of the important centres of the Spiritualist movement in
London, and where Minesta went several times a week. Her
task now was mainly to help and convince recently bereaved
people of survival. Many of these were torn by grief and
sometimes so embittered that it required a great effort to raise
them out of despair.

The Stead Library was situated in Smith Square, Westminster, and a few hundred yards away in Victoria Street, facing the Abbey, was Sir Arthur Conan Doyle's 'Psychic Bookshop', which he had opened some years before—aiming not only to supply the general public but animated by the hope that clergy from the Abbey might drop in to purchase psychic books. It is doubtful if any ever did. The bookshop, which was in the charge of his daughter Mary, must have involved Sir Arthur in a very considerable loss for several years. It was not long before such near-neighbours as the Stead Library and the Psychic Bookshop—and also Minesta and Miss Mary Conan Doyle—became acquainted. A friendship soon sprang up between the two, resulting in an invitation to Minesta from Sir Arthur and Lady Conan Doyle to visit them at their home near Crowborough in Sussex. Sir Arthur, on hearing about Minesta's work for Spiritualism, and about White Eagle (and especially the latter) was deeply anxious to meet Minesta.

This happened during the summer of 1930 when Sir Arthur was a very sick man. A weekend visit was arranged, and then suddenly cancelled because a turn for the worse came. Soon followed the news of Sir Arthur's passing—a great shock—for he seemed a very part of the Britain of those days.

Every one of these seemingly trivial details about Minesta and Sir Arthur have their significance, for they denote a linking, a drawing together of the two even before his passing. They never met; but they had a community of interests, a likeness of purpose at that time. To the world and to themselves they were as strangers; and yet their lives were interwoven even then by ties destined to draw them closer in the near future.

CHAPTER IV

THE HERMIT OF BAGNAIA

THE third tributary story which merges into the main current of events is that of the hermit of Bagnaia—a small town near Viterbo, about sixty miles north of Rome. This account is translated from the *Bulletin des Polaires* for 9th June, 1930.*

'Following many enquiries as to the circumstances which surrounded the transmission of the Oracle de Force Astrale by Father Julian to his successor, we have much pleasure in citing briefly where and how this moving episode took place:

'In 1908 a young man found himself during his vacation at Bagnaia, a pleasant country town of the Viterbo area in the neighbourhood of Rome.

'No sooner had he arrived than his attention was drawn to an old man wearing the coarse monkish habit. Tall, ascetic, sunburnt, his eyes deep set, he passed along the streets as though in a dream.

'The lad made enquiries from the country folk. Was this man a godly hermit? No. After listening to what was said, he gathered that this individual, who was called Father Julian, was considered by the dwellers in this little town as one who could cast magical spells—a sorcerer. Although nothing

---

Le Bulletin des Polaires was published from 9th May, 1930, onwards by the 'Groupe des Polaires' during their existence in Paris (their headquarters being for several years at 36 Avenue Junot, 18e). For additional details see the book published earlier: ASIA MYSTERIOSA: *L'Oracle de Force Astrale comme moyen de communication avec les 'Petites Lumières d'Orient'*, par Zam Bhotiva (Paris, Dorban-Ainé, 1929).

definite in the way of accusation could be brought against him the "presumptions" seemed grave—it would be as well, they said, to beware of this strange person, who lived as a wild man of the woods in an old ruined hut and fed on herbs and fruits; who was scorned by all good Christians and was, moreover, one who had never been seen to cross the threshold of the House of God. Things had come to such a pitch that finally it had been pointed out to him, and not too politely, that it might be as well if he did not loiter in passing by the vines or cornfields, for very potent spells, capable of drying up the ripe grapes or of destroying the cattle by a mysterious disease, can be quickly cast.

'In spite of these tales of magical charms and evil spells the young man was greatly drawn to the recluse, by a strange sympathy, and one day he decided to visit him in his hut. He was received as one who had been expected for a long time. The lad offered money ... clothing ... a more suitable shelter. The hermit refused in his curiously deep and slightly guttural voice (a voice, nevertheless, full of great sweetness); he intimated that he found all he required in the woods around him; the herbs and fruits necessary to him as food; the running streams to drink from. Besides, he must stay where he was even in spite of the hostility of those around him, until the day came for him to set out on a long, very long, journey.

'The next day the young man paid another visit with eagerness; and never a day passed without a meeting— during which the hermit would speak of goodness, of true love, and of brotherhood. Truly, this young Roman boy, firmly attached though he was to the things of the world, saw in the recluse an initiate and partly understood the gentle foolishness of his self-imposed isolation—his way of life— hard and painful though it appeared outwardly, as well as his firm resolve to refuse all outside aid.

'The boy was moved by such sympathy and profound pity for the recluse, so good and of such sweetness of nature, that he felt it an almost sacred duty to continue his daily pilgrimage to him.

'One day on going up the path to the hermit's dwelling, he found Father Julian lying unconscious on the road, badly wounded in the knee. He dressed the deep wound as well as he was able, and then assisted the old man to re-enter his hut. The next day he found the hermit up and about; three days later the wound was completely healed.

'What mysterious herbs had been the means of obtaining this complete restoration to health? The young man did not dare to inquire. Many a time the recluse, when questioned somewhat indiscreetly by his young friend, would remain silent, lost in a dream, the reflection of which shone through his large, dark, far-seeing eyes.

'The link which united the two men grew stronger and stronger. The visits to the hermit's cell became more frequent, the conversations between them of greater length and of a more intimate nature. The old man spoke meaningfully of pain and sacrifice to the younger man whose eyes were still fixed on the dreams and illusions of life. At length the end of the holidays was at hand. With a saddened heart the youth made his way for the last time to the hermit's abode. It will never be known what the recluse murmured "from mouth to ear" to him whom he called for the first time his "son". We can only say that at the moment of leave-taking, he handed to him some leaves of paper yellowed by the passage of time. These were "a small fragment from the Book of the Science of Life and of Death".

'The recipient of these mysterious pages will remember to the end of his days the last words spoken to him by the Sage: "Should you at any time require help or counsel you have only to follow the instructions which are contained in this old manuscript—*you will receive your reply*. It may even occur that one day *I myself will reply to you*. But remember never to divulge to anyone in the world what is written on these pages, for in so doing you run the risk for yourself, as well as for the one who obtains the knowledge, of madness or death."

'The pages contained an arithmetical system which

permitted an answer to whatever question was formulated. The youth, who had little or no inclination to dive into occult mysteries, put away the manuscript in a place of safety, without even having had sufficient curiosity to consult the marvellous Oracle.

'It was not until two years later that the young man, who was then in great distress of mind, made use of the strange power which had been confided to him by Father Julian. He consulted the manuscript. It was necessary first to dwell very strongly upon one's wish, to write it down and to supply the surname and Christian name of the one making the enquiry and also the names of his mother. He formulated his question and then spent long hours in the prescribed arithmetical calculations.

'The reply obtained showed itself to be astonishingly correct and to contain great wisdom.

'Amazed at this result the custodian of the Oracle some time later spoke to a group of his friends, who were students of the esoteric, of this strange method of obtaining information. Thus the groups came into being. In 1923 Father Julian kept his promise. He replied himself.

'In April, 1930, by means of the Oracle de Force Astrale he sent his last message in the flesh "to his well-beloved sons".

'And now the Lord Buddha has opened to him the Path of Light.'

Here the account of how the Oracle de Force Astrale came to be used comes to an end. A complete outline of how it worked cannot now be given. This no-one knows. The system was communicated, fulfilled its appointed purpose, and has now ceased. It could only be operated apparently by someone possessing the requisite psychic or soul vibration, which perhaps one in ten thousand might have, the youth being one of these; doubtless for this reason he was brought to Father Julian. This is why what follows must seem somewhat sketchy and inadequate. What is quite certain is that the Oracle worked and that its message had a cogency and power which made it unique.

It was operated, as has been said, by arithmetical calculation. So does the ancient science of astrology operate, although the intuition of the astrologer plays its part. No doubt the intuition of the operator of the Force Astrale was equally important when he was sending or receiving messages.

God, it is said, geometrizes, for He is the great Geometrician of the Universe. In other words, the universe of God's creation could be reduced to a geometrical or mathematical formula were there any mathematicians capable enough! In a like manner man's own inventions have to be reduced to formulae before they can be constructed. Much the same principle lay behind the Force Astrale.

For instance, any person asking a question through it had to think out the question very clearly and write it down in the fewest possible words. He had also to supply his full name and date of birth, together with his mother's maiden name and her date of birth. The question had then to be translated into Italian, because the Force Astrale operated only in that language. The first task of the operator (now a grown man, and known to his intimates as the 'Mage' or magician) was to turn each letter of the words of the question, together with the names of the questioner and his mother, into arithmetical figures.

He then, by intricate calculations and by use of his own psychic power, 'sent out' this question and obtained an answer to it, the latter coming in as a mass of figures meaning nothing to the Mage until translated back into letters and so into words. From a short question a long answer might come, and vice versa. Sometimes even a long course of instruction or advice would come through. It was claimed that the mind of the operator in no way influenced or affected the quality of the message as might the subconscious mind of a medium. That is as may be. What is certain is that the instructions were accepted without question.

It can be imagined how dumbfounded was the young man at this discovery and how eager he and a friend were to communicate again with Father Julian. What they wanted to know now was the why and wherefore of the secret and why it had been entrusted to them in particular. Many hours were spent in communication, which must, by reason of the procedure entailed, have necessarily been slow and laborious.

A later message through the Force Astrale bade the two men go to Paris and there establish a group which should be called the Polaire Brotherhood. They arrived—strangers in a strange city, and almost penniless. Mysteriously, people introduced themselves and became friends. Money was supplied, and soon the Brotherhood occupied handsome premises in the Avenue Junot on the western slopes of Montmartre. The *Bulletin des Polaires*, a monthly magazine, ultimately reached a circulation of ten thousand copies among adherents of the Polaire Brotherhood.

All this was happening, it should be noted, some few years after the first 'war which was to end war'. At that time the nations were too busy putting their world together again to bother themselves much over the possibility of war in the future. Armed forces were everywhere being disbanded. It is therefore disconcerting to find that the early messages communicated through the Force Astrale referred to the 'Year of Fire' that was surely coming on the world (if it did not change its ways), and which would involve an era of destruction and privation far exceeding that just experienced. But after these particular communications no more came from Father Julian, who, having as it were established relations, disappeared.

Thereafter the communicator was someone carrying greater weight and authority, who became known as the Chevalier Rose-Croix, the Chevalier Sage or the Wise Knight (he has been later identified as the Master 'R' who, it is believed, was at another time the brother Francis Bacon). The Force Astrale had been entrusted to the young man by way of preparation against the coming of the Year of Fire. Henceforward the Wise Knight was to be leader; the Force Astrale his means of communication.

A word about the 'Masters'. Long ago, an occult tradition tells us, the area of land and sea around the North Pole was not only habitable but possessed of a warm and genial climate. It was referred to by the Greeks as the hyperborean region, where there had once dwelt advanced men (and, of course, women) known as Masters; that is, having become masters over themselves—over their human weaknesses—they were no longer subject to the limitations of time or space as men know them. They were masters of time, and over age, illness and death. While they could live as man lives on the physical plane, they could also lay aside their physical bodies (leaving them in a profound slumber or trance, as do some of the Indian mystics today), and function in unseen worlds such as the after-death states. Long, long ago when the earth was young and innocent they ruled it by loving kindness.

Theirs was the golden age to which tales such as the Garden of Eden story refer. But then, the stories go, some interstellar convulsion shifted the earth on its axis, and a tide of ice and snow followed, which slowly enveloped the polar regions; and coincident with this, the golden age chilled and hardened into one of materialism, before whose advance the Sages retreated to the mountains of the Far East, where in secluded fastnesses they are established to this day, no longer mingling with the world of men, unable to endure man's present vibrations.

Tidings of these Masters occasionally reach the peoples of the East, most of whom have heard about and believe in them. Some years ago the writer met a professor from one of the Indian universities visiting Britain, and in conversation heard him tell of his meeting with a Master. When asked what he was like, the professor simply answered, 'He is all love.'★

In these words we have the keynote of a Master or initiate. Since they no longer mingle physically with men, their love is now expressed by a projection of light, which is a ray of love; for love takes the form of light when sent out to mankind— and also to certain chosen and responsible individuals, who may or may not be aware of their contact with a Master. By this power of projection which they possess they are able to inspire, to strengthen, to raise such people (if they be willing) but never

★This story is told at greater length in Grace Cooke's THE SHINING PRESENCE, pp. 28–29.

to influence unduly or override the freewill choice and volition of any human soul.

The symbol of the Polar Star given to the Polaires was therefore an ancient symbol descended from hyperborean times, countless centuries ago, and still possessing some of its ancient power. The Oracle de Force Astrale may date back as long. So also might the method and organization of the Polaire Brotherhood itself be modelled on one far in the past. In any case instructions were given how to make use of the methods of projection employed by the Masters—but with a difference: for the Brotherhood groups must perforce work on a human ray or wavelength instead of the purer ray of the initiates. Thus, when at its meetings, the Brotherhood received the ray of the Masters it was able to 'tune down' the latter and project it forth again on another wavelength likely to be efficacious with more worldly men and women. We have to recognize that any group of some sixty people such as this, who were animated by one purpose, who had been trained over the years, who were unified and harmonized by methods which enhanced that purpose and fortified by greater powers behind, could not be without influence in the land.

We have to bear in mind that well before the late 1920s the Sages never doubted the coming of a second world war. They knew also something of its extent and horrors. Their plans to help must have been made at least as long ago as the boy's meeting with Father Julian, which resulted in knowledge of the Force Astrale being given to the boy.

Before the reason for the formation of a Polaire Brotherhood can be realized we have to recognize the real nature of war. Most people think it is primarily waged with armies, navies, or in the air; with bombs, guns and every devilish device man can exploit. But any armed conflict is but an effect resulting from some underlying causes which must first possess men's minds and hearts and rule their emotions. When over a term of years men's minds are inflamed, their fears fomented, their distrust and presently hatred of other nations aggravated, the whole condition one day reaches boiling point and expresses itself in conflict between armies. This is but a plain sequence of cause and effect.

War really originates, it is here suggested, in men's minds and souls years before its actual outbreak. Maybe this reveals the reason not only why the Masters were sure that war was coming—since they have power to read the collective consciousness or soul of the nations—but also why they formed a brotherhood trained to work on that same consciousness.

They did not promise at any time that the war would be averted. The karma of the world by then had almost ensured its coming. They said only that the margin between victory and defeat for the forces of the light might be so narrow that the work of the brotherhood could turn the scale.★

The Polaires were, as has been said, engaged in 'good works', which differed widely from the 'good works' of orthodoxy. They did not pray aloud as at a prayer meeting. They did not make great mental efforts to project the light; theirs was rather a relaxing, an opening of themselves to receive the Master's ray so that it might flow through them. To whom or what was the ray redirected? To help someone in trouble occasionally, but mostly to groups or communities or nations threatened or smitten by misfortune or catastrophe in any part of the world. Or the Brotherhood projection might be directed to individuals or to groups of people working for peace, for freedom, or for any other good cause. They worked also for lost souls after death. The tasks which engaged the Brotherhood were of this nature; while in their daily round or common task the individual brothers tried to fulfil their obligation to be helpful to their fellows.

Part of the Polaire 'charge' or 'obligation' was that the Polaires must strive to remove the *mad fear of death which haunts the brain of man*—mark, the *brain* of man; perhaps his heart knows better? This brings us to the year 1930 when news of

★White Eagle and other spirit guides actually did appear to say that war would be averted. With hindsight, it feels that this was said in the knowledge that the thought element was so strong it actually *could* turn the tide in favour of peace, if the fear element were reduced. For further comment see THE STORY OF THE WHITE EAGLE LODGE, pp. 13–14.

Sir Arthur Conan Doyle's death reached France. Towards the end of 1930 a long message was received through the Force Astrale from the Wise Knight relating to it. Sir Arthur, the message said, had communicated with the Sages, seeking their aid. Since his arrival in the spirit land he had found that much of what he had previously thought true about Spiritualism (of which movement he had been the leader) and of the conditions of the next life needed revision. He desired to correct any errors which he had sponsored. At the moment he was not in a position to do this, as certain ties still held his soul to earth. His passionate desire was to make these corrections. This he could not do alone. Such was the importance of his message that everything must be done to ensure its accurate reception. This could not be done through the Force Astrale. A certain member of the Brotherhood was therefore directed to proceed to England and to get in touch with Lady Conan Doyle, who would then introduce him to the medium through whom the Wise Knight desired the message to come. This medium, it was stated, had been long chosen and trained for this particular task. When he met her the Polaire brother would recognize her at once. Let there be no delay.

CHAPTER V

THE MESSENGER FROM FRANCE

'To give religion a foundation of rock instead of quicksand, to remove the legitimate doubts of earnest minds, to make the invisible forces, with their moral sanctions, a real thing, instead of mere words upon our lips, and, incidentally, to reassure the human race as to the future which awaits it, and to broaden its appreciation of the possibilities of the present life, surely no more glorious message was ever heralded to mankind.'

Arthur Conan Doyle, *The Wanderings of a Spiritualist*

THESE lines are written on 27th January 1956. Twenty-five years ago, again on 27th January, a group consisting of Lady Conan Doyle, her family and three friends, a Monsieur Zam Bhotiva from Paris, Minesta and her husband, met at the Stead Library in Smith Square, Westminster. Whether there is any significance in the fact that this account is being written on the same date in January depends on how far *numbers* influence human lives. For some people become aware that their lives react to numbers in a strange way. For instance, things mostly seem to happen to them on certain days of the week or month. We receive a number at birth—our date and year—and we vibrate to it; each of us being a unit in the mathematical, or geometrical, scheme of the universe.

The Force Astrale, for example, was intimately concerned with numbers and depended on arithmetical calculations for its efficacy.* Indeed, it operated on a three–six–nine vibration (nine being thought to be the number of the initiate). The six-

---

*For a review and illustration of the workings of the Oracle, see chapter XII.

pointed star given to the Polaires as their symbol was of course a *six* vibration. This is why the Brotherhood, aware that it must conform to the three–six–nine vibration for its best work, usually chose a three–six–nine day of the month and hour of the day for its principal activities, and at first adopted a diagram depicting the figures 'three–six–nine' as an emblem for the heading of the *Bulletin des Polaires*.

Minesta was born on the ninth day of the sixth month, and she was also a ninth child. Here again we have the three–six–nine vibration evident in her life. Sir Arthur Conan Doyle was born on 22nd May: May is the fifth month of the year; the two twos of the 22nd added together make four, and the four coupled with five make nine, so here the three–six–nine vibration becomes evident again. It is perhaps worth mentioning that the compiler and editor of this book [that is, Ivan Cooke] was also born on 22nd May, because this three hundred and sixty-five to one chance might have significance. Finally, we note that all the Conan Doyle work and messages began on the 27th day of the month, which is a day of three times three, making nine, and three times nine making twenty-seven.

The first message from Sir Arthur—whom we will call 'ACD' henceforth for the sake of brevity—came on 27th January 1931, and initiated a long series of messages in which he set forth a full restatement of Spiritualism; making it clear once and for all that death and survival (and occasional communication between the worlds) can be regarded as a normal and natural experience, as much part of human life as the love between man and woman or the birth of a child. Those who read his message intelligently and receptively should lose the fear of death.

Within a few days of ACD's passing, the Spiritualists held a memorial service at the Albert Hall to commemorate their leader. Many hundreds were turned away. It would be interesting to know how many of the thousands gathered there to demonstrate their very genuine grief and their reverence for his service to their cause had been convinced of survival by his own mighty effort for Spiritualism over the years. They might well have numbered half of those present, so powerful had been ACD's advocacy for Spiritualism. About this time many of the leaders of Spiritualism met to discuss proposals designed to commemorate ACD's work for the movement. A million shilling fund was one of these, and nobody saw a limit to what might be accomplished. We shall return to what actually *was* accomplished later.

Ten days after ACD's passing Minesta paid her first visit to his home in Crowborough, where she was welcomed by Lady Conan Doyle and the family. Shortly after a death the soul of the person concerned can be readily seen by a sensitive or psychic. This was the case with ACD, who joined his family in their welcome to Minesta, but was seen by her alone. ACD spoke to all of them that night through Minesta, not yet himself controlling the medium, but with White Eagle acting as his spokesman. The message was both intimate and detailed. A family reunion took place so strong that none present could doubt or question it.

A stranger in these matters may want to know how a 'dead' man can speak to his family. The process is natural enough; but it can only become possible through a close cooperation between medium and guide, which comes only after long training and constant practice. It should be explained that communication between White Eagle and his medium takes two forms: either he may draw very close and bring her under a powerful ray of thought or inspiration, when she will speak the message he desires to send through; or he may bring her under his control, so that she falls into a state resembling the natural sleep of a child. This is by far the stronger, however, being a trance-state so deep that she has no knowledge of what is said while it lasts and no recollection afterwards. It is then that White Eagle himself speaks through her. Her voice changes, deepening in tone; and she speaks with a slight accent, a changed delivery and choice of words. Moreover, the mind and personality of the speaker is strongly marked and there is even a facial change, so complete is the fade-out of the personality of Minesta.

Minesta on the platform at Pembroke Hall, first home of the White Eagle Lodge in Kensington, London, during the period soon after the messages in this book were given.

The awakening out of this trance-state is as natural as the awakening from sleep. Minesta normally remembers nothing of what has happened. If she shortly afterwards reads a record of what was said through her lips a faint memory stirs, much like the recollection of a dream during waking hours; and that is all.

On some occasions White Eagle stands aside for someone other than himself to speak through his medium; but more usually he passes the messages on himself. White Eagle thus played a major part in the transmission of the earlier messages from ACD to his family; but this is no less convincing because not only the personal message but some of his mannerisms, habitual terms of expression and so forth, would come through from the communicator. This was the more cogent proof, since Minesta had not met ACD during his lifetime.

As a result a prolonged correspondence followed at irregular

*These are the letters which are sadly now lost, not those quoted in the introductory chapter.

intervals between Minesta and Lady Conan Doyle. Sir Arthur evidently meant to keep an eye on the happenings at his home, for many a word of advice or caution came through with his messages of affection to the family. Lady Conan Doyle's letters show how well these were understood and appreciated.*

Nevertheless, even at this early stage there was an element of dissatisfaction in Minesta's mind. The messages themselves, she felt, despite their detailed precision, had not the drive and force which might be expected of someone like ACD. Probably this passed unnoticed by everyone but Minesta herself. Meanwhile, a representative committee of Spiritualists was meeting to discuss the Memorial, and after weeks of debate, during which public enthusiasm cooled, more or less reached a deadlock.

About this time, Minesta spent a few days at the Conan Doyle family 'cottage' at Bignell Wood in the New Forest; and during her visit ACD spoke with some vigour about the Memorial, saying it was necessary to get down to business. He then named those whom he wished to serve on the Memorial Committee, the most notable, so far as this book is concerned, being Mr W. R. Bradbrook of Ipswich, who became Honorary Secretary. Despite the latter's enthusiasm and drive many difficulties held up progress. The appeal was not launched until the Armistice Day of 1930, when a copy lay on every seat at the Spiritualist Service of Remembrance at the Albert Hall— where ACD had dragged himself a year before to deliver what was almost his last message to the public.

What was the result? Appeals were inserted in twenty-six psychic journals in many countries. Forty thousand copies of the appeal were distributed in magazines to which ACD had been a frequent contributor. Some hundreds of letters were posted to 'key' persons, asking for support, and the several hundred Spiritualist churches in Britain were approached. Sixteen months later the net result stood at about two thousand pounds, a sum which included an anonymous gift of several hundred pounds. This meant that funds were insufficient to attempt to carry out the aims set forth in the appeal, and to all

* According to Mr John Dickson Carr's LIFE OF SIR ARTHUR CONAN DOYLE the total expended was about £250,000 [note in 1956 edition].

intents and purposes it had already failed. It must be remembered, of course, that not only had enthusiasm cooled through the delay between ACD's passing and the launching of the appeal, but that many people had been hit by the world slump of that year. But though these factors may account for the meagre response, most people in Spiritualism felt sorrowful and a little ashamed, especially when it was recalled that Sir Arthur had spent huge sums to forward the cause.*

A strange feature of some mediumship is a capacity to see into the future. In Minesta's case, this power seems to serve the purpose of preparing her mind, or her receptivity, for whatever may be coming her way. A few examples will serve to illustrate both this power and its purpose. They are taken from the book, THY KINGDOM COME, where both the time and the names of those present to corroborate all that happened are given. Sometimes the words quoted were spoken by White Eagle, sometimes by Minesta herself. Thus, on the morning of the day of ACD's passing a friend of Mary Conan Doyle's was told 'that the foundations of the bookshop were crumbling' (this meant, of course, the Psychic Bookshop at Westminster). As she had not heard how serious was ACD's illness until she saw the posters announcing his death a few hours later this friend did not realize what was meant. It might almost be said that at this time the foundations of Spiritualism itself were crumbling, so grave a blow did ACD's death prove to the movement; so sad a decline had followed his loss.

Again, Minesta's mind was carefully prepared before the coming of the messenger from France. She was also informed about the existence of the Sages in the Far East, usually referred to by White Eagle as the brotherhood. This was a message given by White Eagle on 7th October 1930, Mr Bradbrook acting as recorder:

'Again I impress you that the underlying principle upon which the work of the Memorial must rest is that this brother's name (that of ACD) must be used, not for the furtherance of a personality but, as his life was spent, for the establishment of truth and justice. Thus will his name, after the death of his body, bring to the brothers the power they need to build on earth a temple of the spirit. So much seems to centre around a name, but that is but a means to an end. He, too, throws himself into this work with all joy and zest, because he has been shown the future—of an earth reborn, of truth set free.

'And so the great White Brotherhood is at work. You will learn, brothers, that there are those in other parts of the earth to whom the organization of the White Brotherhood has reached. *You will come into contact with another society in France, and you will find great support from there.*'

These words were spoken nearly four months before Minesta encountered the messenger on the 27th day of January, 1931—January also being a significant month, in that the forces of death or negation end with the old year, and the forces of life or creation arise with the new; so that it was on the 'Master's' day of that New Year that this work began—for the vibration nine–nine–nine is usually considered that of a Master.

On 9th January 1931, White Eagle said to a group of four friends: 'I am directed to tell you again that the helper is near.'

About ten days later Minesta was asked to arrange for a special meeting on behalf of Lady Conan Doyle and her family, together with a Monsieur Zam Bhotiva, who had come from Paris with the sole object of getting in touch with Sir Arthur. As has been said, their meeting was held on 27th January at the Stead Library in Westminster. Conditions were not as good as might have been hoped. There was a certain strain, due possibly to the large number of people present, or possibly to the great power which seemed to be focused on the group. Minesta entered, crossed the room and seated herself. At once M Bhotiva rose and crossed over to her. (Neither had met before.) He said: 'Yes, I know you. We have worked together long, long ago—that was in former lives in ancient Egypt. See—I have brought you this little star. It has been sent to you by the wise ones for you to wear.' He pinned it onto her dress, made a gesture of blessing and protection, and returned to his seat.

CHAPTER VI

THE 'NINE–NINE–NINE' DAY
AND ITS OUTCOME

'The work was there, and the work was to be done. If not me, then someone with greater powers. My own personal powers were little enough, but when immortal forces are behind you, your real personality counts for nothing.'

Arthur Conan Doyle, *Our American Adventure*

AT this stage it will be of interest to know what manner of man this messenger was. He is not easy to describe. Someone who once met him by appointment at a London tube station during the rush hour said that he stood out among the crowds like 'an eagle among pigeons'. This is true, but to say why is not so easy; he was, perhaps, slightly under average height, about forty years old, with a mass of hair so dark as to be black, dark penetrating eyes, strongly-marked features which when he was touched could soften to an almost Christlike expression; yet when he was stirred to anger he looked formidable indeed. His English was of the sketchiest, so that it needed some concentration to follow him. Yet such was the power of the man that he seemed to drive home his meaning—and that meaning was always something very well worth listening to.

In all he was a man of mystery, an Italian by birth, and had been, with the 'Mage', one of the founders of the Polaires. His love and respect for his Chief, the Knight of the Rose Cross in the East, was profound, and he lived to further his Chief's cause and that of the Polaires. He accorded to White Eagle almost a like respect, seeming to recognize early a wisdom in him and power of love, which in later years have been made manifest to a great number of people. Monsieur Bhotiva paid many visits to this country during the Conan Doyle work, often crossing from France and arriving in London without notice by the customary letter or telegram. Minesta, however, was nearly always aware when he had reached this country, saying that she could even 'smell' the particular brand of cigarette he smoked.

What brought him over to Britain in the first place? Here we must turn to a message from their Master which appeared in the Polaire *Bulletin*:

'Brother Arthur Conan Doyle has appeared to us (to the "Wise Ones"), and among the many interesting things he communicated, he expressed the wish to interest himself in the group Polaire. He has promised his friends to give proofs and manifestations of the afterlife. Today he let us know, through the medium of the "Wise Knight" (the Chevalier Rose-Croix), that he will hold to his promises.

'The spirit of Sir Arthur waits in his beautiful Scotland for the meeting of the red and violet rays, which will enable him to reveal himself and to speak to his friends. We advise those who will participate to use during the seance a dark red light, in order to aid Sir Arthur. The medium must carry a six-pointed star to give her the necessary strength.'

When Minesta read this she naturally asked for an explanation. His own particular mission, Bhotiva then said, was to help Sir Arthur to give his message and his proof of identity to the world. Before Sir Arthur could speak with knowledge and authority he must be shown, or even traverse, a wide range of the heavenly kingdom. When the average man dies his soul is held within the astral world for a long time, a world which is still close to this world, and is still 'material' although composed of a finer matter than this.

The soul of ACD differed from most souls because it had incarnated under certain 'earth' rays of great power and significance. No common destiny lay before such a soul once it was able to assert itself. The 'gripping' power of those rays had remained unbroken by his death; that was why it was necessary, according to instructions received from the Sages, for Minesta and Sir Arthur's family to go to Edinburgh (where ACD was born), to hold there a special meeting on 22nd May, the day of his birth. By this means, in conjunction with the red and the violet rays—which were the rays corresponding with the time of his birth, and the place of his birth—the soul of ACD could be set free from its astral limitations.

M Bhotiva continued,

'We know Sir Arthur in France, he loved our country and its people. So too we know what manner of man he is. The Polaires call him the "Great Brother", our great brother. Nevertheless, no man, however great, however strong, however good, can escape his destiny. Remember, not even Christ could escape His cross.'

Minesta pondered these matters for a long time afterwards, as well as the fact that Bhotiva had said that Sir Arthur earnestly desired to restate the case for Spiritualism; that he wanted to correct many of the beliefs to which he had formerly subscribed, in the light of what he had himself experienced after his passing; and began to realize that her contact with his family, with the Polaires and their messenger, with the Wise Knight (the Chevalier Rose-Croix) on the inner planes, was but the preliminary of a major work to come.

It must be made clear that these talks with Zam Bhotiva *followed* the meeting held at the Stead Library on 27th January when he and Minesta first met.

The group waited until the white light in the small chapel was switched off, the ruby light switched on. The hour which followed stands out and is not lightly to be forgotten. By my side sat the medium, on my left was Miss Estelle Stead; the red glow fell on the earnest and reverent faces around the circle as the guide White Eagle rose. Few can realize without sight or hearing the wonderful transformation and dignity which comes upon his medium, the deep measured voice with which White Eagle speaks, his tenderness and humanity.

M Bhotiva's account of what followed, as recorded in the

Polaire *Bulletin*, reads:

'The meeting was strictly private. The medium was a Mrs Grace Cooke, well known to English Spiritualists. She wore a silver star, symbol of our fraternity, and the room was lit by a deep red light.

'The medium went into a deep trance almost immediately. She rose, crossed the room, and in a masculine voice recognized by several present as that of her guide, White Eagle, she began a long conversation with Lady Conan Doyle and her sons, Sir Arthur speaking through the mediumship of White Eagle. (On such occasions the guide speaks on behalf of some other spirit, he being the more practised control.) We shall not repeat the long conversation, which was strictly personal. After nearly an hour, however, the medium rose to search for someone else there present. With closed eyes and a firm step she approached Zam Bhotiva (Z.B. writes of himself in the third person) saying, "There is a gentleman here whom I have not known during earth life, but with whom I am now linked in view of a common work."

'The medium stopped at last in front of our brother, held out her hand, and a joyful, manly "I am glad to meet you!" rang through the small room. A long and low-pitched conversation then took place between the "dead" and the "living". Conan Doyle made himself known to Zam Bhotiva as "Brother", and then, speaking again to those present, spoke of the Polaires as "a group destined to help in the moulding of the future of the world.... For the times are near." He then said, turning towards Zam Bhotiva, "I must speak with you alone in six days. I have some important communications for you; the work, to which I can set no limit, begins."

'It was thus that a man whom the world calls "dead" made an appointment with Zam Bhotiva.'

When Minesta returned home on that night she felt somewhat disturbed on account of the unusual nature of what had happened. She then received the following instruction from White Eagle: 'This man (Zam Bhotiva) has an important part to play. He is our servant. No harm will come if you give yourself to our work. Great effects will result from the contact, and these will be widely felt and will shatter the doubts of the many who cannot believe in the life of the spirit.

'There are many conflicting influences ... this man is of good faith and will not harm you.... *This messenger is sent because of instruction from Tibet, and [he who sent the message] knows of you from there.*'

The following account of the second meeting with the messenger six days later is again from the Polaire *Bulletin*. The group consisted of four people.

'The guide of the medium again takes control and the same manly voice issues from his lips. The room is lighted with a deep red light, and the medium wears the six-pointed star.

'*White Eagle*: "I speak now of 'Nobleheart', as I have called him before, known to you as Arthur Conan Doyle. He recognizes now that his passing on was for a far greater purpose than the ordinary mind can realize. He is to be used to bring to the earth fresh truth and light. He was brought into contact with his brother in Paris (Z.B.) ... so that he might find a medium through whom Nobleheart could speak.... Conan Doyle holds out his hand to you (to Z.B.) in brotherly love. He is ready to help your Brotherhood. His name is a power—if it be a power for good take and use it for good."'

The report goes on: 'Another entity [communicator] takes the place of White Eagle. The voice changes [it would appear that Z.B. now believed the speaker to be no other than the Chevalier Sage, but hesitates to say so directly]. "Conan Doyle and the Wise Knight in harmony—in harmony and brotherly love. Conan Doyle is a great spirit now released from flesh to serve in all spheres of life. Keep from the personality if you would contact spirit. Only in the impersonal spiritual power can you receive divine inspiration for your work. The personal must become divine.

"'The star rises in the East—it is the sign of the Polaire, the sign of the two triangles!'"

The message continued with details about the 'years of fire' or disasters then drawing near to mankind, coupled with an appeal for friendship between France and Britain for 'the link is now made'.

Z.B.'s account continues: 'We do not comment on these seances. The Polaires hold no dogmas, but have a deep respect for all the faiths and beliefs of man. We have summarized and have reported as faithfully as possible the first two meetings which took place, and can only say that according to the communications of the "Wise Ones" received through the Oracle de Force Astrale, Sir Arthur spoke to us through the mediumship of White Eagle.

'With regard to these two meetings it must be distinctly understood that neither the medium nor those present [except Z.B. himself, of course] knew anything about the Polaire organization, nor of what it sought in London. We went to London to obtain certain definite evidence, and employed every safeguard to guarantee that evidence. Moreover, the Wise Ones informed us that at the end of our second seance the medium would give us direct proof of being in communication with our Chiefs. When she awoke from trance she told M Bhotiva that she saw a lofty mountain and a man with a luminous dark face and great dark eyes who held out to her a six-pointed star. Here was the proof for which we waited.'

Here ends the Polaire *Bulletin* account of what must have been a notable display of knowledge on the part of White Eagle, such knowledge being entirely unknown to the medium and her husband, who had acted as recorder during the two meetings.

Another factor which increased the bewilderment of these two was that, unknown to themselves, they were being brought under the ray or projection of a special Polaire group in Paris which had been detailed to help ACD in his mission. This group sat for months at regular intervals to project a ray illuminating both Sir Arthur and his medium.

It must always be understood that in their work the Polaires were forbidden by their Chiefs to constrain or overrule the freewill of any man. They must not attempt to dominate, impose or influence anyone to adopt or follow any particular line of conduct, however admirable it might seem to other people. To illumine a soul—for this Brotherhood was working with its own soul power and not with minds or bodies—and thereby to help it to recognize and follow the light within itself was to practise a white magic; to attempt in any way to overrule the volition of that soul was a form of black magic bearing terrible penalties in this life and the next. No pains were spared to make this crystal clear to every Polaire. May it be as plainly expressed in this book.

Only the recipients of this ray of illumination are in a position to testify to its reality and power. Here Minesta and her husband were in a peculiarly favourable position, since both now wore the little Polaire star which formed a link or point of contact, and both were sensitive enough to be receptive to the Polaire ray. It is no easy matter to describe their reactions. We have all seen an actor on a darkened stage picked out by a spotlight. That is how it felt to these two. They were picked out; something was reaching them, something which was affecting them during the weeks and months that followed, and which was greatly helpful in its influence.

CHAPTER VII

'MORE BEAUTIFUL THAN ANYTHING HE HAD CONCEIVED'

AFTER a further sitting on 2nd February, it became clear that little more could be done to help this soul, which (as White Eagle said) had been 'captured' at birth by the earth rays,* until 22nd May following. The missioner was not yet ready to commence his mission. The little group of people selected to receive his message were still in process of being attuned by the ray from the Wise Knight, passed on through the projection of the Polaire group in Paris; during the many months that followed they were always conscious of that ray, linking them with affection and sympathy to ACD and with respect and devotion to the Wise Knight.

What came next? A series of preliminary sittings were held in a little upper room furnished as a chapel in the home of Minesta. Here is the message White Eagle gave at the first sitting, on 20th February 1931 (taken from THY KINGDOM COME), M Bhotiva being present. Like the others, it has been slightly abbreviated.

White Eagle speaks first:

'You are right; time must elapse before ACD is ready for his destined work. But the day is drawing near when the two forces, the rays of blue and the rays of red [those of the time and the place of the birth of ACD], will contact. You will love Arthur. He wants you to know that he waits to throw all his

---

*See below, p. 97, and for a further note see the introductory chapter (pp. 49–51).

power and service into the work which has been shown to him.... There is a very big bright star here, a six-pointed star, and a great white "House" out in the East from which a great white light is coming—coming here into this room. There is a writing I can see—I forgot to tell you about this. There will be something to be put into a book, not only in English but in French. You will have to put something into a book which has come from (was originated by?) the Wise Knight. Brighteyes knows nothing about this.' We had then, of course, no thought of a book.

Here is an extract from the next record—again taken from THY KINGDOM COME:

'So strange and wonderful have proved some of the hours spent in that little upper room that their memory sinks into one's consciousness never to be erased. As I write again the glow of the red lamp falls on the gracious presence of Lady Conan Doyle; on Denis Conan Doyle, as big a man as his father but as dark and "southern" in appearance as was his father fair and of the North.

'Beside me sits the medium, eyes closed and in deep trance, so palpably a woman to the eye; yet to look away one forgets her womanhood. Wonderful are these gestures! Is it not said that the American Indians reinforce speech with gesture so subtle that it is possible to follow with but slight knowledge of their language? Thus the guide will point his meaning as gracefully, as naturally, as bends a sapling to the summer winds.

'He prays to the "Great White Spirit", Source of all, for His blessing and His presence in our midst; then continues:

'"White Eagle greets all his friends. He is now a spokesman *only* for those who come here to serve. The number six is given; now the presence of the White One, the Wise Knight—he comes to bring a message. He greets you, my son (M Bhotiva); you know him; he brings brother Nobleheart. He would have White Eagle say to those here who love the beautiful soul and personality of ACD—he would have them know that he comes to serve both him and you, dear friends. I am the servant of the Wise Knight.

"'He would have you know that ACD is greater than even you have realized, and has yet a noble mission to perform. You must know more concerning his exact position in the spiritual realms. Do realize that we, too, have a true love and devotion to him.

"'He has a mission more vital than anything [he has] yet accomplished. He calls to you, his dear ones, to help him in his service.

"'He loves Spiritualism because his whole desire was to give comfort to the aching and the broken of life. Therefore he went across the world to bring that consolation and hope to the helpless. Released from the fleshly bondage yet still limited by certain surroundings of an astral nature, he still desires to press forward.

"'The love, deep and sincere, of ACD to his beloved family! He will have a clear channel and only a clear channel through which to work. He is determined to have no conflicting influences—his will be a power, his will be a strength! No-one, when Sir Arthur is in full possession of his powers, will doubt; no-one will doubt. For this is no mediocre man, and only through the purest channel will he manifest. This is no personal matter. It is of the Universal.

"'We repeat, there comes a great sorrow to humanity. Humanity is working up to a catastrophe. As this man realized truth before when the earth most needed help,★ so also he is being prepared and is preparing himself to give to humanity a clear statement concerning the conditions of life after death. He spent the latter part of his life teaching the people from an earthly standpoint; now he will speak from experience of the spiritual life. You will have all doubts set at rest. You will understand later why there have been difficulties and contradictions. The manifestations will come, so be prepared. Just live your days quietly in accordance with his ways as he would have you, and all will be made clear.

"'The Wise Knight, the one in the shining raiment, shows

★Conan Doyle's THE NEW REVELATION shows this to have been the time of greatest loss during and immediately after the first world war.

to us all the star with the six points. He speaks of numbers to us ... three–six–nine; he shows the red cross and the heart of a rose (the Rosicrucian symbol) and says, *Let your light so shine before men!* Oh, it is the greatest thing which has ever dawned, this light! There will come to you, brothers and sisters, the Great One himself in the body ... someday.

'"Arthur has been in close contact with those he loves—an intermingling of love. He finds now a different condition of spiritual understanding coming to him. He is reacting to wonderful revelations, far more beautiful than anything he had conceived or had been given to understand. Will you also try to grasp these *universal* conditions of the life spiritual?

'"It is so simple, not beyond the capacity of any, but rather a problem to put into words. There is to come no revelation of some seventh sphere far away, but a dawning right within man's own soul, so that it separates him not at all from his loved ones, but brings a greater link, a closer bond.

'"You must all realize the power, the love which surrounds you, the truth and the sincerity of the purpose behind. You have been told of big things. Oh, how little this expresses the shattering thing which the world will receive! And this is where the messages of Arthur will come in. The time is not yet ripe, but in due course they will sweep aside doubt."

'(*To M Bhotiva*.) "You have received a communication from your Source concerning this brother Arthur? Wait.... You know that he is linked with the Great Ones? You know that he waits to be enabled with the aid of friends to give that clear account of the life beyond death. But you must hold a special meeting for the purpose. Remember, it must be on a 'two–two' day (the 22nd day of a month) because his spirit was captured a long time ago by earth on a 'two–two' day, and on a 'two–two' it must be set free, like a bird without trammels or hampering. So far he has been able to get through only little bits, but what he gives will come through with such fulness and power that your hearts will be overjoyed."

'(*To M Bhotiva again*.) "I show you a symbol ... now I want to build on four. There are Four. I build on the Square of Four

... concerning the revelation which has been promised. This work will deal not only with the life beyond death but also with the coming of the Christ-spirit. There will follow a very definite change of thought, an upliftment in what you call on earth 'religion'; a revival of the spirit in thought and literature. The government of man will some day be directed from the spirit. The curtain which shrouds you will be rent, and light will dawn so that men and women will see so differently, so truly.

"'That is enough.

"'Reflect well. I cannot impress you sufficiently with the significance of the words spoken tonight.'"

The idea of building on a Square of Four will be familiar to all Freemasons. It so happened that all the sitters (Minesta and Silver Star included) were Masons, as was ACD. It also happened that the group finally decided that four members made the ideal number, members of the Conan Doyle family and Zam Bhotiva being only occasional visitors.

One more significant incident will bring this chapter to a close. In the month of April 1931, a photograph was published in the London *News Chronicle* of a message written on a photographic plate in Sir Arthur's own unmistakable handwriting and signed by himself.

It read:

'My dear all of you. I have greatly looked forward to this, but I cannot come in contact as I ought. There lies my difficulty. My greetings to you all. You are indeed doing God's work.   *Arthur Conan Doyle*'

This photograph was obtained through the mediumship of Mr William Hope of Crewe, a most trustworthy photographic medium, who obtained many of his results by merely holding an unopened packet of photographic plates between his hands; or else by exposing in his camera a marked plate which had been taken from a new packet by someone who had marked it and who oversaw everything which subsequently happened to that plate, so that there was no possibility of mistake or fraud. What lends this incident value is that it provides a completely

independent proof or corroboration of the message of the Force
Astrale, '*I cannot come in contact as I ought. There lies my difficulty.*'
These words substantiate the Polaire message.

CHAPTER VIII

THE NEW MAN IN A RENEWED WORLD

A LATER message through the Force Astrale somewhat altered the plan for 22nd May, as it had been found impractical to transport so large a party to Edinburgh for this one meeting.

Instead, it was arranged for it to take place at a large country house near Bletchley in Buckinghamshire, to which Minesta journeyed early on the morning of the day appointed, and spent hours of quiet preparation for and dedication to her task, among gardens and fields luxuriant with the spring. As the link with Edinburgh was still necessary it was arranged that three friends would sit in that city, tuning in with the group at Bletchley; while a large group of Polaire brothers met to project their ray from Paris direct to the group at the time fixed.

Perhaps only Minesta was aware how great an ordeal was this meeting, for she felt that everyone's hopes and expectations centred and depended on herself; on her poise, her stability and quietness of mind and spirit, her strength and courage; as indeed it did. Nor did it help when those who were to sit in the group seemed strained and over-anxious when the cars drove up, the first bringing Mrs Miller,★ Monsieur Bhotiva, and the Chief of the Polaires, Monsieur R. Odin (who had come from France for this sole purpose). Shortly afterwards came Lady Conan Doyle, her sons Adrian and Denis, and Mr Bradbrook. To the latter we owe our record of what transpired.

★The owner of the Buckinghamshire house and a medium friend of both Minesta and (latterly) Lady Conan Doyle; see the introductory chapter, p. 22.

At the appointed time the group met. Here is a slight précis of Mr Bradbrook's description setting the scene, followed by the words spoken, as in THY KINGDOM COME:

'A beautiful room—a group of graceful and delicately tinted tulips catch the glow of a crimson-shaded table lamp. A similar lamp diffuses subdued illumination upon and around the open piano.... The bright embers of a low fire complete the Rembrandtesque effect.... [A faint fragrance comes] from an indistinct mass of mauve mist which proved to be lilac blossoms.

'Silently and unobtrusively seats are filled.... Three figures seem to dominate; two are the Polaire brothers wearing the blue robes of their order, the other a figure in a dress of deep blue. The mellow notes of a dignified *Largo* fall on our ears....★ We enter the Silence.

'The figure in blue rises to her feet: *"Great White Spirit, full of faithfulness we come. May Thy power dominate all creatures; may humanity be illumined by the glory of Thy light. May these Thy servants who bow before Thee be so filled with truth that they may give light to the world. May Thy Light guide them to the path leading to Heaven. Amen."*

'White Eagle speaks:

'"White Eagle's voice holds Brighteyes, but not White Eagle's words. You know he, personally, is White Eagle. He loves you all, but the Great White Spirit shines through his individuality.

'"There are great Presences with you at this time. The Wise Knight is present. He sends the Light through White Eagle. The White Chief, Arthur Conan Doyle, is so happy to come and speak with you. He asks that every heart here may be filled with tender love. The dear one, Arthur Conan Doyle, will speak to you for himself. There are many things which perplex; but will you leave the perplexities on one side and just hear his word? White Eagle asks that you will keep silent and let the

---

★The 'Largo' mentioned would almost certainly have been the well-known movement from Handel's *Xerxes*, 'Ombra mai fu', always a very great favourite of Minesta's, whether from this moment on or before.

Brother speak. He is closer to you in spirit than you realize; closer now than when in the body, but in a different way. He is become united to your spirit. It is difficult for White Eagle to explain, for spiritual things are hard to put into words. Your hearts must interpret his message. You will know and understand what he means."

'There comes upon the medium a change, subtle, indefinable, yet a distinct change of personality. When next she speaks the voice is different, though still that of a man. The face has fallen into other lines; the gestures, formerly fluent and expressive, are now few and clumsy, as of one too reserved often to employ gesture. The very phrasing is changed, is become that of one who has some mastery over his choice of words; neither is the speech broken, nor the sentences clipped, as when the Guide speaks. There has come, too, a burr, as of a Northerner ... the voice as of one from far places, amazed, broken with wonder, but gradually gaining in power.

"'Yes ... yes ... yes.... I am coming—I am coming....Yes ... thank God! A large gathering! (A realization as of some mighty concourse of beings of brightness and splendour there present seemed to dawn.) I seem to be amongst a great company of friends ... the light is very bright; this is grand ... grand! ... Speak! Speak!"   (A murmur of voices, "We welcome you!")

"'Arthur speaks to you *again*—my wife!" (Here a portion of the record is omitted.)

"'Thank God! God bless you! I am here—I am here! You must forgive my emotion. [It is] not like me to feel emotion, but it is so marvellous to speak with you. You do not understand what this means! I have come back!... Yes, it is all coming to me. I have spoken, of course I have spoken before, but not with such power. I have passed through wonderful experiences. I want to tell you. I want to tell you *all* ... it is difficult. I have heard ... [name omitted] calling me. I have been so close, and yet there seems to have been some difficulty. Now I have been given power. I must keep calm, as I have a definite message, my friends. Will you follow what I have to say with close attention?

"'I would thank those who helped me ... I seemed to be very puzzled when I first realized where I was. My one desire was to get back—and then ... oh, there is so much to explain and tell you! I have been to my home, I have been in my home, I have seen my dear ones. What is it that has prevented me from doing all that I intended?... I see a mission. I have to give a message to you all.... It is difficult."

'The figure of the medium lay back, exhausted. For awhile it seemed as if the speaker had lost his control. With growing apprehension we watched: was this the end? Surely he would tell us something of his mission, give us some indication of his message? The minutes slipped away: five ... ten ... fifteen.... When the spirit spoke again, there was more than a timbre of White Eagle's voice in his words, as if the Guide was also upholding the medium, a timbre which gradually disappeared, as again the voice gained confidence.

"'Still here, gathering power to speak with you.... I have not left you, but there is confusion [in me] surrounding manifestation. I have learned a considerable amount concerning manifestation from the after-death side. Much that is erroneous must be cleared away [from existing beliefs]. I find there is a part of me which can manifest to a slight degree in various places and under various conditions. I see now that some of the phenomena in Spiritualism are attributable to astral projection and astral memories. Thus it is possible to pick up these astral memories which are registered in places and conditions of thought, and can be manifested to the people of earth as coming from their loved ones. There have been a variety of communications as from myself, not always projected consciously from me. You know and understand, J—? I so desire to clear up this point.*

"'I have passed through what you know as the astral life, and have now been freed from the condition which was hampering my work. To clear the astral vibrations was not altogether an

* This perhaps refers to the many communications claiming to come from ACD which the post brought almost daily to Lady Conan Doyle at that time [note in 1956 edition].

easy matter; but do not be misguided with regard to this state; it is a necessary evil. To be loosened from astral ties does not sever one from his loved ones. It frees the spirit man and allows him to enter into the full realization of his own nature.

"'You do not yet know one another as you will when you pass into the illimitable consciousness of God; and those same material ties which bind you here on earth will bind still when you leave the earth condition, until you wake to the glory of God's love.

"'In other words, we mean this: a loosening of the personal and an entering the impersonal consciousness of the creative essence called God, and in that consciousness realizing the 'perfectness' of all you love.

"'I must work—I must work. I must go forward. For it is shown to me the mission which we have to fulfil. I see so clearly now, whereas before I saw through a glass darkly; and now I see you and all men face to face. Most of all I see *myself*.

"'I thank God for the many opportunities he gave me to help my fellow men.

"'I see certain things in which I was mistaken. No man can have the entire truth. In some respects I was misled. I had before had my suspicions regarding astral memories, and I knew that a certain amount of spiritualistic phenomena was attributable to these memories. But I do not believe that all communications are of such cause; nor are they! I tell you definitely, that it is possible for the spirit … for the real man, if he has a definite mission to perform for the good of humanity … to come back and execute that mission and help forward the evolution of the race.

"'Survival is a proven fact; is unquestionable. But the world is waiting for a greater demonstration and a clearer proof of this mighty truth. Humanity must realize that communication with the astral memory and with the real man are vastly different. It is necessary for the spirit of the loved one on earth to be raised to the consciousness of spiritual reality, before he can hold true communication with his beloved in spirit.

"'So much is futile in the [Spiritualist] movement today; but the glorious truth of survival must be given to humanity in clear and perfect form.

' *"Personal responsibility and the redeeming power of love*. Personal responsibility is irrefutable. I find it is not only a man's actions that count, but man's inmost thought. The spirit world is a world of thought, an internal state rather than an external condition of life.... Thought promotes action; the actions of an individual again promote thought in his fellows. Thus we return again to the thought world. Truly it is said that *as a man sows so he shall surely reap*.

'"In the broad sense the seeds [of thought] he sows are interpreted as actions; but I find thought to be actually more powerful than action, since one of the first things that a man is faced with on his escape from earth life, is the world of his own thought.

'"Let us pass from this condition to the next. It is not always pleasant to be isolated with all the thoughts one has projected during a lifetime—but God is Love, Wisdom, Justice. I would not have it otherwise, for it has been revealed to me in a most marvellous way how the love of God manifests in the deepest heart of his children.

'"Personal responsibility and the redeeming power of love—this one great lesson I have learned, and I pass it on to you all. No man lives or dies apart from God: God ... Christ ... love—call it what you will. Earth has seen a supreme manifestation of that great power of love, in one, no, in several personalities."'

'A long pause ensued. The speaker had been under deep emotion and agitation throughout, and his power was now obviously flagging. He continued,

'"Yes ... yes ... yes. The redeeming power of love! I must conclude my message with this. Love! Not personal ... impersonal. Love for all men. I see the great need ... the Master."★

'The Guide [White Eagle himself] interposes. "I think White Eagle can help just a little, as the Brother is not able to finish.

★There is a note about this paragraph in the introductory chapter, p. 52.

White Eagle is now the spokesman. If you did not understand these things, I have to say that the Brother is so pleased that you make this meeting, so happy to get into touch with his 'Heartsease' (the character name White Eagle had bestowed some months before on Lady Conan Doyle), so happy you welcome him with so much love on his birthday. It is indeed his birth day—his second birthday, because from now he gathers power and power and power. He is to help you more than ever in the work of God's truth on the earth plane. Vibrations are very strong, and he is overjoyed. (Although he says, 'Nonsense, I did not lose my head!'; but when you are dealing with a condition of life absolutely unusual, you will understand.) He is so full of enthusiasm and desire to serve, to work, to fight on, and to win. He does so want it 'all on a level'!... He is sensible of the token of love and remembrance of his old body. He thanks you all for that which you gave him this morning. [This apparently refers to flowers laid on the grave.] He is much more satisfied with the new. Truly I am to say that he gets younger and has a new body, strong, and 'full of beans', he says.

"'This you may think peculiar. He was very fond of life in the woods and gardens, and of the pet squirrel. He loves still to watch its little ways, and is quite friendly with it. He has a heart full of love for 'the little people'. So boyish, so simple, and yet so big, so honest and sincere in desire to help. He would not utter one word he could not prove. His one desire is to give proof and comfort to the broken-hearted. There is one thing he wanted (he stands on my left amid a group of shining forms) he says, [and that is] with respect to the prophecies of catastrophes on earth. He says, 'Do you not see how linked up we are with this new age. We have before us a mighty work. There must be a great effort put forward to help humanity in its crisis. So we have to spread the truth and then prepare so that souls may not come over here to darkness, and fall back into.... ' I will not complete the sentence.

"'Unto the Great Spirit we give our hearts....'"

Thus a brief blessing completes the record of that day, spoken under conditions of extreme emotional strain. Already we see that the dominant urge of ACD—beyond even that of family and affection—was this imperative message waiting to be delivered, this mission to which all else must be subordinated.

ACD managed to strike a keynote. He laid, as it were, a foundation on which all that followed was to be built when he used the words *As a man sows so he shall surely reap*. To this he added, 'In the broad sense the seeds he sows are interpreted as actions; but I find *thought* to be actually more powerful than action, since one of the first things that a man is faced with on his escape from earth life, is *the world of his own thought*.'

CHAPTER IX

DEFINITIONS; AND
THE 'MATERIAL PROOF'

IT SEEMS necessary here to break the continuity of ACD's message in order to define one or more of the terms employed, such as 'soul' or the 'astral world'.

For what does the word 'soul' mean? It means *ourself*; that is, man's inner self apart from the body physical that we drag around, which demands nearly all our strength, time and energy to nourish, clothe, house, protect, transport from place to place, amuse and exercise; and eight hours' sleep in order to rest it every night. The soul is *ourself*. We are apart from our body only when we are carried away from it by something which absorbs us—by music, poetry, flowers or scenery, by drama or the ballet, by deep meditation, aspiration or spiritual illumination. Then do we function in our soul. We are that soul in all the higher reaches of our being, and our memories, interests, enthusiasms, thoughts, feelings, aspirations, comprise it. Sometimes we are all *soul-ful*; but more often, when the body is sick, sorry and complaining, we are mostly body. Nevertheless, our soul is ourselves as we really are, and as we shall be after the death of the body when we shall first migrate to astral realms.

Not that there will be anything very novel in our astral environment, since we go there every night when we fall asleep. Sleep being a little death, we are well practised in dying, and in this fashion die three hundred and sixty-five times yearly. With each new day we awake. With the same certainty we shall presently awake after death, since both sleeping and dying are natural functions of our being.

Why then do we not remember anything about the astral places which we are said to visit during sleep? But we do, though we store our knowledge in a different compartment—or department—of ourselves, away from the self of every day. We are often ignorant of the extent of our ignorance. We know hardly anything, for example, about this physical body. We don't know whether physical matter is real, or what electricity really is. (The two may be very closely linked—who knows?)★ We don't even know what our world looks like, because our physical senses have so narrow a range that there are colours we cannot see, sounds we cannot hear, scents we do not register.

This being so, man has a distorted and incorrect impression of the world in which he lives. We are, however, *aware* that everything in it is in a state of vibration, and that we ourselves vibrate in accord with a host of other vibrations. This we believe and accept scientifically. We need therefore only one step further to believe that there are other vibrations around us, not necessarily physical but ethereal or astral.

There are indeed astral worlds encompassing this, each in a differing state of vibration from coarser to finer. 'Encompassing' is the word, for they are not distant planets like Mars or Venus, but are additional departments or colonies of this world, which they encase—much as an onion is encased by its various 'skins'; and yet also interpenetrate our world with themselves, much as water soaks through a sponge.

These astral worlds are mostly of a higher vibration than the physical, and therefore consist of a finer matter. Human life is less burdened, since the astral body worn over there by man does not weigh down its wearer, but is a thing of beauty, health

---

★Ivan Cooke of course wrote these words in 1956. Today's reader can now turn to the discoveries of the particle physicists, in which matter and energy are indistinct from one another and the whole sense of linear time is largely defunct. For our own purposes—allowing the heart's simplicity rather than the mind's abstruseness—it may be more helpful to turn to White Eagle, who constantly takes us beneath the crust of physical seeming and reveals a world which he calls the real world totally interpenetrating the so-called physical one.

and joy. This is the Summerland beloved by Spiritualists. Souls go there (souls being humans freed from the flesh but otherwise unchanged) and inhabit an astral body. They do not at once become greatly wise or spiritual. Rest and refreshment after the toils of their earth life is the first necessity. This they obtain, and they remain in the astral world while time slips past.

Some will say this is too *good* to be true. Nothing is too good to be true. Therefore it is perhaps a pity wilfully to believe, habitually to believe, in things too *bad* to be true, of which there are many varieties, most of which are only bogies. But if people find this makes them happy—well, why not? What matters to us is that the astral worlds are very close to us always; because they interpenetrate our world and even influence our daily life, whether we are conscious or unconscious of the fact.

Because these worlds are so close, the majority of spiritualistic contacts are with people of the astral, who are little changed from their former selves, except that their life is more serene than ours, less limited, less burdened, and their world more beautiful. They are not greatly wise, and their message lacks power. Great things are not demanded of those living in the restful Summerland.

There is, unfortunately, another side to the picture. We have considered the higher astral worlds (or planes, to be more accurate). But what of those of a slower, of a lower vibration; perhaps even lower than this earth? These are not pleasant places, for they are peopled by humans whose lives have attuned them to such planes. They are grey, misty, dark-November-fog places, good to get out of. That is why they exist; to spur their folk to get away, by their own spiritual efforts. Some are worse even than the November-fog plane, but it does no good to try to frighten people into goodness. The church tried out this method for centuries without success. Hence the decline in the popularity of hell-fire preaching.

Whither is all this leading us? To a better understanding of the 'birthday' message of ACD, when he said that 'to clear a soul of the astral vibrations is not altogether an easy matter'. This was surely an understatement when it meant so great an act, so great a surrender, on his part. For at that moment he must have relinquished his promised Summerland of rest, refreshment and recreation which was his due after his strenuous years. Yet, in the Summerland life, there is an element of forgetfulness, forgetfulness of the cry of pain rising from men. For ACD there could be no forgetfulness, no laying down of his burden, no sealing of the heart. A new dedication, a new crusade was waiting to establish a new truth since the earlier truth for which he had formerly laboured proved insufficient.

Therefore he said: 'In the broad sense the seeds man sows are interpreted as actions; but I find *thought* to be actually more powerful than action, since one of the first things that a man is faced with on his escape from earth life, is *the world of his own thought.*'

Consider these words in the light of what has been written about the astral planes, wherein man prepares for himself an abiding place by his own thought and feeling during his years on earth. He migrates to a world of his own thought, a self-constructed home or environment. One is reminded of the saying in the Bible, to the effect that *whatsoever* (sins or blessings) *a man binds to himself on earth shall be bound to him in heaven; and whatsoever he shall loose from himself on earth shall be loosed from him in heaven.* Here the same truth is conveyed again. To the world of our own thought which we go to inhabit, our sins and shortcomings will be grafted, but also the goodness that we do.

It must be realized that this ACD communication was coming to us, not from an astral world of people like ourselves, but from a source wiser, higher, purer, with a message far more powerful and enduring. This being so, what of the medium or instrument through which the message was to come? Surely the transmission of this message entailed some pains? Indeed, yes; for Minesta had to forego much. It is true that the power and light of the Wise Knight made this contact possible, and was continually sustaining her. But that contact was a continually shattering experience. After the Bletchley meeting she was exhausted for some days. What intensified the problem was that she was pledged to speak at or work for numerous spiritualistic centres, and the alternation between the astral contacts of the latter and with ACD soon meant the abandonment of her work for organized Spiritualism—one hesitates to say 'orthodox' Spiritualism, but it is the more accurate designation.

After the meeting of the 22nd, the Polaires returned to France, and the other sitters to their homes. The task of obtaining the ACD message now rested with Minesta and her three helpers—that is, with the 'Square of Four' anticipated by White Eagle.

On the whole we shall find this 'Square' proved steady at its task during many months to come.

★

Those who know White Eagle best are aware that he never comes without prayer, that he is always composed and leisurely, always dignified and serene. 'Why hurry,' he says on occasion, 'when you have all eternity before you?' Perhaps this is why nobody has ever seen him ruffled, hasty or irritable, or heard him speak ill of any man. Only kind words pass his lips.

This being so, the impetuosity with which ACD jumped in in his haste to convince us that none other than he had spoken on 22nd May, was surprising as was the assertion that he had been trying for days to get this confirmation through; he managed also to confirm the salient points of his message of the 22nd, although White Eagle had to help him time and again. It was obvious that ACD had much to learn before delivering his message, and that contrary to spiritualistic beliefs communication between the worlds was proving a matter of much difficulty.

Nearly a month had passed since the last meeting.★

'ACD: "I have been trying for days to come through. Now let me thank my friends—all of you—for your gallant help. I shall get stronger—I shall not give up; I shall stick to it. And this is what you, too, must do—stick to it! I shall improve with practice....

★The date of what follows is 17th June 1931 (at Grove Court, London).

'"I desire to say that it was I who manifested at Bletchley on the day of my birth. I was trying with all my strength to make my dear ones know that I was there. You do not understand the difficulties we have in coming through.... (A spasm of coughing ensued.) All right; I shall overcome this—wait! (A pause of some moments, then:) Hold it, White Eagle, hold it! I want to do it!"

'...As we watched we saw White Eagle's presence 'grow' on the medium. Then followed White Eagle's invocation:

'"*Great White Spirit of the open sky, the wide prairies, and the quiet valleys of the earth: Thou Who dost dwell in the mighty places of the heavens; Thou Who dost speak to the human heart when it waits in the quiet hours. O Spirit of truth and love, we come. We love Thee: may we be worthy to follow! O Father of Love—may we deem it as a gift of Thine that we are given an opportunity of serving Thee, by sacrifice of desire to service.*

'"*O Father God, Thou knowest, Thou weepest for Thy children. May we always see Thee as Thou art in our brother man. We bring to Thy throne of grace those children who are blind and as yet cannot see Thy bountiful love at work through the darkness of their material lives. May they find illumination! O God, we pray for Thy power on our labours.*

'"*So mote it be.*"

'White Eagle continued: "Brother Nobleheart is very disturbed—very anxious to speak with you.... (*To Mr Bradbrook:*) Arthur Conan Doyle wants me to say that he looks to you to see these messages through. It means so much to him that his new realizations should be made known—it means all the difference between heaven and hell. Finding these things are true he must needs give them forth. It doesn't matter about the opponents. God will fight for him. Lady Conan Doyle has no need to be anxious, for he appreciates the wonderfully brave fight she has made. He is out for the universal truth, those fuller truths which he brings back. O! if you could see how small personalities are! Yet since a notable man may be used to bring universal truth into the hearts of man, so far as ACD is tuned in, he will be the channel.

"'The [Conan Doyle] Memorial is not in the hands of the Spiritualists, as they are today, but of the universal light. Until all are united they cannot advance. The noble work he wrought may not be halted, but ever progress, and now that he has found greater knowledge of the afterlife, he will lead its advance.

"'There are many who cannot reconcile the teaching of the seance room with the outworking of laws divine and immutable. When Nobleheart arrived on this side he found contact with earth not the easy matter he had once thought.

"'There tosses a great sea of astral memories—mediums tap these unconsciously. He found the one vital thing to be the secret thought-life of the man. All that he had ever thought was now become his world. Into a world self-created folk enter, and heaven reveals itself as that which is within. Much accepted as evidence of spiritual life can be wiped off the slate. Evidence is to be found in spiritual contact *heart* with *heart*. Man can only see a spirit with his own spirit. Evidence must be spiritually discerned, or else may consist of husks, mere pictures— although there are, of course, exceptions to this rule, for sometimes a spirit having a divine purpose to fulfil can produce a 'pictured' impression of himself, much as a teacher may instruct a class.

"'ACD now desires to make a restatement. He desires to clear out of Spiritualism all which is unreal and confusing. His soul is charged, and has a glorious mission and clearer teaching to unfold. In the light of this teaching must the Memorial be built, for there can follow no advance otherwise."

'White Eagle was asked if he could obtain a clearer outline of what was to come. ACD then spoke. It is interesting to note the change in words and phrasing. Would that print could indicate the change in diction, manner, in the whole personality that now manifested.

'ACD: "It lies in these words: *The Kingdom of Heaven is within.*

"'I see the need of a Master. In Christ you have all. In His teaching rest the secrets of life and death. Man must take up his cross and follow the light of love. The cross symbolizes the crucifixion of all selfish aims and desires—the complete submission of the personal to the impersonal love of God—the Creator of all. This is the secret of life both here and hereafter. Man must live not for himself, nor for his good name, for personal power or prosperity, or his own success, but to contribute to the common good. Giving all, he receives all. Thus, and thus only will he enter into his kingdom of heaven.

"'Truly it is said, *Man must be born again*—not of the flesh but of the spirit. Every man incarnate or discarnate must eventually pass through death of himself, and awaken again into new life, into fuller consciousness of the one all-loving God. Thus only will he find himself and all those whom he loves. From this sphere of Christ-consciousness descend those whom you love, in spirit, so until you can attune yourself to their light, your communication must lack something most beautiful and pure.

"'Consider the gulf fixed between the rich man and Lazarus: the bridgeless gulf, yet of man's own creation. Still there is a way … the way of *love*. But not, mark you, the personal or possessive love, but rather the impersonal love of self-giving, self-forgetting, and self-sacrifice.

"'*Unless a man is born again of Spirit he can in no wise enter the Kingdom of Heaven.* True indeed; yet there remain some bound to earth, who seek to contact earth through channels provided by mediumship. They too need teaching. The veil between this world and yours is thin indeed, compared to the severance between the earthly man discarnate and the man of heaven.

"'The mistake we labour under is that of stressing the importance of persons, of nationalities, forgetting that there must be mutual cooperation in the spreading of eternal truth. [That is why] I desire no personal reference in the Memorial appeal. Remember, you are working not for a person but for a principle, an ideal. Embody the broad charity of the Christian teaching, the pure principles of Christ, or of the Great White Light of truth: it matters not whether it is interpreted through Buddha, Krishna or any other Master.

"'My wife will admit me a man of strong opinions, out of which I was not easily persuaded. Nevertheless, Spiritualism compelled me to admit certain facts. Later I again changed my mind when accepting the leadership of Jesus Christ in the movement of Spiritualism. Yet again I change concerning the after-death state. Surely, surely, my friends would expect a man to have greater knowledge and clearer vision when freed from the limitations of the earthly tabernacle. Else where would progress be?

"'I am not prepared to say more. These things cannot be forced. I am content to leave the matter in the hands of God.... This is the chosen instrument or channel for this work. Other means will be used when the time is ripe to satisfy those who require proof of a more material nature.

"'The Wise Knight, with whom I am in close contact, has arranged soon for another meeting. This, however, is the kind of gathering I like and think likely to bring best results.

"'I am to endeavour to give you a proof on a photographer's plate. (*Turning to Silver Star:*) You are very necessary. There is a special link with you.

"'White Eagle once called me Brother Nobleheart—I should like this name to be mine. This is a triangle of great power.... Tell the brethren in Paris that I am deeply grateful. I am linked with the Wise Knight for a definite mission which will prove itself as time progresses.'"

It will be remembered that ACD said that he was shortly preparing to give a more material proof of his identity—a proof on a photographic plate. At that time only two mediums were available in England for psychic photography. Mrs Miller [Silver Star] managed to secure an appointment with a Mrs Deane, at the Stead Library, on the following day, and to her delight received the picture of ACD as promised [see the reproduction on p. 119]. The photograph itself will be seen to be an extraordinary production, because psychic photography itself is one of the most chancy and hit-or-miss varieties of mediumship. Perhaps once in six or once in a dozen times do the features of the desired person in spirit appear on the plate. More often there comes the face of a stranger, or of someone still on earth known or unknown to the sitter. All too often the faces look as immobile and lifeless as masks or as plaster of Paris casts. This of ACD has been claimed as the best of all psychic pictures. Be that as it may, it is worth careful study for its animation, good humour and benevolence, and for the sense of life which invests it. It differs from any other psychic painting or portrait of Sir Arthur, whom Mrs Miller herself had never met personally. Lastly, the photographic medium herself knew nothing of Mrs Miller's association with the ACD work.

So there the photograph stands, as a testimony not only to ACD, but to the Wise Knight behind him, for it was the latter's power which enabled it to be secured with such ease and certainty and indeed made it possible. Mrs Miller went many times afterwards to try to obtain a second picture of ACD, but in vain. It was again the Master's power which was lending life to this message from ACD, a power which originates from beyond astral realms and contacts, as we shall see later. By this photograph ACD signed, sealed and delivered his message of the 22nd. This was one proof—but not the conclusive proof which was to come later and, as Bhotiva said, would 'crash all critics'; but substantial nevertheless.

A professional photographer's picture of Sir Arthur Conan Doyle (by William Ransford, Belsize Park, London).

The spirit photograph of ACD, obtained through the medium Mrs Deane.
The sitter is Mrs Miller.

CHAPTER X

'I AM A HAPPY MAN'

'People ask me what it is which makes me so perfectly certain Spiritualism is true. That I am perfectly certain is surely demonstrated by the fact that I have abandoned more congenial and lucrative work and subjected myself to all sorts of inconveniences, losses and even insults in order to get the facts home to the people.'

Sir Arthur in a letter

AT the next meeting, on 22nd June, M Bhotiva was again present. It will be noted that the group met when possible on the 22nd of a month, this being a day of power so far as the ACD work was concerned.

White Eagle spoke first.

'[It may interest you to know that] I knew of the big work to come long before Arthur passed out of the body. I knew when I spoke at a circle held about twelve moons ago [the seance in Wales: see p. 19] when I gave a great deal of valuable information. The records are in the possession of the sitters still.... Foundation stones have to be laid in differing times and places, and then connected up. You have to find these stones, for you build a temple. Long after you are gone from physical manifestation the work will go on.

'ACD is so happy....'

Then ACD spoke.

'Cannot you see that by my old face [in the picture]? That is what *you* have produced!... Your power has sent to them [the family] a message so that they—my dear ones—will know how I feel. I am a happy man.

'This you can see: I want you to compare the impression [of myself] which we were able to imprint on a photographic plate with some of the spirit photographs previously received by others. I particularly wish a close comparison. It will teach you much....

'I want you ... to realize the difference between an "astral impression" and the real thing. This is the very truth we are determined to make clear. There is so much humbug [about these psychic things]—unconscious, I admit. What the world needs is a sane discrimination between the substantial and the nebulous, and this is what Spiritualism's critics, good men at heart, stand out for. You must help your people to discriminate between the real and the unreal. By this you do not lessen but rather give them strength to mount to spiritual consciousness.

'This brings me to the very core of my mission. It is to indicate the difference between that which is foolish and nonsensical, and that which is a jewel of eternal truth. The latter will reveal heaven itself; the former makes a fool of a man. So long as man remains enmeshed in intellectual pride he can never find truth. (I am afraid my friends will disagree.) And this brings me to another point: *Except a man become as a little child he can in no wise enter the Kingdom of Heaven.* Again I repeat my statement.... Any questions?'

A questioner: 'Will you define *"except a man become as a little child"?'*

ACD: 'Except a man be stripped of all pride and egotism; except he realize he is *nothing* without the power of almighty Spirit; until a man breaks out from arrogance to the understanding that *of myself I can do nothing*, he is dulled to the glories of Heaven.

'Each soul must eventually be stripped of all possessions, and stand forth naked, an infinitesimal *nothing* bathed in a vast ocean of universal knowledge and power. He must go through the valley of death, not of the physical body, but of *himself*; naked of all....

'Then and then only can the light dawn—for him. So the spiritual sunlight breaks upon the way, which is also the truth and the life. So comes growth in power, peace and joy to the soul entering on the Universal, the babe about to grow to spiritual manhood in the tender and everlasting arms....

'Has it never seemed strange to you that men of force and power, intellectual power, should never return from the unseen to communicate with earth? The answer lies in the foregoing. They cannot.

'I look to you all here to put forward these messages of mine. They will increase in power and clarity as I become more accustomed to using Brighteyes [Minesta]. You realize my dependence on you to give this message to the world?

'I can but hope that these words will clear away both doubt and credulousness from many who question or accept the teachings of Spiritualism. No words of mine detract one iota from the great love and true communion which can assuredly take place between those on earth and those in spirit. Not for an instant would I shake the belief of thousands who have received comfort from knowledge of the spirit life: *but I would give a higher conception of it*, give something not only ennobling to themselves but to the whole community. We work for the impersonal, for a diviner love to be brought into the hearts of men, so that they may live rather than talk of brotherhood. I hold no other desire. May God grant it! I believe He will give me the power and opportunity to carry this message to the uttermost parts of the earth.

'I may not speak of great work or wide success. What is required rather is for you to be as babes, to be guided, to be used, willing channels for the spirit. An ideal, perhaps; but in that alone will you find your joy, your happiness, your kingdom of heaven. You may well thank God for the opportunity.

'God bless old White Eagle! He is one of the shining ones! To you he is just old White Eagle; to us something more; but sufficient be it that he is just old White Eagle, your loving companion.'

Now follows the record of the next meeting.

White Eagle: 'You must be conscious of the power in your

midst. By purity of heart and purpose only you command this
power. Of yourselves you can do nothing, it is true; but by
allowing the purity of God's love to fill your being, which can
only be when the heart is devoted to the service of God, you
raise yourselves and immediately command power from the
celestial sphere.

Grove Court, 2nd July 1931

'In the silence, in your innermost hearts, know God's love!
You cannot fail. It is a sacred trust that those assembled here
have placed upon them. God sees purity of heart and sincerity
of purpose. In spite of the dross and weariness of the flesh, light
will pour through these channels. We desire you to continue
at intervals as the power is assembled. Only a small amount of
material can come through each time, but we shall endeavour
to give quality in the message.

'ACD will be used by his own freewill and desire to give the
truth of the life that immediately follows death of the body of
flesh.' [Long pause.]

ACD then spoke: 'When I can adjust myself to the medium,
we will continue our pleasant little talk. It requires a certain
amount of practice, I find—that is, in the controlling of the
physical body of the medium—to be able to give through her
consecutive and clear ideas. [Taps meditatively with fingers of
right hand on chair.] Yes ... yes ... let us have a friendly chat.
I think it is easier. Yes, we will warm up to the subject later—
a friendly chat is the best with which to commence....

'I used to think that everything was very easy in the spirit
world. In fact, I made a point of painting pretty pictures of it.
I would not take away one iota of belief and hope, but should
like to give a clearer idea of the state to which one passes on
leaving the physical body. The truth is this—that it is so difficult
to explain to the finite mind the actual facts concerning the
mental state of the individual after the change of death; because
to each man comes a different experience, and one cannot lay
down any hard and fast rules. There is a state, or intermediate
condition, lasting perhaps a few days, weeks, months, or
continuing for many hundreds of years. I find that there is so
much on the astral plane of life to interest you that I hardly

know where to commence the story.'

A questioner: 'What was your first impression after passing?'

ACD: 'It was utterly and entirely different from what I expected, and that is what most people, orthodox and Spiritualist alike, will find—a very different heaven, or Summerland, from that which they anticipated. We must clear the ground, and give a purer vision. Of course, it turns largely on the quality of a man's mentality, but more on his attitude towards his fellows, and life in general. That is to say, a man may find himself much better off than he or anyone else had anticipated; or on the other hand, he may find himself in complete bondage.

'The power to create is the gift of every man. On his creative power rests the crux of the whole matter. The man of ability whose bent lies in the creation of characters; the painting of pictures, the writing of poetry; the creation either of beauty or the reverse by positive creative thought: he is as surely creating a world for his habitation when freed from the flesh.

'What of my first impression? Well! Well! I can speak only for myself. One does not at once realize that one has passed away from one's material body. One seems to be leaving, and yet has not left. One is still able to see, and to a certain extent contact earth and earth conditions. It is rather a terrible sensation when one endeavours to express oneself to one's friends, and is unable to make any impression; and when some souls here find their deeds working evil in the minds and hearts of others, it is terrible to find oneself unable to arrest the forces one has loosed.

'That is the main idea; the creations of one's own brain going on and on like the waves of a rolling sea, ever beating against the minds of many. When such creations are beautiful, then it is a heavenly and immeasurable joy to see the good radiating through the human universe. But when it is the reverse … I dare paint no picture.

'I would explain that there are different degrees of mental activity [in the spiritual world]. The more highly developed a soul is mentally and spiritually, the greater the joy or sorrow it will alternately experience; although in lower grades light and shade is not so apparent.

'Astral memories and interferences: I intend to deal fully with that question because there exists so much in Spiritualism of, I would not say untruth, but misrepresentation of actual fact. You have already, of course, a certain knowledge of the power of thought, and are aware that a thought in your own mind can be photographed.... If you compare a spirit photograph of myself lately published [in a psychic journal] with the one which you yourselves received, you will observe that the former lacks intelligence, vitality, life; the latter portrays—I flatter myself—an intelligent representation.

'This can be found throughout the phenomena of Spiritualism—in certain manifestations by means of ouija boards, or materialization, or the direct voice. These phenomena are like bubbles; prick them, and they fall away, for they lack a sustaining intelligence. Prove this for yourselves by observation, and you will prove the existence of a great sea of etheric impressions, which lingers and clings to particular places such as to former scenes of a soul's life. Unknown to the individual, such thought-forms, if very intense, will live. For instance, in a house much loved by a former owner, people may feel "presences" passing them on stairways, hear "whisperings" in rooms, and even the apparition itself may scare the inhabitants. These phenomena are not spirits, of course, but memories that live and cling. In churches and old buildings with an accumulated power, there will be found many such forms and lingerings, frequently seen by clairvoyants and described as spirits. Not so at all; they are merely the thought-vibrations of a bygone day.

'I do not wish for one moment to take away from the value of spiritualistic phenomena. Undoubtedly there is genuine manifestation.... There remains, however, so much that is merely shadowy.... The many spheres of thought and manifestation have all to be considered; but it must also be remembered that unprincipled spirits can manipulate astral thought-forces to suit their own mischievous purposes.

'The crux of the whole matter is the quality of the mind, or the aspirations of the communicant. If attuned to the spiritual sphere of love and intelligence, there will follow a perfectly intelligent communication; but if his mind is merely nebulous, untrained and without spiritual understanding, then comes trouble....'

Speaking of his personal self, ACD continued: 'It is not *that* part of me that I want to live in the spirit world. I want to forget personalities. Personalities, although very sweet and dear to us all, must take a subsidiary place. It is the great Christ light that we follow, to bring this into clear and perfect expression through the medium of men's own hearts. When I think of past errors in thought, when I see the results of those errors, oh my anguish! Oh my despair! Oh, to be able to give a clearer conception of truth to others! Only one thing in life matters, which is for men to realize the redeeming power of Christ's love in their lives. If the Christ-spirit is awake, if it is abiding within, they live! All the phenomena, all the continual running to mediums to keep touch with the dead, is all wrong. Men must seek rather for the living light of truth, the redeeming love which the demonstration of survival will help them to understand. Only with this object in view, should men seek to lift the veil.'

CHAPTER XI

COMMUNICATION AND COMMUNION

*A*T THE *next meeting** ACD returned to this important theme.* 'Confusion—that is what we see sometimes. We see those who are mediums as you see a light radiating through the fog, and we make contact with that light. Picture yourself in a London street on a foggy night, and it will give you some conception of the difficulty. Yet it is not always so. Sometimes we return and find things clear-cut and true, the mind of the medium happy and bright, with no ripple of depression or worry to disturb reception, and so we are able to sail in and make a clear impression on the brain.

'It is comparatively rare, however, to get a perfectly clear and definite message through, since there lingers usually a remainder of the mentality through which we have to press. Mediumship is a fine art, and as humanity is only waking to the value of the spiritual life, mediums themselves still remain ignorant of the powers which might be theirs. It is necessary for a medium to be well-balanced, but also to be flexible and easily influenced. It is no easy matter to attain and retain that combination of self-control, combined with the sensitiveness of the visionary and idealist. All this is essential, however, before a perfectly attuned instrument opens to receive the perfect message.

'The majority of communications received by the Spiritualist come from the denizens of the higher astral spheres, from souls both good in intention and pure in motive, although of

*Wembley Park, 22nd August 1931, recorded not by Bradbrook but by Silver Star (Mrs Caird Miller).

limited knowledge and outlook. Remember, they pass on, more or less, but personal opinion and personal experience. For this reason we find so many controls in Spiritualist circles detailing only their own viewpoint and outlining their own ideas. He who dwells in the astral sphere narrows experience, much as a man voices set opinions, political or religious. Maybe he thinks he possesses the whole truth, and that his convictions are final. Every soul, however, must eventually enter that path whereon he becomes at length cleansed from all assertion. It is of this heaven-world I would speak tonight.

'The Spiritualist may not declare that in his contact with the first three or four, or even seven astral planes, he has found all. He has yet far to go, and there are, moreover, many pitfalls, snares and illusions in his contact. The psychic or magnetic forces about the human environment are responsible oft-times for phenomena too readily accepted as an evidential communication from a spirit. So much can be found in the sitters' mentality and magnetism to account for such, and then there are deceiving spirits, who find their amusement in the impersonation of higher personalities. (I have witnessed this myself, with some disquiet.)

'Sometimes a medium himself or herself will create a thought-form which becomes so endowed with animation as to attach itself to a medium, be seen by a clairvoyant, and actually give messages. This also I have seen.

'This is not necessarily conscious fraud. Many, when they come into Spiritualism, strongly desire to become mediums. Developing circles are formed, and the sitter having been told that he has mediumistic powers, a condition of self-hypnotism takes place. A thought may become so 'backed' and clothed that it becomes realistic. We have said that astralities are merely dead things, or masks which can be easily detected. The true spiritual communication holds always its own ring of truth.

'It is certainly not wrong, nor is it undesirable, for you to seek communion with those in the spirit life. Neither is it wrong for you to give your friends an opportunity of returning to communicate. In many instances such communication is of the utmost value and help to both of the parties concerned. But having had that experience, the man in the spirit world having been able to send his messages of reassurance, both of those concerned should realize that there is work to be accomplished in the next world which cannot be done if the spirit is continually being held back by those who mourn its passing.

'It may help you to understand me better if I give my own experience of control.★ I find the easier way to use this particular medium is not through her subconscious but through her subliminal mind.† We have already said that man—broadly —can contact two planes of spiritual life. If he be attuned only to the lower grades of astral life he cannot expect to receive knowledge of an uplifting character; but if a medium can be induced to raise his or her consciousness, to open up that subliminal channel, true spiritual contact is established.

'My best work through this instrument [Minesta] has always been through her subliminal self, and not when controlling or endeavouring to control through the brain…. Although I cannot hold her by automatic or hypnotic control, I can pour facts and teaching through this medium's spiritual intelligence. Therefore do not confuse her conscious mind with ideas. Leave her alone and mentally isolated. Then I can do my work.

'Seeing clairvoyantly, you would witness an illumination around the head which projects for two or three yards, of which the upper part tapers into a golden beam of light like a channel or trumpet.

'In many communications through mediumship you may get automatic action or control. You may witness much which on occasion reminds you of departed friends, or hear short sentences so like in style and manner that proof seems certain,

★From the sitting of 27th April 1932. The previous paragraph does not appear in THY KINGDOM COME, and was inserted into THE RETURN OF ARTHUR CONAN DOYLE.

†[Note from THY KINGDOM COME:] By the word 'subliminal', ACD denotes the spiritual mind or divine intelligence of man, as distinct from the subconscious mind or repository of the thought-product of memory and intellect.

these being the product of the automatic trance control
employed ... [which is a kind of] hypnosis of mind and body.
Remember that in such cases little more than an automaton
functions, and the flow of inspiration is definitely checked.

'On the other hand, with control of the subliminal self of the
medium, can be obtained a clear and satisfactory reflection of
the nature and personality rather than the mannerisms of the
communicating spirit.

'There is but a small percentage of what is called "subconscious mind stuff" coming through Spiritualistic communications. What is often called "subconscious" can be attributed
rather to the *conscious* mind of the medium interfering with the
spirit control. The core or inner life of the subliminal self
remains always in contact with the universal life and thus can
be, and occasionally is, influenced by greater beings, which
usually operate in a band rather than singly.

'In our own particular instance★... the messages are transmitted down through the spheres. Sometimes we obtain a clear
channel, and are able to express exactly the idea desired, while
at others there seems a certain crossing of currents and
vibrations, so that when we read our message we feel a sense
of dissatisfaction and sadness. Obviously our thoughts have not
reached you with the clarity we could have wished....
Sometimes we find it impossible to convey our exact meaning.... In spite of all these obstacles the veil thins between the
two worlds. Proof of survival in the years to come will not so
much depend on communications through recognized mediums, but rather will win acceptance because the majority of
men and women will have become awakened and alive to the
unseen powers around them.†

'I impress it upon you§ that in certain conditions only will
a shaft of clear light come through. Unquestionably mediumship can be developed, but I would not advocate the development of mediumship for everyone. Only the chosen vessels.
That is the mistake made in the Spiritualist movement: the

★4th May 1932.   †In 1994, it feels this is being proved true.
§22nd August 1931, Wembley Park.

wholesale advocacy of the development of the mediumistic faculty. As in the days of old, so today—there are those chosen, and the dangers of forcing psychic development cannot be too much emphasized.

'Some think that a medium becomes as an empty vessel when in a state of trance. This is not so; for although the medium's body serves to express the communicating spirit, there is retained a residue of its owner's personality and mentality which has to be cleared; and in the clearing the message given becomes coloured more or less. Thus can a medium be of the greatest help or the greatest hindrance.

'If the medium cultivates both mentality and spirituality, then that medium can become of infinite use and importance. It is untrue that a totally ignorant medium makes the best instrument. If an unlettered or ignorant medium has been chosen for a specific task, this choice is due to some spiritual quality or faculty inherent in the medium. Let me, however, impress this; the intelligence must never be overbearing but rather so docile that it lends itself to the communicator. An ignorant medium, while useful in so far as the mind does not dam thoughts brought through, labours under the disadvantage of being unable to bring forth with clarity and force.

'We are dealing with thoughts which can only be expressed in words, and we clothe them with such language as we find in the mentality or comprehension of our medium. Therefore you see the necessity of the mind being well trained, to enable us to give clear and precise teaching. We are hoping to use this medium: Brighteyes will forgive an old man for saying that it is no easy matter to play a fine tune on an instrument with one string, and that she could help much.

'In later days you will find I shall finish many a theme commenced at the beginning of our sittings. In that you will recognize the handiwork of an individual and outside communicator. Do not judge until you see the finished article. Before my passing I did not understand the difficulties of communication, but became convinced on cold evidence which I recognize now might not be so valid as I once thought. When

I come back hundreds of ideas attempt to pour through—I must learn to regulate this overcrowding....

'I find over here that it is difficult to get the human mind to receive, though it eventually accepts the idea. I want to link you all together for there is so much for you all to learn.'

★

M Bhotiva was present at the meeting (9th March 1932) from which the following extracts are taken, and Lady Conan Doyle and her family arranged to 'tune in' from their home in Sussex.

ACD: 'You have been asking for proof, my friend [Bhotiva], that this is Conan Doyle communicating, that it is Conan Doyle who has come back to his friends to bring them the glad truth of life after death. I do assure you that these proofs are at hand; not only are the proofs lying in my words, in the talks which I have given concerning the life after death; but even so, more tangible proofs than these are yet to come. I have expressed a desire that our friends should first receive the teaching, and after the message has been delivered, then will proofs be given of a physical nature.

'People will accept my message, they will—they must—for so much depends upon this teaching. Conan Doyle is the spokesman for the great ones, and when my mission is finished I shall leave the earth plane and advance. I have not hurried my own family in this matter, because I know that they find it difficult to accept the changed man that I am. I want you to recognize, however, that it is not Conan Doyle alone, but the powers behind which enable me to bring these proofs and this message back. While the power here is good, and there is sympathy from all, I feel a certain difficulty in tuning in to the extra vibrations tonight....'

[A lengthy pause.]

'I am brought back by the thoughts of my family to the personal plane. I cannot hold that vibration of the celestial sphere, my friends.... [ACD had spoken throughout with considerable agitation.] But it is good to feel a reunion with them. What a strong personal link I am feeling in this room tonight—quite different, quite different.

'You remember, friends, I have told you before that we function on these different planes of being, and even from the earth plane you can touch the astral, the mental, the universal? I have explained all this, and coming back to earth conditions it is for me also exactly the same. We attune ourselves to the different degrees of mental life of those we contact. Sometimes I speak from the astral plane, sometimes from the mental and at others from the celestial; but I have to attune my vibrations always in accordance with conditions provided....

'I am directed to speak tonight about the work which lies ahead. You have been prepared for years, much as I myself was prepared, although I did not then realize my mission. I did not realize that I must pass from the earth into the spiritual life in order to be a servant of the White Brotherhood. I am under the direction of the Wise Ones. I am their servant, their instrument, and I have to organize this group, this work, in London. This teaching, these messages, are to be the foundation. I come back to amplify those teachings I gave whilst in the body. I have to reveal that finer life, a nobler path than ever dawned upon my earthly conception. All must be put right. Men must be taught the truth concerning the life after death. I have given it. Send it out to the world!

'No man who knows me, my thoughts and my writings, will doubt these words: they will recognize me therein; they will understand; they must understand.

'Why was I once inundated with all those prophecies of disasters and catastrophes to which humanity is heading? Because, as I see now, I was the pivot, the central point. Thousands then hung on my words. Because of this I was destined to be used for the Great White Brotherhood to bring a clearer, truer, and more exact teaching about the life beyond.

'In this connection, you wonder why the Conan Doyle Memorial has been kept in abeyance, why such an organization has not travelled faster? Had it gone ahead it would have been likely to have got into the wrong hands, been run on the wrong lines. Men's minds have to be prepared. Communication has its place, the proving of survival is necessary, but must not be abused.'

White Eagle said afterwards: 'Evidence is not always what the human minds consider to be evidence. The spiritual brother-hoods have their own way of producing evidence, and the spirit of man must be ready to receive it; otherwise it means nothing to him.... The foundation of the English group of the White Brotherhood lies in your records. When the message goes out many will accept its teaching. People will say, "This is true; we will follow!" All classes of men will be brought to believe.

'Your faith and loyalty will carry it through. You will never fail—never fail.'

CHAPTER XII

RETROSPECT

I

THE PRECEDING chapters have established the circumstances in which the messages of ACD—the main part of this book—were given, and have provided a foretaste of them. People who had known ACD personally—his family, Miss Estelle Stead, Mr W. R. Bradbrook (the Secretary of the Memorial Fund)—realized by every trait of his personality, by his mannerisms, his old energy and masculinity, his sheer force of character and warm-hearted enthusiasm and affection—that this was the man, Arthur Conan Doyle, as he was in life, though with his character now more sublimated by his experiences. On the other hand the medium, her husband and friends, had never met Conan Doyle before his passing. The personality who spoke through the medium possessed a knowledge and power of expression, and a literary style quite foreign to the medium; and the change of semblance in the medium, both facial and in habits and gestures was remarked on by everyone present. Moreover, there was no question of telepathy; here was a man speaking in precise detail, and at the end of his discourses taking up and replying to any argument or query. Nor was there any question of it being the higher self of the medium speaking and answering; the personality of ACD was felt as strongly as was his presence, his character, and the spiritual power and upliftment that were given him to bring through his message. It was the sense of *life* that was so convincing—of free, untrammelled life, the marvellous potentialities and expansion of our sense of life beyond bodily limitation. This sense lifted the discourse above the ordinary mundane or mental level. Here was no phantasm, no ethereal and temporary projection of the mind from its inner recesses. Moreover, the work continued over a long period and the man was intensely alive and real throughout. In fact, his character was far stronger than that of any earthly person present: vibrant, forceful, integrated, yet wider in range of human understanding and sympathy. This was no longer the sick, worn-out and ageing Doyle who passed in 1930; but a man whose force and vitality impinged upon everyone present in the room.

What should we rightfully expect from the dead if they returned? Mere memories about their former life? We should surely expect, if they were still living, to hear something about their new experiences. If this man had formerly been competent, of fearless mind and upright character, disdaining all that he thought shallow or untruthful, then in his case an exact account of his experiences might reasonably be expected. If, moreover, during his life he held some misconceptions regarding life after death, would he not strive to put them right, particularly if they were of consequence to those people who had shared his former beliefs? Indeed, he would leave no stone unturned to give his new message. In sum, if the man lived, then his validity and character should survive death; for these, it is commonly said, are the only attributes a man is left with on his deathbed.

This then was the Conan Doyle who came back, changed in some of his opinions, full of his new experiences, uplifted, and in every sense alive; yet still retaining the character known to all associated with him. To his family he remained still their father. But he wished and he was determined that his message should come through to the world at large. Furthermore, he intended his message to be self-evident.

For one cannot go into a court of law and say, 'I have irrefragable evidence that one Arthur Conan Doyle is still present and alive; here he is; let him go into the witness-box

himself and give evidence.' Yet Conan Doyle, discarnate, put
himself in the witness-box, not before a court but before the
world at large—or at least before those who would pause to
hear his testimony. He said, in other words, 'This is I, Conan
Doyle; I cannot come to you in a material body such as yours,
but yet I can by certain means render my evidence. Let my
evidence be recorded and read out. My affidavit is given in the
presence of those who knew me, who would testify to my
identity if I were in a material body. I give you a proof cogent
and reasonable. And if it is I—then with a fair and open mind
listen to my testimony.

'This very testimony that the dead live and therefore have
identity, naturally I could not give while I was in a material
body. But now I have made it circumstantial. If it be the work
of a forger or imitator, judge for yourselves. On the other hand,
if it does not conform with people's views—or absence of
views—on life after death, or their religious preconceptions,
you cannot expect me to offer as my sole evidence an array of
facts which were already known to me and others during my
lifetime. There must indeed be something new if I have gained
in experience. And yet any novelty that I bring can be seen in
perspective, if you will study the scriptures of world religions,
and the writings of the mystics; or if you will open yourselves
to the realization that God is a God of Love, and that there is
harmony, order and reasonableness throughout the universe.
Then you will see that the progression of man through death
to the afterlife is based on a man's own nature and deserts; that
his after-state is the logical outcome of his own growth and
expansion, and the development of the life within him. Finally,
that after death you live still in a rational and not a fanciful
universe, where facts are yet facts.'

★

A further matter of considerable interest was the evidence given
to a representative from the Polaires in Paris. White Eagle
dictated certain figures in a cipher which was able to be

comprehended by the Polaires alone. This, in itself, constituted an objective and mathematical proof of the veracity of his statements, and one notable in the whole range and history of Spiritualism.

In addition to this proof there are other considerations. The Polaires, it will be remembered, obtained their knowledge of the Wise Knight and his brethren—together with their directions to take part in the reception of the messages from Conan Doyle—by one means alone, the Oracle de Force Astrale, which operated solely through a series of numbers translatable in strict accordance with an arithmetical key. When a question had been transmitted, the answer resolved itself into a series of digits, which were then translatable into perfectly spelt words. These words were, however, still in an incomprehensible or-der, and it required a further calculation by the operator to place them, however numerous, in correct sequence. The result was now an intelligible message.

Both question and answer had perforce to be in Italian, for the key was for that language alone. The Polaires themselves did not possess this key, which remained throughout with the original possessor who kept its secret undivulged.

The Polaires, who had received through the Oracle in November 1930 precise directions concerning the messages about to be given by Conan Doyle, now required proof that White Eagle had access to the spiritual Chiefs who directed the Polaire Brotherhood, and that his words concerning Conan Doyle were valid. This proof he gave first by a brief description of their leader in chief, then by describing a vision the import of which was plain to the Polaires, and finally by dictating a series of digits, the reason for which was comprehensible to the Polaires and to no-one else present.

First, as has been said, this cipher was in itself a remarkable piece of cross-evidence, for numbers, unlike words, to mean anything must be all of them exact.

Secondly, as we have shown, the code which gave—to quote the words of the Polaires—a *very precise* check' was almost certainly that of the Oracle de Force Astrale, in which the answers given by the Sages formed in the first place a series of digits. As White Eagle was himself, it was afterwards disclosed, a Tibetan Sage, the hypothesis is not unrealistic.

As a counter-check, it may be added, the Polaires sealed and deposited with a Paris notary the communications regarding this very sitting which they had themselves received through the Oracle. Having obtained the necessary proof, they published the results of the sitting in their magazine—from which the following extracts are taken.★

(*White Eagle is speaking of the spiritual leaders of the Polaire movement, and of their Chief, the Wise Knight, the Knight of the Rose Cross:*)

'The great beings are near me. Now White Eagle is in contact with the Chevalier Sage. What a marvellous being! White Eagle perceives his great black eyes and his white robe decorated with a red cross. It is he who directs the Polaire movement. It is he who projects love and brotherhood upon the world.

'…Now I must describe to you a vision. I have to indicate to you the numbers 3 and 9, which are of very great importance: 3 x 3 = 9. There is the entrance to a cavern. On the dark rocks shines the six-pointed star. On the floor a sword in its scabbard. A serpent entwined about a staff. The creature speaks: *Man has descended through his own self-will into the mire. He has now to break loose from his circle of sorrow and darkness. Of his own freewill he 'lost' his paradise, and he will not regain it save by his own will and by an immense effort.*

'…My brother, you know the reason why White Eagle should dictate to you certain numbers? This is no easy thing, but I will do my best to communicate those which I see inscribed for you. I must make them known for a purpose which only you will understand. Then write XXV, now XV, next IV, and then III. Write down V and II, afterwards C and LV. Finally a V and a I.'

★*Bulletin des Polaires*, 9th March 1931, from which these extracts are a literal translation. The details of the numerical code are taken from M Bhotiva's book ASIA MYSTERIOSA, pp. 38–40.

Regarding these numbers, 'B.Z.' (that is, Zam Bhotiva) added the following notes. Of the 3 x 3 = 9: '*These numbers relate to the series of digits in Roman numerals given later.*' And of the series of Roman numerals themselves: '*These digits were given for the purpose of a* VERY PRECISE *check, which has enabled us to take account of the source of these communications.*' The message concealed under these Roman numerals was not made public, but this much may be disclosed—that White Eagle was working from the same centre as the Chevalier Sage, in close cooperation and complete harmony (as they work still); and the proof that this was so lay in the particular numerals given to Bhotiva.

★

The writer believes that the latter part of Chapter 1 in Part Two deserves special study, for in it ACD gives the key to the nature of the next world. That key is the word 'externalization'; for here and now we are continually externalizing ourselves in all that we do and are, and do so from infancy onwards. The result is that our homes and families, our hobbies and habits, our trades or businesses are all exact expressions of ourselves; as are our face and its expression, our state of health, our body, its gait and bearing, our habits of thought, our speech and mannerisms. All proclaim exactly what we are because they are externalizations of our real or inner self. This may be a truism, but is one often overlooked. What few of us realize, however, is that with the same unfailing accuracy we are externalizing ourselves on the invisible world around us. By so doing we are preparing both the condition and environment to which we shall go after death, and this by a process which might almost be called automatic. Truly, man makes his own heaven. He also makes an alternative place, if he so wills.

Secondly, what is the key which opens up contact with the next world? It is love. By love is meant loving kindness not only to a few people, but as a habitual expression of ourselves to all living creatures, to the world we live in, to life itself, and to God. Love such as this alone bridges the gulf between this world and the next, and itself governs the quality both of communication and communion with those in the life beyond. Those who seek contact with relatives 'over there' through a medium will truly succeed only if they have loving hearts—if they are broad and big-hearted, warm, loving and wise in their loving. Then the gates are flung wide. So also with those who would so raise themselves that they may commune on the plane of reunion. Warm human love is the one factor which will raise them. No amount of mental strain or struggle will avail; for there love alone prevails.

'Externalization', then, is the keyword which makes the rulings and conditions of the next life comprehensible. We externalize ourselves into that life. It in turn reflects back into our mortal lives while we are living here, so that we can always be in touch with more worlds than one. 'Love' is the second keyword which ultimately means the difference between hell and heaven both in this life and the next. Although these matters are serious, we need not be too gloomy about them, because an element of mercy, of compassionate understanding, pervades all worlds. We can be far harder in our judgment of ourselves than God will ever be. But these two momentous words contain the essence of the ACD message; and for this reason they are stressed.

II

THE publication of Conan Doyle's message in THY KINGDOM COME in December 1933 was, moreover, by no means the end of the story, but part of one much longer and no less significant. Its events, which can here only be summarized, began after the 'two-two day' meeting on 22nd May 1931. The cause was another message through the Oracle de Force Astrale. The Polaires were told that a certain 'treasure' was concealed at a ruined castle in the French Pyrenees; for the lofty hill on which the castle stood had once been a sacred temple, a secret shrine of the Albigensian brotherhood. This treasure, whatever it might be, they were instructed to recover.

History has almost forgotten about the 'Albigenses' or 'Cathars', a people, it is known, who came from the East and spread westward across southern Europe early in the eleventh century.★ In the south of France they received the name of Albigenses. Though their origin still remains largely obscure, mystics believe that their original founder (though many centuries earlier) was John, to whom are attributed the Book of Revelation and the fourth gospel—the gospel which mystics declare will be that of the New Age. The following account is quoted, partly summarized, from THE RETURN OF THE MAGI by Maurice Magre,† who devoted many years' study to the history of the Albigenses.

'It was in the region of Albi, Toulouse and Carcassonne that the mystic revolution took place…. [Afterwards, for nearly a century and a half the doctrine spread over the south of France and into Italy and Germany, where it found many adherents.] Buddhist renunciation became a moral law which spread among its followers with astonishing rapidity. From Bordeaux to the borders of Provence, in stern Languedoc, under the chestnuts of the Albi district and on the moors of Lauragais, the roads were full of ascetics walking barefoot, eager to tell their brothers what the spirit had revealed to them. It was always the humble in spirit who received inspiration…. In the poplar avenue and the stone cloister where walked a hundred shaven-headed monks, it breathed sometimes with such contagious power that it caused the gates to be shut and the garden and the chapel to be abandoned…. Estranged more and more from the God of the churches … the God of rich prelates and pitiless barons, the Albigenses worshipped the inner God, whose light grew brighter the more they lived pure lives filled with love for their fellow men.'

Within the sect were distinct grades. There were the ordinary adherents, among whom many of the nobility of the

★Since these words were written, there has been an enormous amount of interest resurfacing about the Albigenses or Cathars.

†Translated from the French, London (Philip Allan), 1931.

south of France were numbered; these corresponded to those who followed the 'middle path' recommended by Buddhism for the majority of men; and there were the *perfecti*, or the adepts, who sacrificed all ease and comfort of body for the spirit.

Through the *consolamentum*,* the adepts had power to open an approach to the heavenly worlds; for these adepts were heirs to a lost secret, a secret which had come from the East and was known to the gnostics and the early Christians. It should be understood that while St Paul had provided a basis for, and even founded, the Christian church for the masses, some mystics believe that an inner group or brotherhood was also established by Jesus Christ, the leader of which was John, called the Beloved of his Master. He it was who had first been entrusted with the *consolamentum*, the secret of which was the transmission of the supreme power of love, the rite itself being the material and visible means of projecting this power. Behind it was hidden the spiritual gift by which the soul of the dying was helped, was able to cross without suffering the gulf of death, to escape the shadowy astral lands and merge into the light.

'Never has any people at any period been so deeply versed in magical rites concerning death,' the author continues. 'The *consolamentum* must have possessed a power which to present-day people is quite inconceivable ... the inspiration of the dying must have been actually visible to the onlookers, for the adepts had knowledge which today is lost....'

In other words, the true cult of the Albigenses had been that of the Holy Spirit, the divine Paraclete—that is to say, of the *principle* which enables the human spirit to attain to the real world (of which this world is but the reverse side, the shadow) —the world of pure light, the 'permanent and unalterable City'.

For nearly two hundred years the Albigenses gained in numbers, but the end of their movement was tragic indeed. A campaign was launched by the church of Rome early in the thirteenth century, aided by the king and armies of the north

*Precisely what the Cathar sought or believed deep in his heart to have found: in one sense the Grail; in another, 'the peace that passeth all understanding'; in another, 'the jewel within the lotus'.

of France, together with mercenaries from other lands. Adherents and adepts alike, all must die, for all were heretics. Hundreds of the 'heretics' were walled up in caves to die of hunger and cold, were thrown into the flames, or cast from mountain heights into chasms below. Man, woman and child, they each met savage deaths, mostly without flinching and in a spirit of calm heroism. Not even the bodies of those who had previously died naturally could escape desecration; they were dug up and maltreated. And after it was all over—after twenty years of bloodshed—even the few children of the 'heretics' who remained alive were cast out and so clothed that men might know of their parents' shame. In all, this is known as the greatest and cruelest massacre of mediaeval times.

It is said that none of the adepts escaped, but certainly some of the adherents did, for again and again something of the faith and freedom of thought brought by the original brothers from the East manifested, and was again and again savagely suppressed and thought to be exterminated by further massacres and by the holy inquisition. Some think that Protestantism itself had its beginning with the advent of the Albigenses. This is as may be. What is quite certain is that no religion of past or present, the Christianity of Paul not excluded, has ever brought such tidings or such consolation to mankind about death and its aftermath as did the revelation of the Albigenses. Neither Spiritualism nor occultism have any such contribution to make; for it is said that even those Albigenses who were walled up to die in caves or flung into the flames saw heaven itself revealed and were caught up in its glory.

Nor must it be supposed that those who killed the adepts had any power over their souls—especially these illumined souls. During mortal life they were pent up within their personal selves. Afterwards they were freed, each in his degree (as was Jesus set free) to serve in a more subtle manner, but more widely.

So the souls of these adepts should be thought of as intensely alive, albeit invisible, exerting an influence which can still be felt within the mountain lands they once inhabited. They bless them still with their unseen presence; the passage of years means little or nothing to them; despite the centuries their influence still reaches mankind. They watch, for they have still power to assist men as the occasion arises. Such an occasion was undoubtedly the coming through of the ACD message. The invisible powers ever work in conjunction; and theirs may have been the inspiration behind the original instructions which came through the Force Astrale. They may have worked in conjunction with the Wise Knight—the Knight of the Rose Cross. Certainly the complete ACD message might be considered as something akin to the *consolamentum*, and as preparing the way for it someday to be restored to men.

If this be accepted, then it is indeed natural and reasonable that they should send for Minesta, that she should be brought to that particular mountain on which had been their shrine, and there be blessed, there initiated into the lesser mysteries, in order that the knowledge and power thus imparted might facilitate the coming through of ACD's message concerning the heavenly life.

Because of her belief in the Sages, Minesta journeyed to this hill, which was over three thousand feet high, rising above a deep valley, and ringed about with greater heights which were still snow-capped in summer.* Once among the ruins of the castle on the crest of the hill, she felt that she must isolate herself from the rest of the party. They were hurried, over-eager to find the treasure. By now she was not convinced that any material treasure existed. Day after day while the party pursued the search, Minesta became more aware of the presence and reality of the unseen brethren on that height. Many of the

---

*The chateau of Lordat (shown in the postcard reproduced on p. 12) is perched on a cone of rock which stands 370 metres (about 1200 ft) above the floor of the steep-sided valley of the Ariège. The height above sea level is 956m (3100 ft). Behind (that is, to the north, and blocking the view towards Montségur) is the Pic de St-Barthélemy, 2348 m (7700 ft): presumably, the snow-capped peak of the text, although the main ridge of the Pyrenees is visible to the south from Lordat, and will certainly have had snow on it as late as July, which the other may not. Today's tourist leaflets confirm that after the fall of Montségur, the castle was asylum for the last of the Cathars.

Albigenses had perished there. Human bones were found here and there only a foot or so beneath the surface of the ground.

But the *perfecti* or adepts still watched over their shrine. They came close and spoke to the soul of Minesta, telling her whence they had come and what had been the faith for which they had died. It was true—John the Beloved had been their Master—John of the fourth gospel—John who had been entrusted with the gnostic wisdom, and bidden to found an inner, mystical brotherhood or church of Christ, much as St Paul had been called to establish the outer church of Peter. During the centuries to come, the message of John would enter and inspire the hearts of men. The secret of all secrets which was theirs had been the *consolamentum* for the dying, which alone had power to lift men literally from earth to heaven by unveiling heaven itself before them; and this even by a word, a glance, a touch of the hand from an adept. Yet not in words alone could that secret be imparted—perhaps it could never be written down in words. Power to impart that secret could only be gained by living the life of renunciation—such as had been their life.

In a measure, they told her, they had entrusted their secret to her soul. She must go from there preserving it secure. Hers had been a minor initiation into their mysteries. It remained to see what use she might make of it in the modern world. She had in fact been called and initiated there because it would help the ACD message to come through with greater purity and force.

Meanwhile the rest of the party were busily delving into many places and finding many strange things, but not a treasure either material or otherwise. The time came for Minesta to return home. Ostensibly the expedition had failed. Yet had it failed? The Oracle de Force Astrale had only promised that Minesta should find the treasure. No mention had been made of others. What had she brought away as the result of her visit?

Succeeding years were to prove. We mortals are apt to think that we ourselves decide our every course of action. This may be so on occasion. Mostly, it would seem, in every important action we are *impelled* to do this or that. Most certainly it was so with Minesta during the years which followed. In the first place she had felt impelled to undertake the work for ACD. Then she felt she was bidden to go to the castle where difficulties and dangers abounded—for there were grave dangers there quite apart from those to life and limb. For long months after her return she laboured with ACD's message, now constrained to do so by an impulse she could not resist.

Shortly after the return from the Pyrenees, a branch of the Polaire Brotherhood was started in England under Minesta's leadership. Its title and method of working were subsequently changed, and it is now believed that these became more in accord with the ancient Albigensian methods. Two years later, with the publication of the book THY KINGDOM COME, a considerable problem arose.

Merely to publish the ACD message was not enough, it was felt. For any book is soon forgotten. How could the ACD message be kept alive? As with the messages of earlier teachers, there seemed only one way, which was to make it a basic faith for a community, and thereby to test it out to see whether it worked. This was done; under White Eagle's guidance a humble beginning was made at a small hall in west London, opened in 1936. It was named 'The White Eagle Lodge'—the word 'lodge' denoting a place where a 'family' might gather; and the initiating and sustaining power behind the work was that of White Eagle, under whose guidance and with whose cooperation and assistance the ACD message was given; and upon whose subsequent teaching the work has gone forward. Yet in those early days ACD's message was its foundation.

III

SINCE 1936★ the White Eagle Lodge has grown far beyond anything dreamt of in those early days, and through many a 'miracle' has proved again and again the guiding hand of the

★The section that follows (to the end of the chapter) was written for the 1975 edition of THE RETURN OF ARTHUR CONAN DOYLE by Ylana Hayward.

Sages. When in 1940 the original premises were destroyed by a bomb, new premises, more suitable in every way for the ever expanding work, were soon found, and the work continues there to this day. Later, under White Eagle's guidance and instruction, a country centre for spiritual retreat and instruction was sought and found at New Lands in Hampshire. The London Lodge, New Lands, and the rapidly growing third branch of the work, the White Eagle publications, all became registered as Charitable Religious Trusts, thus not only safeguarding the future of the work but also ensuring that no private profit could ever be made from it.

It was realized from the outset that with a horizon as wide as that opened up by the ACD message many subjects were dealt with far too briefly and this has been rectified gradually by the publication of books of White Eagle's teaching which expand ACD's original statements. Many thousands of 'White Eagle' books are despatched each year from New Lands, which has become the administrative centre for the work of the Lodge and Publishing Trust. There must be few, if any, English-speaking countries in the world where these books are not being read today, and it is felt that they carry an influence with them, a ray maybe, from the Mage or from the Brothers of the Mountain.

What started as a venture of faith has continued in faith until today its influence touches thousands of lives through its books and through the Lodges at London and New Lands and daughter lodges and small groups in many parts of the world. Spiritual healing, originally based on the chapter on the 'Healing of all disease' in the ACD message, has ever been an important aspect of the work of these Lodges and groups, and the White Eagle healers now treat hundreds of patients every year, with some outstanding results.

Establishing the fact of man's life after death is a vital part of Arthur Conan Doyle's message, and so one asks, what has been done about this in the White Eagle Lodges? In the early days of the Lodge individual proof of survival was given to numbers of people, especially to the recently bereaved; but as the years went by, it became clear that White Eagle and the brothers wished to help people to find their own contact with the world of spirit through meditation and spiritual communion. Now, individual messages are seldom given, but countless sad, bereaved people have found their own consolation and certain knowledge that their loved ones are still with them. This knowledge, which we can surely call the *consolamentum*, and the certainty that all life is one, is strong in the Lodge, strong in the lives of its members and friends and many who just read its books. It is now plain that Minesta was taken to the mountain-top all those years ago to establish the link with the ancient *consolamentum*. This was the treasure she brought away.

There has been a perfect plan behind all that has happened, behind the bestowal of the Force Astrale, the formation of the Polaire group, their linking with Arthur Conan Doyle, his message through Minesta, and the founding of the Lodge. In 1966 another stage of the plan was revealed. The Sages directed that a White Temple should be built on the hilltop by New Lands, and that this Temple was to be the focal point, from which the spiritual light and teaching was to be given to the world. The White Temple was eventually built and opened to the public on 9th June 1974, but preparations for this (although unknown to anyone on earth) began many years before. In 1956 Minesta again visited the Pyrenees, impelled by a hidden spiritual purpose.

Again she climbed to the crest of the hill—almost a small mountain in itself—and found the shrine of the adepts, despite other changes in the neighbourhood, as remote and isolated as before. There were still traces of the excavations by the Polaires twenty-five years earlier, but all sense of their restlessness and haste had departed, leaving the place entirely peaceful. As before, the brethren were waiting for her, seemingly as real— more real—to Minesta's trained vision than would have been mortals standing at her side.

They spoke with her, and through her to a group of brothers who had accompanied her, saying that in the mountains around were certain air currents which made it easier for the cosmic rays to penetrate, and that the pure and holy devas who guard those heights also watch over human evolution. They said that humanity as a whole was about to rise to a higher level of life. Therefore the watchers from heaven were on the alert. It was also literally true that St John the Beloved had once come to this holy place on the heights. This was the source of its ancient power which had kept the Albigenses loyal even to death; the source of the *consolamentum*, the 'consoling', which could overcome the dark veils between the physical and heavenly worlds.

Knowledge and power to use this *consolamentum* had long been the desire of men, who searched for it and called it by various names; it was part of the mystics' attainment of the 'holy grail'; it was the 'lost word' for want of which Freemasonry languished. But it could only be imparted to those who lived in purity and truth; all others would be blind and deaf to its significance.

These brothers of an older time had watched over the delivery of ACD's message and its outcome in London. They saw the effect of that work as a great etheric building already taking shape in the world invisible which interpenetrated this world. They had constantly held that work within their ray of love and compassion, which took away the fear of death from those who could respond to it.

During the great massacre of the Albigenses, their enemies had power only to kill men's bodies. Sometimes this had set souls free to inherit a greater power, a more vigorous life; and this power they retained for service even in the world today. They had been able to sustain Minesta in the same way that they were behind every true and dedicated brother of those or earlier times.

Much more was said but these words epitomize the message. Minesta came away exalted by the wonder of this experience; and yet it was but a preparation for what was to come. For in 1966, when she was in Italy in a simple chapel of what was once a monastery, the contact was again made with the Sages and the plan for the building of the Temple was revealed. The 'etheric building' described by the brothers in 1956 was to take physical form; and so it did, in the summer of 1974.

Anti-clockwise from top left: Minesta at Lordat in 1931; again, with Mrs Caird Miller and two of the Polaires; return to Lordat in 1956.

It is so difficult to compress any account of the history of the Lodge into a few pages, but at least this brief synopsis helps to demonstrate that the tangible proof promised by ACD at the end of his message has indeed been given. The ACD message has proved itself and continues to do so with every passing year. Every patient healed is a living testimony to the scheme of healing he set out, every person who finds that ACD's message provides a good working philosophy of life, a practical and hard-working religion which answers his questions and resolves his doubts, by so doing testifies to its truth. The existence of the Lodge, its expansion and the birth of many daughter groups, and then the building of the White Temple, these are all the promised tangible proofs.

The White Temple, its design a subtle blend of classical and modern architecture, a symbol of the Ancient Wisdom restated for the new age, is surely a fitting memorial to the spiritual work of Arthur Conan Doyle. The Conan Doyle message laid the foundation stone upon which the White Eagle Lodge and teaching has been built. As the light is sent forth daily (its focal point, the Temple) in prayer, meditation, healing of individuals, nations and the world, so his message lives on; and it may be that in time to come men will look back on this message and deem it the greatest and most significant among the works of Arthur Conan Doyle.

★

All that needs adding to this account, perhaps, is the opening of similar Temples, dedicated to the same high purpose, in Australasia (at Maleny, Queensland) in 1990 and in the Americas (at Montgomery, Texas) in 1992: an indication of the worldwide spread of the work.

PART TWO : THE MESSAGE OF ARTHUR CONAN DOYLE

Line illustration by Selwyn Dunn from the
book THE WHITE BROTHERHOOD

FOREWORD TO PART TWO

LITTLE has yet been said which can give any real idea of the conditions ruling when ACD spoke at the later series of meetings when he gave the full import of his message. That which follows is an eye-witness account taken, slightly abbreviated, from THY KINGDOM COME.* It first describes the room, furnished as a chapel, in which the meetings were held, the great power which gathered there, and the spiritual upliftment of all present as White Eagle opened the meetings with prayers of deep sincerity which filled the listeners with the wonder and awe of God.

'It will be remembered that a circle of four people was advised, and as, to our regret, Mrs Miller found that ill-health prevented her regular attendance, an old friend of Brighteyes filled her place, Mr Bradbrook making the fourth and acting as recorder throughout....

'Figure to yourself, then, the tiny upper room in a suburban home. Facing the East sits the medium, while on her left the glow of a shaded lamp falls on the notebook of Mr Bradbrook, on his attentive face, on the quiet presence of our friend opposite. By my side sits the medium. Strange to witness the day by day personality of Brighteyes sink to abeyance and fade out as entrancement steals over her, strange to see the grip of mind and personality sink away, to see her body sitting loosely in her chair, emptied of herself; and then to witness the overshadowing of her guide, White Eagle, the transformation wrought by the greater personality. Strange to listen to a woman's voice which has become man-like. There is dignity about White Eagle as he rises to pray: *"To the Great White Spirit, Lord of the rolling prairies, the wind-swept sky, the still waters, the*

*It is, however, like this Foreword, by Ivan Cooke himself.

silent night." Not yet have I heard any man pray with the same depth, sincerity, the wonder and awe of God.

'Then again, a changing: White Eagle's presence has fallen from the medium, and she becomes again stilled. There comes upon her the personality of another. Now her form settles in the chair, the hands fall loosely, as if in characteristic attitude; occasionally her hand may lift to stroke and smooth meditatively the upper lip, as if a heavy moustache hung there; and then again the figure settles. The face is now utterly changed, it is re-moulded, it is become—so far as a woman's face can so become—like unto the pictured features of ACD. The voice is different from that of White Eagle, for now it holds a northern burr, whereas the speaking voice of Brighteyes is clear, her words a little clipped. Now the voice somewhat slurs its words, and one could well imagine that heavy moustache as being there, for this—may I be pardoned—sounds like a heavily-moustached voice.

'Slowly fall the words at first, each sentence building one on to another. How still we are! As the words come, the pencil of Mr Bradbrook follows with little curls and dashes, dots and lines. The glow lights the wall beyond, where hangs an engraving of Our Lord. How wonderful grows the power gathered within these four walls! Still the voice continues, now swept along as if by a torrent, now stilled as by the glory of some vision which the voice is striving to pinion; now, stroke by stroke, steadily, steadily, as a smith at his anvil, beating thoughts out into expression. Then after a period will come a check, heralding always a change of direction, of subject; a pause while the mind behind switches over to hold its new theme, and then again the steady torrent of the words. Perhaps there would come a mistake, the commencing of a sentence to which the mind could not see a clear and logical ending, or the use of a word other than the one intended. Then a crisp "Stop!—score that out!"—or perhaps the voice would check itself, searching for a word or phrase, and then, failing to find the exact meaning required, retrace and recommence.'

Yet all this time [Ivan Cooke added later], one side of my

mind was noting how strangely formal, even businesslike, the gathering was. Apart from a few words of greeting, it was obvious that the speaker was continuing a theme from where it had ended a week or more ago, and that every atom of power, every moment of time must be utilized to the full. So also, when the meeting drew to a close and all the power was spent, the speaker would conclude with just a word of thanks, a message of affection or a blessing, and a brief farewell.

I shall long remember—indeed, I shall never forget—the passionate earnestness of the speaker, his purposeful voice, his forceful gesture as he attempted to emphasize some meaning not wholly clear in words. This was in truth a wonderful experience.

★

The period of reception for these final messages was about seven months, ending on 1st June 1932; which was almost two years since the first contact had been made with ACD after his passing. The account which we have just quoted will, it is hoped, serve to set the scene for the reader; so that from now on—throughout this second part of the book—the messages can be given without further comment or interruption. For the convenience of the reader, the brief words of greeting and farewell with which ACD began and ended his discourses have generally been omitted, and the discourses themselves arranged in a logical though not necessarily chronological sequence. Some of the prayers with which White Eagle opened the meetings, before ACD took over the control, have been placed at the head of the chapters. Apart from these all that follows in this part proceeds from ACD himself; it is he alone who now speaks.

CHAPTER 1

MAN'S REALIZATION OF HIMSELF, AND OF A LIFE EVER MORE ABUNDANT

25th Nov. 1931

'We call upon the centres of Love, Wisdom and Power, and we worship at the foot of the Cross, the Emblem of Sacrifice and renunciation of all personal aims and desires. We seek to be at-one with Thee, Divine and Living Christ—the Great White Light. We await Thy coming, O Spirit of Love. We worship Thee, and through Thy Love may the Truth of Life beyond death of the body dawn upon man so that all fear of death be lifted from man, woman and child. May they hold clear vision of the progress and beauty which opens before them. Thus shall man come to know his brother and to love him, even as Thou hast loved ALL. So mote it be!'

I

18th Nov. 1931

I FIND myself in an unspeakably beautiful 'heaven-world' at the present time. I desire above all to bring this reality home to my friends, but realize only too well I can share it only if they understand the 'heaven' to which I have gone. And this has made me feel a deeper urge to spread the truth concerning the afterlife. I believe that I have won some reputation as a missionary. I carry on my work still upon earth, but by diverse means and ways from those I once followed. O the difficulties of coming into touch with the earth plane! It is all so different from what I anticipated. The true conception of the life of spirit has yet to dawn on man. Thank God, the mists thin, and I can see with a clearer vision than once seemed possible. My friends expect me to talk of the trivialities of the earth life, but I have done with trivialities, having found the realities. Is it possible for me to paint, with the language at my disposal in this medium, an adequate description of heaven's glories and beauties? It can but be attempted—it shall be done.

★

It is fact that after passing through what is known as the astral plane we do actually shed a 'shell', shed the 'dress' or 'envelope' which once contained the soul, and which ... remains in that astral condition from which we die to rise again to true spiritual life. And that same 'shell' or 'raiment' can be reanimated or resurrected temporarily by psychic powers. Be it noted, such is purely an artificial animation, but can appear to a medium as a reality. We would raise people's minds to the true life of the spirit, wherein alone they may make perfect contact with those who have passed on. Let us remember, however, that a large percentage of those in the spirit world entertain no desire whatever to return to the earth plane, being neither interested in its progress nor in the people they have left behind. It is not for everyone to seek or try to force communication between the so-called dead and the living.

I repeat, in this new life intercourse between the two worlds proves not nearly so simple as I had been led to think, but communion can be a finer truth and more glorious reality than is yet understood. Communication must come to mean a true communion of spirit. Of the personal aspect of such communion, I would agree that while personal affections and manner-isms endear one to one's friends on earth, it is well to remember that these may be also a pitfall to man's relationships with his brother man. There exists too much of the surface relationship and insufficient of the deeper understanding of the needs of man's spirit.

Here lies the basis upon which much of the future Spiritualism will evolve. It must no longer be that free-and-easy, happy-go-lucky contact of personal memories, of earthly pleasures and desires, but growth into deeper understanding and recognition [of the spiritual needs of each soul]. What I am driving at must become the bedrock of Spiritualism. It is not enough, this free-and-easy contact of personalities. Spiritualism and spiritual contact must grow to an abiding reality. When such reality becomes part and parcel of the soul life, all fear of death, sickness, and poverty will be wiped away. This same spirit—the very spirit of the living Christ—can heal the ills of all. *For He shall wipe away all tears … and there shall be no more weeping or wailing or gnashing of teeth.*

With all the strength of my spirit I desire to reveal to my friends the new man [that I am]. I am no longer concerned with the trivialities of earthly affairs, except so far as these experiences affect the spiritual development of the individual concerned. (Not that I can help the individual save in teaching the foundation of the spiritual life.)

Yes, the old Doyle seems to be passing. But I will prove to you all that while I die yet I live again! There are no trimmings on a man when he has passed the Second Death; only pure spirit remains. O! that second awakening! One thing only was I conscious of—and that was the Allness, the infinitude, the wonder of God's love. In that supreme moment I knew no such thing as separateness of existence. Personality had died, but individuality was reborn. Into that great celestial throng of pulsating spirit life have passed all those who lived in innocence, in forgetfulness of self. In this mighty living host men and women who have passed through earth-death *live*, and give of all that is most beneficial to God's plan.

★

25th Nov. 1931   Not for one moment would I have you think I destroy the beliefs of Spiritualism. No! Rather am I trying to bring back a larger, wiser and finer understanding of this glorious truth of immortality. Some pass weary in mind and spirit, to a condition of dreaminess wherein they live, just breathing, as it were, for long periods. Others speedily traverse the lower spheres, shed that dense body which is theirs on quitting the still denser physical body, and enter the heaven-world. Realize this—only in *this* state of consciousness is man brought face to face with 'judgment': with God. When faced with the 'judgment'— which is but the realization of *himself*—he is able to look once and for all into the deeps of himself. Knowing at last his own frailty, as set beside the glow and glory of the God-life, his soul is filled with compassion towards all: with love, that redeeming love of Christ.

Now the ways open. He can go forward, leaving the earth plane far behind, forward into ever higher realms of spiritual consciousness and understanding, ever opening to the inflow of life more abundant; or else he is arrested by the cry—the anguish of those sorely struggling in darkness and sorrow on the earth plane. Is it for him to ignore the heart-cry of humanity?

Rest in peace! Yes, friends, I understand now…. If you had experienced the peace, the tranquillity, and the beauty of the heaven-world you would realize that there are many who prefer to rest in peace. Does not man also rest after strenuous labour?

I do not like the personal [that is, singular] pronoun very much, for it has become 'we' now—*we*. And that is how men will all feel upon entry to that spiritual life wherein there exists no separateness. Although individuality becomes greater than you on earth can conceive, in its greatness it becomes unified with the whole. Therefore no individual speaks of himself as 'I', because the individual is become no longer 'I' but 'we'. This is the teaching which will come to men's hearts—*we*. Man will know then that he can neither think, speak, not act entirely of himself, for every thought, word or act must bear its effect upon the entire community.

We—WE! Did not the Master Christ say, *Of myself I can do nothing?* Does not the great man say, 'I am nothing'? And being nothing, he becomes everything—he becomes all-infinite! Is it humility that speaks here? This is one of the first lessons a man learns when he passes the Second Death.

Spiritualism brings a vital message for this reason. There are thousands of souls released from physical life who need contact with their dear ones when they first come here. Then communion is right and true. The fault lies when there results [from that contact] a clinging to that soul when it would else pass onward. To establish true communication, man must seek the pure spiritual contact, never obtainable through the more crude psychic phenomena.

I trust we bring a message of happiness and beauty. Carry on patiently and you will see far deeper into the truth which these messages convey. Meet soon! God bless you all!

II

22nd May 1932

OH, the ineffable longing in my heart to bring back the greater truth of this heaven-world and the world of the discarnate!

It seems an age since I left my body, and yet today comes to me an increased power. Today, I believe, was my earth birthday, and although men may consider this long past and finished so far as I am concerned, yet indeed the links of earth seem to hold. Be it known that the day of the spirit's incarnation in flesh is a day of power for that spirit, and can be used either for good or evil. Thus on the anniversary of a death, a birth, a murder or a suicide, of any happening tragic or otherwise which vitally affects man's soul, comes a recurrence on the earth plane of psychic vibrations about the scene of the experience.

I seem to be far removed from earth memories—that is, up to a point. Experiences which were spiritually trivial fade and only those conditions which deeply affected my spirit remain. Much of which I wrote has vanished, while yet other works of my pen and imagination live: live sometimes, friends, to sadden; at others to inspire. Thank God that many a writing of mine dwells in my heart as a glowing memory of happiness and joy!

As I am speaking—or, shall we rather say, am pouring my spirit through the channel long prepared for this especial labour—I am again caught up in a ray of power, and can express with increased vigour my experiences since my release.

In very truth *a man does not fall into a honeypot when he passes from earth to the spirit world!*

Of course, all depends on the man's mentality and spiritual development at the time of his release. He who has lived a life gross, material, sensual, or selfish, finds himself in 'queer street'. [that is, in trouble]. Understand this, my friends; the soul must pass through every condition and phase of desire once encouraged and gratified: pass through, still [as] the conscious self, grown so familiar—longing for, yearning for, desiring with all his being to gratify the thirst and hunger for similar experience now torturing his newly-released astral body; and unable in most cases to attain even alleviation. Eventually the man becomes shattered, as it were: so driven by unquenched longings, until at last realization dawns that the grey astral is barren of anything to gratify or satisfy him. No picture can paint, no description attempt, the driven life of the underworld.

Of course, inevitably and eventually he reaches the point of exhaustion, once the fire of his being has all but flamed away. As a last resort his soul cries upon God. Where else can a soul turn in desperate extremity?

So soon as aspiration has found birth—*My God, my God, why hast thou forsaken me!*—so, according to capacity, awakes such tiny essence or germ of God sufficient to enkindle the desire for more.

He passes onward, through the underworlds. Every step towards salvation must be earned. Even in the next sphere, although lighter, clearer, brighter, there operates the law of salvation by effort; not even there will he attain satisfaction, but onward and upward must he strive.

My friends, there is always the other side [of the picture]. Whilst man may traverse hell and suffer tortures of mind and body both on the earth and in the spirit, there remain times when we can and do attain the heights: you there [on your world] and we here.

[Remember that from spirit] we come back by our own volition. By *right of choice* we accept conditions such as we, the ego—the true innermost of man—know will yield most valuable experience. Never imagine that the time of birth, the place of birth, or man's condition of birth to be an accident. The whole of the earth life—I say the 'earth life' because that forms a focal point from which the succeeding spiritual life evolves—must fall into accordance with definite and divine plan.

With what precision spoke the Master when He said, *Not a sparrow falls to the ground but your Father in Heaven knows. Even the very hairs of your head are numbered!* Such is very truth. The whole lies in the mind of God, for He holds you in the cup of His hand.

What man has to learn is to support himself by courage and effort. He must find not only himself, but control of his own being. Until then, man cannot realize his own tremendous potentialities: which same realization forms the object of life's discipline.

By 'life' I mean life, not as you understand it through mortal eyes, but as a whole, as one vast experience, passing from apex around the cycle, to return to the apex.

Yes, yes; I was given a glimpse of those heaven-worlds. Sometimes I seemed lifted up, to be borne on angels' wings to catch a glimpse of surpassing wonder.

Do not however mistake me. In many cases those conditions in the lower worlds, in the underworlds, are never experienced. The newly-released spirit can rapidly transverse those planes in an unconscious state, much as when at night you dream. To such they remain only a dream, thank God! Many wake on the plane known to Spiritualists as the 'Summerland', and there find a comfortable place, a very good place, waiting....

On this subject you may have queries.... I will try to give you lucid answers.

Question: I assume from your teaching that the seventh astral plane, the denser, is the underworld of desires and lusts?*

The lowest astral plane consists of a plane of desire, burning and persistent desire, the which the man has fostered during his life on earth. Those who migrate thither are such as hold neither affection nor love for any creature save self.

The plane above? Well, there we find life a little brighter. Although still dark, there abides more a greyness like a foggy English November morning. A dim light penetrates, because the inhabitants have developed some affection, some love, albeit merely love of nature or of animals. Throughout the journey of the spheres, light comes only from the waking within. In the greyness are seen stunted trees and vegetation, while forms of men live and dwell in mists damp and thick, being themselves clothed in grey; being in fact so wrapped up in themselves, in self-centredness as to create about themselves environments unpleasantly cold and repellent.

Thus self-centredness becomes outwardly actualized in a perfectly logical and natural manner.

Question: *What about the next astral plane* [the fifth]?

Now here we find brighter conditions, a desire to do something for the fellow next door, a waking interest in one's neighbour. Earth conditions tend to reproduce themselves. We gather in public worship, we dwell in houses not beautiful, somewhat dilapidated, and occasionally not exactly salubrious. Again the interior spiritual conditions of the inhabitants become outwardly actualized. The soul, however, here strives towards the light, and thus conditions grow more beautiful, more hopeful.

We pass into the fourth sphere. Now things are decidedly better. Here we come to beautiful scenery, to happy and on the whole harmonious conditions. Families dwell together; we see the homes described in many spiritualistic books, the lakes, rivers, mountains, flowers and animals: altogether quite a

*In the original text, the questioners rather confusingly numbered the astral planes both from the highest to the lowest and vice versa. For clarity, in this edition we have altered the text so that they are numbered throughout to give no. 1 as the highest and no. 7 as the lowest, and so on.

bright 'second edition' or continuation of a comfortable life on the earth plane. On this plane the soul attains to mental and spiritual development, and having so attained creates these outer conditions of harmony and of beauty, which after all are but the reflex of the soul's mental and spiritual level.

Cannot you understand? Paradoxical though it appears these conditions result because the mental and spiritual advancement of the spirit creates these things *for itself, out of itself;* much as a man on earth contributes to his home life either harmony or disharmony. Thus only our beauty, serenity and comfort come into being in the spiritual realms.

Question: *If the astral planes number seven, how can this be reconciled with the dominant number, twelve? You have given us seven astral, three mental and three celestial planes, thirteen in all?*

There are actually twelve planes. Of the seven spheres which we must call astral, the lowest, or seventh, remains so closely interwoven with earth, so identified with earthly interests and influences, that it cannot be included. To be mathematically correct, one should couple that lowest with the earth plane, for the denizens are still earth-men. The first plane of spirit commences in the first grey sphere. Is that clear?*

Therefore the spheres number twelve: six astral and six heavenly. The last mental plane marks the stopping place, or the *nirvana,* where the soul meditates, contemplates and absorbs experiences of the past. This is the resting-place after every incarnation before the soul returns to gather fresh experience.

Beyond these mental planes, beyond *nirvana,* awaits—we will not call it the 'third death'—but the final liberation from incarnations. Then the soul goes onward through the 'waiting halls' into the celestial or cosmic consciousness.

*An interesting concomitant of this account of the planes, is that the moment a man or woman rises in thought above the densest plane, they are already, in one sense at least, living in spirit.

CHAPTER 2

THE HARMONY, PERFECTION AND GLORY OF THE HEAVEN LIFE

'O Thou Who art Light, Truth and Love, the supreme illimitable 13th
Power of the Universe; Thou who art the sweetness of every flower that Apr.
blooms; of every human love that throbs in the heart of man; of the 1932
wind-swept sky, of the rolling waves and the sweet breath of life!

'O Thou Who art our Father God, we bow before Thy Majesty.
We pour ourselves out in thanksgiving for Thy love. May we be
purified according to Thy desire, that we be servants to Thy will. So
may we live in the eternal with Thee. We call upon the centres of
Wisdom, Love and Power.

'As it was in the beginning; is now; and ever shall be; world without
end. Amen.'

I

AFTER I left my earth body I could not free myself for a *Date*
considerable period, yet it is impossible to describe *un-*
exactly the 'geography' of my condition. I felt strangely linked *known*
with the place of my birth and early years. I could not escape
either to return or to advance to that heavenly plane which I
knew existed and was quite near. Truly I was tied, and all my
hopes of communicating with my friends knew frustration. I
tried and tried again, and yet again, and found the contact most
difficult. I was at a loss to understand the cause. I found myself
only able to give thought-projections, and sketchy bits seemed
to filter through the denseness around me. Such slight messages

gave assurance to my dear ones that I was conscious, at all events.

And then I seemed to be picked up, as it were, in a ray of light. A power unknown came to my aid, giving me a vision of my true state, and I subsequently learned that this ray of light was a projection of love and power from the Polaires Brotherhood [*sic*]. It proved of inestimable value to me, and has brought a clear vision of the actual state of life immediately following death.

Every soul must pass through such a condition, such a period of time, short or long, according to the mental condition of the man when he leaves his body. To some this is a matter of a few hours or days; to others of years. Remember, even the Master Jesus himself descended into a condition of uncertainty and what is described as 'Hades', the sphere of the disquieted spirits.* So, too, must every man on leaving the earth pass through that belt of the disquieted souls of men. As I said before, it is very difficult to escape from these astral attachments, mental and physical—only the enlightened soul rapidly traverses the sphere of astral, lower astral, and denser astral matter.

Time is nothing in spirit life. *In the twinkling of an eye we shall be changed,* as St Paul truly said. *At the last trump*—but this does not mean at the end of the world, as our Christian friends are wont to believe. It means at the end of the soul's world of matter. Then, when the man passes through the grey astral spheres and is touched by the light of the eternal spirit of God, *in the twinkling of an eye* he is changed!—and casts off the old terrestrial body and puts on the body celestial, and dwells in the heart of eternal spirit.

Truly, truly, it is said that a gulf is fixed between the man who dwells in Abraham's bosom, and the rich man imprisoned in the fires of hell. Can this be obviated? Will the gulf always exist between the man of heaven and the man on earth? Always, so long as the man continues to think and house his being in earthiness!

---

*'He descended into hell; the third day he rose again' (Apostles' Creed).

We have dealt of late with the conditions immediately *9th Dec. 1931* following death, and it may appear that we have perhaps enlarged on the gloomy side, by talking rather pessimistically about the grey spheres, the astral memories, and the mistakes of the Spiritualists. We unfold the reverse of the story. I have so recently passed through that state which is disquieting and disturbing that it may have left a rather deep impression upon the part of me which the more readily contacts the earth plane.

The difficulty is to find words in which to describe these conditions of life. The representations of life in the astral planes made from time to time through Spiritualism are often only the actual experience of those souls still closely linked with earth. As you have many social levels of life, so on the astral plane exist various conditions attuned to the desires of those who dwell therein; therefore you will get a variety of descriptions of this particular plane. After passing through the 'death' of the astral body, when the man discards his astral vehicle and enters the heavenly life, we there find a condition of at-one-ment—attunement—a condition wherein the soul is conscious only of the one vibratory note of love and service. In this sphere the soul is cognizant mainly of the great cosmic powers.

In speaking of that Second Death through which we all pass *20th Jan. 1932* after experiencing a period of unconsciousness—which may last for minutes, hours, days, or even years—a period of quiescence of consciousness, we said that the spirit then wakes to life rich, vivid, renewed. Time is nothing over here: the Second Death has taken place, and all that was of earth has passed away. With the Second Death there comes the great awakening—the soul's awakening—when it sees truth, and for a moment gains vision of the mighty salvation through Christ! With that in view a man advances into the mental condition of life.

I would, however, make it clear that the soul passes not through every mental plane, but migrates to the one particular mental plane to which he is attuned. Thus in succession he will work his way up through every plane of spiritual life, not only from that one experience which you understand as the physical life of here and now, but by and through every incarnate life the soul of man has lived. Thus he will mark out during each separate incarnation that place in the mental plane to which he must travel; and so in course of time experience every phase and every condition of spiritual life.

Is this clear? For that particular astral, mental, or celestial plane to which he is destined he lays the foundation in this physical world, the result being that he attains to lesser or fuller degrees of astral life, of mental, and of celestial life according to the aspiration and growth of his soul whilst on earth.

II

9th
Dec.
1931

I HAVE here a most difficult task. I shall endeavour to show the difference between the mental plane, whereon the soul emerges after the Second Death, the mental activities themselves, and the celestial life which lies beyond. The mental body contacts a mental state only, a state widely differing from that known as the spiritual and celestial.

The mental plane is very powerful, and on it it becomes necessary for the soul to use the mental faculties, which become unloosed as it enters this plane of existence. A delicate balance must be attained between the mental and the spiritual before the soul wakes to the celestial. For a period it would seem the soul must grow in quietude. As the seed is sown and left to germinate, so too the man, when passed into the mental world, dwells there for a period of quietness and growth, and then emerges into the celestial, carrying with him the power and equipment gathered.

In the celestial world the work of creation commences. That is the glory and magnificence of that condition of life—that creative art which is the real *becoming* of all creation. In this heaven-world man absorbs some potency from the divine quality of Christ. Almost having become angelic, he dwells amongst angelic beings. Would we could endow you with some flash of intuition by which to gather some idea of the harmony, the perfection, of the life!

Here the soul becomes conscious of its true nature. Here the ego* knows itself as very part of God....

Passing from earth in normal course of development, men reach this sphere of life in about thirty years.† There can be no drive or urge for the soul [against its will], for ever man exerts his own freewill. If he would linger in the astral condition he can stay long, so that a century or longer may elapse, or sometimes he passes quickly onward, anxious, longing with all his soul to be reunited with the God-consciousness.

What then can it mean to a soul willingly to renounce its heaven world, to retrace its steps earthward to serve? Can you conceive a tithe [that is, a tenth] of the wonder, the harmony of life celestial? Yes, there are forms, but forms that one sees are angelic: perfect in beauty, with faces tranquil and peaceful, shining with the glory of a great peace and love. Each mind is softened and becomes beatified. The air is rare and fine. There is a harmony, a divine music, which breathes continually in the soul. The soul finds a supreme joy in service, in self-giving. Do not conceive this as a sphere of rest, albeit it is a sphere of peace: for in peace we learn something of creation's ways, and become ourselves creative.

Yes, there *are* souls who willingly sacrifice even such joys to descend to the lower planes to labour. Like a diver descending to the deep, or a collier into the bowels of the earth, so can the returning soul don its astral garb and wear again something of the limitations of personality. And then they can labour in lower spheres only for a period, after which they ascend, as it were to breathe, unable to sustain for long so dense an atmosphere.

It *is* possible for souls still dwelling in celestial spheres to communicate with earth. There are messengers for that purpose. Few understand the wonderful mysticism of our Bible, wherein Jacob dreamed he saw a ladder placed between

*i.e., the divine spark of the individuated spirit, not an aspect of personality: see the note on p. 50.

†For a note on ACD's fluctuating concept of time from the other side of life, see the introductory chapter, pp. 48–49.

heaven and earth. A childish story, perhaps? He saw angels descending and ascending it—and that is precisely what is still happening. Communications *are* coming from those in the celestial spheres to the earth people: alas, that so much is lost in transit and that so much confusion exists regarding the methods of communication!

We spoke last about St Paul's words, *In the twinkling of an eye, at the last trump, we shall be changed.* This is the call from the supreme power, the Christ-power, the Cosmic Christ, to whom all men shall find [their true] relation. Sooner or later each and all must awaken to that call, the trumpet of the spirit, summoning them homeward. Man will then leave behind all that is of the earth, earthy; the individuality will become preserved, enhanced; the personality will die, and be shed. Regret it not, for although of the earth, and soiled by earth, it has yet been a means to an end—a means necessary to enable contact with experiences invaluable on man's upward climb to God.

Yes; teach the people the truth of communion, but for God's sake teach them the truth! Do not offer a fool's paradise! I can assure you that life after death is a very serious matter, not to be regarded lightly, nor to be glossed over with a varnish paint. I can assure you that when a man passes over from the physical to the astral condition he has to face up to things; there can be no more backsliding. Life resolves itself into a forward march!

Proofs—proofs? People of the earth cry out for proofs! They do not know what proofs are! They only consider something capable of being conveyed to their understanding through any of the five senses physical as proof of spirit power! And yet the great proof of spirit power is manifesting itself at this precise moment in a very definite and drastic manner all over the face of your world!

III

16th Dec. 1931

SO LET us return to deal further with the mental plane: not, mark you, to be confused with the celestial. Although terms almost baffle me, the several planes in the mental world must be clearly subdivided. Thus, after the Second Death, the soul enters to the plane whereon it finds itself surrounded by previous creations of intellectualism. In other words, the chief characteristics of the man find expression in cold, hard intellectual thought.

Yet a delicate balance exists between the intellectual and the intuitional, for on this next plane the soul responds to that intuitional or spiritual light which draws it ever onward, ever higher and nearer to the central focus of its being, the Godhead. On this second mental plane man becomes conscious of an intuitional flow, toning down hard intellectuality, and enforcing purer, intuitional concepts of life. In this condition man himself is becoming creative, since from this plane all the creative activities spring which take ultimate form as art, literature, music, religion, science: the many varying expressions of creative energy. Here man finds himself able to contact the source of all inspiration and creation.

From this intuitional ... but still mental, plane, you understand ... he passes to the higher, the third and last mental plane. Now he enters a state of quiescence.

As the man journeys upward he is ever shedding: shedding that stratum of himself which is of the earth, earthy. Always he absorbs lessons learned in his journey, which are retained by the ego. When man attains to this condition of peace and tranquillity—not lethargy, mark you!—the spirit remains still conscious, although mentally in a state of soliloquy, and he is at last enabled to see himself as he really is: able to gauge the effect of his life, not only as it has affected the lives of others, but in relation to the whole creative principle; able to estimate the magnitude or otherwise of his personal contribution towards the evolution of God's plan.

The third mental plane is a condition of withdrawal from outer form into inner relationship with the Universal. It is essentially a plane where the individual ego contacts that universal sphere of spiritual being. Whereas the past planes have been of definite *16th Mar. 1932* form, when man arrives at this third mental plane there is to a certain extent a lack of form. It is very difficult for one on the earth, concerned only with a life of form, to comprehend such a condition. Yet, my friends, when you consider the universal life—that great Omnipotence which you worship and love as God, you can conceive of no particular form. Yet there dwells within and without you God's pulsating life-power, which you recognize by its myriad manifestations as an individual intelligence proclaiming its handiwork in every creation of its power. When you pray, you pray to a mind that understands, to a heart that loves and is compassionate, yet to try to formulate that heart or mind is utterly impossible. For no other reason the Cosmic Christ manifested to the earth plane in flesh that he might give a form, a nexus, in order that the people of the earth might make contact—according to their capacity—with the universal Godhead.

So when we reach the third plane of the mental-spiritual world, we find that lack of form. That is, the ego is not limited, confined or bound to any particular form of being. The man is rather spending his time, not only by withdrawing into the centre of himself, but also expanding from that centre until he contacts the whole, the Universal.

It is true that from the earth plane men and women contact this universal sphere; but it is so powerful, so tremendous in its vibrations, that it proves oft-times dangerous in its effects on the human organism. This is a vast theme; but you occasionally see advanced souls on earth at whom men wonder—adored, loved and respected by their fellows—and yet for some unknown reason they collapse and death awaits them. They die of disease which the medical world cannot diagnose. Again we say that until medical science deigns to study the laws governing man's spiritual being, it must face and be baffled by obscure diseases.

Do not mistake this statement. We do not [seek to] convey that all who die thus are necessarily people of high degree of spiritual consciousness, whose end is due to contact with the universal sphere. It seems well, however, to explain that this

universal power proves responsible sometimes for the shattering of the physical body unless sought in humility and truth.

You ask exactly what is meant? We reply that there lies an
inmost centre within all, a divine birthplace of the spirit, which
to reach and comprehend is beyond all intellectual striving or
attainment. To attain to this plane by intellectual straining and
striving, without that due attunement of the spirit, or growth
to the spiritual planes of being, must inevitably bring disaster.
Yet if man will strive with heart and mind and spirit to seek
the kingdom of heaven in simple, childlike faith, he must reach
that plane to receive of truth and power and life.

We repeat, friends, that on this third heavenly plane there
is a withdrawing from expression through form into the inmost
depths, and in such withdrawal there follows expansion into
and absorption of universal life.

With this the thought will arise: has man thus ultimately
sunk individuality and lost desire? No, no, my friends, no! It
means that man has become greater, nobler, in his individuality. He has tasted the divine fruits, and *knoweth at last of his
own divinity*. He has become at one, even as the Gentle One
said: *I and My Father are One; I in thee and thou in Me*.

But then, of course, the man, the ego, can still return.
Although he is become as a seed sown deeply in the soil of life,
again to blossom in the spring, the human ego can again
emerge, assume form, and re-enter the various states of being,
until, if he so desire, he takes upon himself once more physical
existence.

IV

I SPOKE of a period of quietness and review before the passing
from the mental plane. Remember, in the mental plane, a man
is more or less concentrated upon himself, strenuously labour-
ing within, concerned now not so much with output as with
his intake.   Released from the mental plane, the ego loses
touch in great degree with earth life, but in the celestial sphere,
it seems, the contact again becomes far more vivid than before.

*16th
Dec.
1931*

To cover the ground again: we have outlined three mental planes—the lower mental or intellectual; the intuitional; and the higher mental which is where man contacts the cosmic forces. We then pass onward to the true spiritual spheres.

The Buddhists refer to the heavenly condition as *nirvana*, which well expresses that peace, the tranquil retracement of the experiences gained by the soul on its long march.

Did I not hear someone speak of the 'waiting halls of heaven'? Let me now return to these waiting halls. The soul whose fulfilment lacks completion dwells for a period in the mental state, an indweller of the 'waiting halls', having then gathered all his knowledge and reviewed his past. There he waits until the call comes or he accepts the order to descend, to take another dip into earth life, as it were, much as a diver to the deeps.

★

20th Jan. 1932

We have referred to the astral, the mental, the celestial, and the Christ sphere. There has been some confusion of terms, and I wish to clear up this point now. I conceive of seven planes of astral life, three of mental, and three celestial. From the celestial we pass to what has been referred to as the Christ sphere (but which I would prefer to call the 'cosmic or universal spheres'). In this condition of life dwell those beings who, freed from rebirth to a physical plane of existence, are now concerned not only with the earth but with the cosmic life of the universe. From this plane go forth creative masters, responsible for the life of the soul on other planets and in other spiritual spheres of existence.

16th Dec. 1931

Thousands of years must elapse, of course, before the ego attains to full expression and development, and only after gaining all knowledge possible through physical existence does it pass onward, beyond the halls of waiting, onward beyond even the celestial, into a still higher plane. What term can prove adequate?—*the Christ sphere!*—the at-one-ment with Christ! The rapture of a perfect love, a perfected fulfilment.

Passing from the mental to the spiritual spheres, the soul becomes conscious of a spiritual element [which was] before lacking, the near contact of the Christ sphere, from which the creative ones, the exalted ones, may descend to merge into some earthly existence by a supreme sacrifice. Such as this happened when the Master Jesus made his renunciation—but you have so much to learn yet of his life and death.

It is unnecessary for man to pass through physical death to contact all the planes of spirit life. Mortal man can and indeed does contact and responds to the influence of all planes of spiritual being, the difference being that when the soul is released, spiritual life gains a sweet intensity: the soul having lost a physical body, all the more surely does the soul-experience afford greater reality.

Again, *all the spheres of the spirit life are, or can be, reached by incarnate man,* who may thus indeed draw experience from a hell of desire or heaven of ecstasy.

CHAPTER 3

THE SPHERE OF REUNION

10th
Feb.
1932

'Immeasurable Might, Ineffable Love! Great Architect of the Universe, we worship before Thy throne of Grace. We come before Thee in humility, duly prepared to receive Thy commands. O Great One, take our will and make it Thine. Beautify our vision according to Thy truth. Inspire our minds with Thy goodness and make our hearts subject unto Thee. O Divine Love, we call upon the Centres of Wisdom, Love and Power. Amen.'

16th
Mar.
1932

AT this stage of our discourse a question will arise: this is all very interesting and very well, but what about that vibrant human love and reunion so long our dream and desire—will this be ours in the spirit spheres of life? What is the use of being a formless mass of consciousness, like an egg without a shell? Very unattractive, very uninviting, it seems, when one dreams of love, deep, rich and full, the fulfilment of which alone can make earth life worth its price. We remember the longing with which man looks forward to that reunion, to peace and happiness such as the world can neither give nor take away. Long have we dreamed that beyond the river Jordan we should find reunion.

'And with the morn those angel faces smile
*That we have loved long since and lost awhile.'**

Are we then destined to some formless condition, far removed from the fragrance of human love?

Oh, my friends, I can assure you that there is indeed a sphere

*Slightly misquoted from Cardinal Newman's hymn, 'Lead, kindly light'.

in the spirit world, a divine sphere of life in the upper regions of the astral plane, far more than the Summerland of the Spiritualist, a sphere of souls united. Mark you, there can be found not only reunion for those incarnate souls who can soar thither from the earth plane, but the reunion of all grades of spiritual life.

Let me explain: this is the sphere of family reunions—might it not be described as a family gathering, where all the dear ones greet one another? But not, be it noted, necessarily *continually* doing this, nor always indulging in a flow of merriment and joy. Duty may be joy and ecstasy or sullen labour, but when the call comes all must obey, migrating to that condition for which they are suited, or to which they have adapted themselves.

There exist periods in the astral world, or 'festivals', when there are family gatherings, much as you hold at birthdays, at Christmastime, at Eastertide, Whitsuntide, and so forth. On these occasions families meet and exchange experiences, meet in wonderful love and happiness and peace. Yes, indeed, a man can find his beloved there, and live and dwell together in happiness and reunion. Then again they mingle in massed concourse, in vast ... not halls or temples, no ... vast open-air cathedrals, as I may term them, where they praise God by song and love and prayer, in gratitude, in profound thankfulness.

Would you [like to] question me about this sphere of reunion?

Question: *Suppose one partner follows another to the life beyond, and is much lower in spiritual attainment than the first, and so cannot reach the plane of reunion: what happens then?*

He or she who has attained the higher spiritual plane can always raise the other, if only for a brief period. Illustrate this by your own experience. Take a woman of a deeply spiritual nature who loves greatly one whom, you would say, seems unworthy. Cannot that woman by her influence and love, at certain times raise that other soul by power of her spiritual presence? It may be but a fleeting experience, but he knows he is become near to her for a flash. In the spiritual sphere the same law operates. Remember, time is nothing over here: but a question of consciousness—that is all. By intensity of experience two souls may live a period in a moment, and the time seem long. A light will then have dawned upon that soul, and afterwards he or she will strive with added desire and zest to reach again that plane of consciousness whereon they two had enjoyed some marvellous moment of bliss and reunion. *There can be no separation in spirit!*

This must be very difficult to understand. Try, however, to grasp this idea of spiritual affinity. Although there may be work to be accomplished in different planes of life, there waits always *one* point at which souls may contact, although perhaps only at given intervals. At times you yourselves can reach heights of spiritual consciousness. True, you fail to sustain them and fall, as it were, with a crash. Nevertheless, you have had your moment. Surely to go to the spirit world does not make a man an angel always, or for ever?

Oh, how can I make you understand the love, bliss and joy souls here experience when they reach at last to their beloved? What joy to know that separation can never again be theirs: although they must perforce sometimes go their separate ways to service and to labour! Or to come to the supreme realization that separation dies forever in the arms of love!

Question: *What of twin souls who are indeed affinities? What is their destiny?*

It is a big question, but here again there follows no question of two souls, twin souls as you term them, merging and becoming one individual. There can be no question of the individuality of either becoming lost and absorbed in the other, or both in one; but there may develop such perfect harmony of desire and understanding that the two life-courses run as one within a single channel. When the soul reaches the higher celestial spheres there remains still the active and the passive aspect, the man and the woman; and each still contributes his or her particular creative ray, his or her ray of life-force, to the Universal.

I want to emphasize this truth again, and yet again. There can never be, with the eternal good, the universal good, any question of absorption; and yet it is all absorption. Here is a paradox; do you not see? In becoming one you become *all*, and in becoming *all* you become One: a most magnificent, stupendous, and transcendent thought!

If you could grasp—if only occasionally—some realization of this, you would find that world affairs run as a perfectly oiled machine. Friction would depart, because man would be translating the individual out of the personal viewpoint into some realization of his true nature. To this realization Jesus the Master and the Christ strove to bring men!

Whilst we are here we would leave another thought in your minds. On this plane of consciousness we have called the Universal—which means the all-ness of all life—man (I have to use the word man, [although I mean something greater]) can control the elements, can create at will by filling his consciousness with the universal creative life-force. Such is the secret which the masters utilize. Through that same vibration they overcome, or rather can control, all material elements, be they the physical atoms or those of the astral and the spiritual world. The Master, having realized this plane of consciousness, would by an effort of spiritual will (not physical will, mark you, but spiritual will) raise himself, and so quicken his vibrations as to attract to himself spiritual atoms. When they are accumulated, he can lower their vibrations, lower, lower, and yet lower, until they become no longer spiritual but physical atoms, to be formed by the force of his desire. Many question the record of the 'feeding of the five thousand' with five loaves, and two fishes. How did the Master accomplish this miracle? By raising His consciousness to the Universal, holding His thought *at one* with God, and attracting to that thought those spiritual atoms, slowing them down, and by His will determining the particular form of matter that these atoms should take. Thus He fed the five thousand.

We were speaking last about the sphere of reunion, that condition of spiritual understanding upon which all could meet. We spoke of family reunions on festive occasions which

30th Mar. 1932 (two weeks later)

obtain also in this spirit life. We tried to show that even from the earth life there can be reached this common 'plane', 'sphere' or 'condition' of spiritual harmony and contact. In preceding talks it was indicated that the life which is described as 'the life after death', is in reality *the life of eternal spirit*, so that these realms of spiritual consciousness cannot be limited to the life discarnate, but are with you, here and now.

This is the crucial point to be brought home; that this life of spirit, erroneously referred to as 'the life after death', is the life of the present, the life of the future, the life of the past—in fact, the life eternal; the life which every soul is living and contacting every moment, whether he be conscious in a fleshly body, or functioning on any one of the planes of spiritual being.

This inner spiritual life will harmonize and unite every school of thought, every religion that has held the hearts of men. It is indeed the full gospel of Universalism.

CHAPTER 4

CONCERNING NATURE
SPIRITS AND ANGELS

'Great Architect of the Universe, we assemble again with one accord 6th
to receive from Thy ministers divine truth of life and being. We, Thy Jan.
servants, being duly prepared, present ourselves before Thee, awaiting 1932
Thy commands; and we remember that with Thy wisdom in our hearts,
Thy beauty in our vision, and Thy will in our hands, we may go
forward to complete Thy work in Thy name, to Thine honour and
glory, for ever and ever. So mote it be.'

NEITHER pen nor brush can paint the beauties of the
heaven-world. Man glimpses but faintly the wonders of
the spiritual life, and but few there are who, by aspiration and
actual contact with high spiritual spheres, catch fleeting visions
of the glory of these lands. Such are the artist, the writer, the
musician, the man of fervour and religion. But these glimpses
are not sustained, and soon must fade when the man returns
to the mundane affairs of earth.

It is true: the spirit world and the physical world are
inextricably interwoven, and it is impossible for man to
separate these two states of being. When man has advanced to
such a degree of understanding as this he will live no longer
in so dense a material world. The very matter or fabric of the
world will become so refined, so etherealized, that man will
enter more or less to the astral condition of life. Such will be
the future, and even in your day will commence the gradual
etherealization of the material atom, so that the world becomes

more beautiful as humanity advances on the path of divine evolution.

We touch now upon another side of spirit life which seems much neglected; that is, the *nature spirit* line of evolution. We have been concerned hitherto with human life incarnate and discarnate, to the exclusion of physical nature. We must take into account also the life of the plant, the animal, even the life in the elements, of all those planes of pulsating life distinct from the human. Let us remember that nature also continues its evolution beyond earth to the astral, the mental and the celestial planes. Natural life fits also into the plan of creation in a perfect manner.

Strange as it may seem, I was always a follower of the 'little folk' and loved the fairy tales which delight the children—fairy tales possibly, to the hard-headed, but actually the most delightful little realities one could imagine. I take joy in visiting the great underworld—shall I call it undergrowth?—of nature life. It is the greatest joy to see the little people, the gnomes and fairies, at their work in the gardens of the earth plane, and in the gardens of the astral plane; and on the higher planes, a-weaving their dreams and aspirations (to be some day captured by someone dexterous with brush and pen); to see the little people creating their representations of the divine love and beauty of God.

This perhaps sounds rather flowery, and no doubt you will expect us to come down to a more practical and concrete description of these planes of nature life! How sensitive is the plant world! How wonderful it is to see little fairy creatures busily carrying spiritual life and sustenance to the plants! Without the fairy aid your plants would surely wither and die. Without the powers which are controlled by the deva, your physical world would fall to chaos. Man speaks complacently of the law and order governing his universe, without under-standing of the mighty power which holds the sun and the planets in their courses. Man speaks trustingly of a divine plan and loving Father who orders all things aright, but fails to take into account the marvellous organization of the spiritual spheres or the control, sustenance, and retention of these laws of nature.

Science regards these happenings [that is, what happens in nature] as normal, the outcome of certain laws named but never understood. Science proclaims that if a seed be planted in the earth, given certain conditions of moisture, sunshine and warmth, that seed enters upon a certain process of development to become a plant. Mankind accepts this outcome not as a miracle, nor as a wonderful manifestation of divine power, but as a commonplace; much as man accepts the ordinary routine of nature as a matter of course, almost, it seems, as a matter of right, refusing tribute to that infinite care and love and patience, the causation of all.

So: lying behind every manifestation of life, broods this great world of spirit. I wish, my friends, that you could open your spiritual sight as you walk in your gardens, to see the innumerable little folk. Maybe they would ignore you, since all are busy builders, creating their part of the temple of the earth life.

Yes, I catch a thought. There are in touch with the earth plane souls of angels who have evolved not through the human but through the nature line of evolution. True, these become sometimes attached to the human race that they may impart certain knowledge to bring power or accomplishment to the individual they serve. For instance, there are angel beings attracted to ceremonial. (This is no fairy tale: I give you facts.) I have myself seen such present at religious ceremonial or sacred functions. Some more or less nebulous knowledge of the angels of life and death has filtered through, and maybe you have regarded these beings as evolved spirits once of human men or women? You are wrong. There is an angel world apart from the human race, apart from the human chain of evolution, formed of souls never incarnated in a human body, souls advanced through a process of natural development, souls in close contact with inner laws of creative service.

Of such are the angels of music. Here I would interrupt my theme by comparing the 'little people' with the 'tones', their labour forming one mighty union and swelling the sublime harmony of nature. There will come a time, friends, when the brotherhood of men and angels will be better understood. To such end the whole of creation and evolution labours: to complete understanding and harmony between all God's creatures.

Why not? You are [all] one and we are [all] one. When man has passed that Second Death and is reborn to the realization which comes and grows for evermore, as an expansion of consciousness—the realization that in the giving and the serving of his brothers and sisters of all kingdoms of life, man becomes at one with the Universal—in that understanding he grows to become at one with God, and loses himself only to find in his submission the Christ himself.

To talk with you is a very pleasant service, but sometimes so difficult that I feel not unlike a man on a very hot day with a collar unduly tight and a head almost bursting. Can you appreciate the conditions? We must be patient and do the best we can.

Do not imagine any one plane, be it of nature or heaven itself, to be far above the earth in illimitable space. All wait within your own consciousness. Did not a wise and simple soul say,

'Closer is He than breathing, and nearer than hands and feet'?★ Such is the lesson we have all to absorb, that the kingdom of heaven is within.

It requires no great intellectualism to enter that kingdom, but only the simplicity of a little child. Teach your children about the fairies. Look for them yourself, and hold communion with this universal spiritual life.

Our brother, White Eagle, knows far more than he has ever told you about the nature spirits! Ask him! The Indians, bless them, lived nearer their God than any of the proud intellectualists of the western world, did we but realize it.

Here, then, is my last thought: simplicity. That is the key-note, simplicity. Life is not complex. Only the ignorant

★From Tennyson, 'The Higher Pantheism'.

themselves—a sweeping statement, but true—only the ignorant make it complex. Life is great in its simplicity and simple in its greatness. God bless you. My tender love to you all and all you love.

CHAPTER 5

FREEWILL AND
DESTINY: BOTH EXIST

10th
Feb.
1932

IN ANSWER to a thought—no, I am not working singly in this matter. I am but one of a band, but have been strengthened and taught many things. It is my particular task to be the spokesman, and to bring these messages back. Much that I pass on has been given to me, although my mind has caught a glimpse of these outer glories which I describe. I know these things *are*, but cannot truly say I have experienced such wonders; yet it would seem as though the whole panorama of life at times opens, and I see not only into the past but into the future of the world. Great changes are coming, a wonderful light streams upon the earth, humanity is responding. As that humanity quickens to this light, so it will become more spiritual, more etherealized.

Maybe you would like us to speak of something nearer to your own life, something more simple, tangible, understandable? *Dear friends, these things of which we speak are the simplest of God's gifts to His children!*

★

2nd
Mar.
1932

We would speak tonight of the harmony of the spheres of life. We have already dissociated ourselves from the idea that the spheres of spiritual life necessarily mean life *after* death. We have explained how these same spheres of spiritual life interpenetrate the astral and physical planes. We cannot sever these spiritual spheres from the physical, a most important lesson yet to be learned by man.

We would refer you to our talk a few weeks ago about life in the nature kingdom. We spoke of the marvellously intricate life of the nature spirits; of the rhythmic harmony and attunement between the varying grades of life in the natural kingdom.

Compare these marvels with that wondrous thread of cosmic life which penetrates and interpenetrates every aspect of each man's being, and try to realize the splendour of the love with which the Father God endows each and all of His children....

You little realize, my friends, as you take your way daily, how marvellously you are guided and cared for at every step. You do not realize that those dear ones whom you take as a matter of course—we speak of the beloved 'guides'—labour sometimes for years, even for half a lifetime, to produce some spark of divine light within your consciousness. They work persistently and consistently to piece together the broken fragments and disharmonies of human life, to bring to the human soul some degree of the Christ-consciousness. They labour continually on the earth plane, and also beneath your earth—that is, in the denser astral planes—as also in the higher astral planes.

From the lowest rung of the human ladder to the highest there is this same transcendent love and care exercised. You question: if this be so, where does freewill come in? How then are we to be judged? by the measure of our own desires, our achievements, and our failures? If this mighty power binds even the outer framework of our daily life, surely we are as mere puppets in the game of life?

Ah, no, my friends; although ordained by the great Lord of Love, this does not detract one iota from that freewill choice of action which is man's. You are continually making choices, either of the upward or the lower path. If, however, you choose the lower, the passive or nugatory aspect, then you must needs, through suffering and tribulation, experience the effect of that course—*by yourself chosen, remember.*

Freewill choice versus destiny: what a mighty problem! How little is it understood!

These problems find solution only by gradual growth into knowledge of God, and never by a straining of the physical intellect. There exist *both* destiny and freewill choice. Destiny, so far as man is concerned, stands for certain physical experiences through which you must and will pass: choice lies *in your own reaction* spiritually to these conditions of physical life.

We pass in our consideration to that great power which interpenetrates every moment of life and being.

Consider again the wonderful organization which exists in the natural kingdoms; in the creative life of nature, forever building, unfolding, encouraging, and forcing the growth of the plant; consider that same creative force which continually holds the stars in the heavens, the planets on their courses; that same creative life-force which is causing birth and life, death and rebirth, life and death again, like a rhythmic wave through all creation.

Can you now conceive a tenth of the power of that infinite intelligence which creates and sustains through aeons of time this indomitable life-urge into being?

Then, my friends, think of our wonderful human life, of your own individual lives! Of the power which supports, bringing you through these physical life-experiences and which weave some pattern of spiritual beauty into the warp and woof of man's very being!

If you could glimpse for one moment those gracious and beautiful beings living a life of tranquillity and harmony in celestial spheres; if you could see the beauty of face and form, it would bring some conception of that wondrous inflowing life of the Christ-consciousness, which has been working through aeons of time, through the many lives to produce eventually such radiant beings of glory.

Remember, step by step, every man is thus gradually trained, is developing towards his own illimitable mastership and Godhead. Think well, then, that every effort of mind and will, every action, every experience from the smallest, goes to the building, to the creating of such a Man....

Alas, when such realization flashes upon one's understanding, one is appalled ... appalled at the ingratitude and selfishness of one's own heart!

CHAPTER 6

THE PROBLEM OF
GOOD AND EVIL

20th Jan. 1932

'Most high and perfect Spirit of the Universe, Great Architect, we come before Thee praying that Thou wilt guide us in all our ways. May the wisdom of Thy mind inspire our work. May the beauty of Thy form be made manifest in our work; may Thy love inspire our every thought and action towards our brethren, and still may we pass through life's journey in safety, and come at last into Thy glorious Presence, perfected through Thee. Amen.'

27th April 1932

GREETINGS, my friends. Power comes with such dynamic force that I am almost swept off my feet, rather like a straw before the blast. This seems a good simile by which to describe the power of the spirit upon the earth plane at this precise time. With this onslaught you will witness national calamities and international distractions; withal, will be seen a remarkable rebuilding of a humanity which indeed will be inspired.

The same was told me during my earth life; I can but repeat them. There will be physical catastrophes; yet even now we see creative powers at work. The fiat has gone forth! There will emerge a great continent where now exists ocean, and there will follow the equivalent subsidence of land. There will arise a new continent, upon which will evolve a race of humanity in advance of that of the present day. With these changes there will come a refinement of the physical substance of the earth and the spheres surrounding the earth.★

★

The main theme we wish to develop tonight deals with the spiritual spheres above the astral. We again refer to the first mental sphere, the intuitional plane, and the plane of divine intelligence or wisdom. [To give you an example of the nature of this plane, we would say that] Christian Science as a 'church' draws its power from the first mental plane of the celestial spheres. When we pass to the next plane, the intuitional, there comes rather a withdrawing from the hard intellectual state to a more inward or intuitional condition of mind. And so to the next sphere, where the first two spheres become so perfectly balanced and interwoven that we arrive at that state of consciousness which may be described as divine intelligence.

We would differentiate between *intellect*, which is the condition of mind existent on the first mental plane, and that consciousness which exists on the third plane of the mental sphere, [which I shall call] *intelligence*. We re-emphasize the vital difference between intellect and intelligence. Intelligence is a very part of the divine mind. Alas! so many men, intellectual and clever, lack intelligence—indeed, often possess little intelligence whatsoever. From the sphere of divine intelligence or wisdom we draw creative power—not the creative power which produces form in the astral planes of life, but the power which creates actual *substance*.

★No time factor is given for the apparent prophecies of disaster, which may lie in the distant future (the birth of a continent, we can be sure, does not happen overnight!). In part, ACD was presumably anticipating the war years, the 'years of fire' (and in this respect the concentration of the Polaires upon this subject, for which see the introductory chapter, p. 36, is interesting). But he also speaks elsewhere of in life having been inundated by prophecies of catastrophe and even casts round for a reason for this (see above, p. 133). In the context of his message generally, one wonders whether he might also be saying, there is a plane from which these disasters seem indeed disasters: maybe as the consciousness develops, such things appear in an entirely different light, not just in their meaning, but in the way we experience them? But that is to stretch his stated meaning quite a long way.

On all planes of being dwell angels of light and angels of darkness. Do you grasp this? Do not imagine the angels of darkness flung down to some uttermost pit of degradation, nor conceive the angels of light as raised to the highest, 'sitting at God's right hand'. Nothing can be more erroneous than such a conception, which has long falsified man's outlook upon 'good' or 'evil'. Tonight it is my mission to endeavour to wake the realization that these conditions of intelligence—or, if you will, 'light' and 'darkness'—work and evolve side by side, and are the actual complement one of the other.

This must be driven home, so that there may dawn a clearer concept of good and evil. Always men have conceived that good must oppose evil. Again, nothing is farther from the truth. 'Evil' stands always as the complement to the condition you call 'good', so without evil good could not be.

So we return to the angels of light and darkness. These powers, hand in hand, labour unceasingly to bring to perfection that divine intelligence which ever strives to manifest through all form and substance. Now then! From each plane of spiritual activity, even from this third mental plane, the sphere of meditation and soliloquy, the work goes forward. From this plane can be drawn power, which, shed upon the earth plane, penetrates lower forms of creation, much as rays of sunlight and sun-power light upon the earth. The lower the sphere, however, the less active it becomes.

From all planes of spiritual consciousness can be drawn power which can be and is in use by man: power for good or power for ill. Never run away with the idea that all spiritual power must necessarily be good or 'white'. What, then, of the 'principalities of darkness', the 'adversaries' and 'princes of the shadow'? (You recall St Paul's teaching on the subject. Being a disciple of the Ancient Wisdom he knew both 'good' and 'evil'.) With this in mind we can also recognize many an instance in which men and women utilize such powers for selfish and even evil motives. One might instance many a warlord and conqueror, many a great financier.

Is this difficult to credit? Take for example a man desirous of accumulating wealth. Something within more forceful than himself ever spurs him forward, once embarked on his path— once he has attracted to himself such powers. Despite any wish to cry halt to his money-grabbing he cannot stop, though perhaps he is beginning to loathe a wealth that enslaves. Control is lost. Like an accumulator of limitless capacity, the cash flows in an influx he is actually unable to arrest, though no man now knows better the burden and the curse of wealth. Such an example may also be found in the writer, the dramatist, the statesman, in *any* who lust for power, and have that in them which can contact the power sphere. Beware, lest the driver become the driven!

Beware! The angels of darkness are at work! I but give the idea, the concept, the realization. You yourselves can trace this shadowing power in many a life ending in failure and disaster. Would it not be better, then, for evil to be wiped out and only good remain? If such be conceivable, is it desirable?

We cannot see such a happening making for a perfect universe.

Can we help you to visualize two great wheels, two rings, two cycles revolving one against the other, each keeping and holding, as it were by a magnetic force, the position of the other? We see an enlargement and a working of perfect harmony.★

We would impress this upon all: *that which you call 'evil' is also of God; the universal Intelligence which man calls God contains both good and evil!*

Such a statement must create much controversy. I give, however, such as I know and see the truth to be. We must live and strain and strive, all and each of us, for a perfect balance, so that darkness shall never overcome the light; but rather that good and evil together shall, not as masters but as our servants, work out in us the perfect law with perfect precision. At the

★[Note from THY KINGDOM COME:] Here ACD failed to get across in words his actual meaning; but by gesture also he endeavoured to show us the concept of two cycles, one turning ever against the other, in perfect rhythm; by such time and rhythm maintaining the moral balance of the universe, much as centrifugal and centripetal force poise a planet in the solar system.

present time comes an overshadowing, an overruling, by the powers of darkness. The earth has to readjust, to find and maintain once more her moral balance, such being perfection: greater than good, greater than evil. Good and evil must become your servants, even as they are God's servants. That is the ultimate.*

4th
May
1932

Only when a man becomes raised above the physical and the personal thought-life can he view life as one stupendous whole; see it as one comprehensive *all* of God wherein can be no difference between good and evil, black and white.

Now the question comes: *If what you say is true, do you not rob us of all impetus towards good? What need is there of striving to improve the world, or to raise oneself, if after all there be no difference between right and wrong? We might just tumble along any old way, for all will come right in the end.*

We remind you that as the stars are poised in the heavens, so also is every human soul poised in the cycle of life, is held there within the consciousness of divine intelligence. Whilst that soul has been given a degree of freewill choice whereby to accept or reject good or evil, so also it can never break its link with the great Soul, God. To God there is always an upward pull. For a time that soul may divide, deny, reject, but can never escape, at the last it must surely yield. Then: *I will arise and return unto my Father!*

What follows if for a time the soul resist? It means that by his own freewill he takes the left-hand instead of taking the right-hand path. Remember, he hasn't escaped! The magnetic force of the divine intelligence must ever hold him on the path

---

*The notion that the powers of darkness were, at the time, 'overruling' the powers of light *is* controversial, though largely because in spite of Conan Doyle's insistence, we still tend to see that light and darkness in conventional moral terms. Seen in the way he clearly intends us to understand it, the comment is in some ways very reassuring: it shows all suffering and so-called negativity as being within the divine love—not only in a way that suggests the sufferer is in some way protected and loved, but inasmuch as it shows the whole process of life to be moving towards an end which is, in the over-riding, single and not dual, sense, *good*. This, if we understand ACD correctly, is the meaning of the next paragraph: that there is a Oneness wherein this duality is entirely contained.

of eternal progression. Through many transgressions he may take the easy path of evil, downwards, downwards. Then comes the turning, the lifting, the upward climb with bleeding feet. Thus no man can escape his destiny, which is ultimate perfection; ultimate *return* to the God of his creation.

Truly, before man can become Godlike, he must pass the lowest arc; must bottom the depths of evil, as well as reach the heights. To win to perfection man must pass through the deepest hell, and climb to heaven. When at last man can grasp this tremendous truth he will cease to condemn. The bright ideal of a perfected soul towards which brother man evolves, to which he is even now striving through good or through evil—will hold and fill his heart. My brother's path is his—my path is my choice. What matter?

Thus only does the ego attain to mastership, master of himself and of all the powers whereby this earth life is encompassed.

★

We touch here on the spheres of cosmic life. In the past we have described mental and celestial spheres, but now we deal with that cosmic life which is the highest, from which must descend and ascend the outermost and the innermost plane of spiritual consciousness in touch with man.

When a man can by continual effort reach that cosmic consciousness he will be able to get into touch and receive clear communications from inhabitants of other planets. Although man has for long striven to invent an instrument [in order to obtain such communications], he will learn that only in spirit and through spiritual understanding can communication be established. First man must attain the brotherhood of man with man in social and national life; and then brotherhood between nations. Later will follow an interplanetary brotherhood, born of the interplanetary communication which will become possible to the raised consciousness of humanity.

First, however, we have to learn the elements of brother-hood. *Man cannot live by bread alone, but by every word which*

proceedeth out of the mouth of God. In other words, man can
accomplish, can attain to the fulness of life only through
contact with spiritual verities.

★

We are aware that the statements we have made about the
problem of good and evil might evoke a good deal of criticism.
Nevertheless, we re-emphasize the fact that these two forces,
'good' and 'evil', are not so opposed as appearance warrants.
Marching in step with the creative powers of good must always
tread the destructive powers of evil. Even as in your earth life
it is necessary to consume and to destroy rubbish and garbage,
so it is also with the economics of the universe.

Might we not then describe the angels of darkness as the
individualized powers of evil, as great destructive forces which
consume that which is unwanted in the scheme, a perpetual
absorption from actual being of those things which prove
undesirable? Thus we suggest that the powers of evil cloak our
ultimate good. Being negative, it is true they absorb from life—
the human life, the universal life—absorb that which is
unwanted, cast off, and discarded. Appearing to destroy,
actually they do not destroy; though we have said they
consume, rather they *transmute.*

So let us conceive them as transmuting the undesirable to
the eventually beautiful. Let us recall the two mighty cycles—
shall we say of evolving purpose?— which men call 'positive',
or 'negative', or roundly 'good', or 'evil', [and see them as] each
the complement of the other; and both as being necessary to
perfect the scheme of the Absolute. As night follows day, so
with the same certainty does evil balance good, and good evil,
while always there proceeds the transmutation—good to evil,
evil to good. Thus the great cycles of God's evolving purpose
roll onward, through aeons of time, eventually to clothe the
soul of humanity with perfect balance, and perfect harmony.

Eternally this perfected attainment means the putting forth
again of God's energies for the creation of fresh worlds,

destined for the habitation of new races of men—for the house of God must ever enlarge as His children return from their wanderings.

It is utterly impossible for the finite mind to comprehend eternity. Again we can only suggest eternity is best represented by the great wheel, continually revolving, never checked, never stayed in its course.

Yes: God is both good and evil. It is but your conception of 'evil' which is wrong. Shall we suggest evil to be rather a concept of thought than actual reality? If a man thinks and lives but to satisfy his own desires, so also he lives from a one-pointed sense, or selfish attitude of mind, in darkness or that which men call 'evil'. If, on the other hand he lives and labours, desiring to give all, to unite himself with the common brotherhood, he dwells then in the light, and draws to himself light, happiness and all those attributes which are of the heaven-world.

Cannot you see that merely a reflection of the man seeks the evil or the good, the two being one and the same to the inmost man?

Man looks about him, seeing cruelty, evil, ignorance, and declares, 'You cannot ignore or deny evil!' Such a conclusion is based on false premises. By what possibility can man judge whether his fellow serves good or evil? Mostly is he guided by the conventions of the country, by the customs of his people. 'Good' to one seems 'evil' to another, and vice versa.

★

We would speak of an order of beings seldom described. Indeed, I think that to some they are not even known about— that is angelic beings, winged beings. Yes, they *are* winged beings: the great deva who holds the ordering of so many lives; who commands such wondrous power that without her, man's life would lack all sweetness.★ I speak also of the angels of birth

★ The devas control the group-souls of the nature kingdom, of which ants and bees are a prominent example, but their powers extend beyond the insect to the vegetable, animal and bird life [note from THE RETURN OF ARTHUR CONAN DOYLE].

and of motherhood, of the angels of death; of the angels of music, of art and literature. Has man ever dreamed that the emotions of which music, art and beauty are the outcome, vibrations which are so fine, so delicate, originate from spheres beyond grey earth, from ranges beyond the compass of human mentality? Spiritual beauty must emanate from the spiritual world and the spiritual beings thereof. Such angels are dual personalities, crowned by the love which they bear to each other—and not only to each other but to the whole universe.

Yes, yes—we have not dealt sufficiently with the heaven-world. We have occasionally painted pictures of rather gruesome character, I fear. It is profoundly difficult to express spiritual reality with words fitted only to explain and describe material and physical conditions of life. I would hold out to all a hope beautiful and true beyond compare. I would assure them of progression to be won by desiring and striving after beauty, love and wisdom. I would describe a life perfect in expression of all higher feelings and attributes which lie in the depths of man's nature. There is not one soul of earth—black, white, red or yellow—but that it finds providence in the vast universe of spirit. I would paint if I could a picture that must *satisfy desire and fire imagination for evebnvgry living soul on earth;* were the words mine, I would show a world of spirit ever evolving and opening to new vista upon vista of beauty. As one attains one sees, endlessly, heights beyond. Ever the air grows finer. Exultation fills and floods one's being, nerving one to fresh effort and attainment.

CHAPTER 7

'AT TIMES THE WHOLE PANORAMA OF HUMAN LIFE OPENS BEFORE ME'

I

WE HAVE reminded you that every phase of life in the spiritual realms interpenetrates the planes of physical life, and that man, whilst in the physical body, is still active on the spiritual planes, astral, mental or celestial, to which he passes on leaving the earth plane. This brings us right to the heart, to the very core, of spiritualistic philosophy, indeed to the very nexus of every religion which has ever been or ever will. The basic truth of all ancient religions lies in this teaching of the life of the soul, not only during earth existence, nor when it passes into the unseen, but during the whole soul life, from when it first became a separate ego, a projection from the great Sun of life.

Such teaching comes from the very birth of time, when man dwelt in his highest form of spiritual consciousness, before the descent into the depths of materialism (from which he now struggles on the upward arc of evolution). Yet through those ages of his descent, man has never been bereft of inner consciousness of his true being and his relationship with the Godhead.

The life of the spiritual realms represents always the inner life of man. In man's descent from God, that inner life becomes less evident, since the life-urge then becomes a 'putting out'

3rd Feb. 1932

into form, the formation of a personality; in the ascent there comes a withdrawing into, a seeking and finding of his own true nature, his own vast heritage.

I want again to emphasize this point—that during man's life on earth he is acquiring that quality of consciousness whereby he can and does manifest on the numerous inner planes of life. Thus, when he is freed from the prison of flesh he will automatically migrate to that particular plane in the different worlds for which he has fitted himself. With this vision and this knowledge, life becomes orderly, no longer touched by chance nor subject to accident, disaster or injustice in any form.

When people express loathing of the thought of reincarnation, it is indicative of a closed mentality. It would seem that a shutter has come down on half the spiritual mind, as though a dark curtain hangs between the seeming outer realities and man's inner, deeper intuitive knowledge. When one reviews life and examines closely the long experience inevitable before man draws near to spiritual completion, one recognizes not only the necessity for reincarnation, but the tremendous importance of the smallest detail of life.

In the world of spirit all is law, order, and harmony. Few dispute that in the world of nature everything reacts to an exact law, and physical as these laws seem in their outworking, they originate from the spiritual universe.* There are no haphazard methods, for nature is very drastic in dealing with delinquents. So also in the spiritual spheres; the smallest action calls forth an exact reaction, and thus man's thoughts, his creations, become like his angels of good or evil. When he views his life from a higher plane of existence, he well realizes the disaster of those mental creatures of gloom and depression and selfishness which were and are his children.

I touched this some time ago. It has affected me deeply since my arrival, for I was wont to create characters, scenes and word-pictures. Mine was a vivid imagination, and whilst I gave forth many a picture of joy, loveliness and beauty, on the other

---

*Since these words were first published, physical scientists have of course quite considerably changed their views about the laws of nature.

hand my pen also depicted ugliness, crime, crudity and horror. Whilst recognizing that such by their very contrasts teach their lesson, on the other hand creations of ugliness and terror live in a man's mind and fill it with vibrations which are violent and unhealthy. Now I gaze into the lives of men and women who have been thus considerably influenced by me. This I tell you only to illustrate the lesson.

Some day man attains the joy or terror of seeing the effect of his creations, be they beautiful or the reverse, no matter whether these creations are merely fictitious characters, or actual conditions of life resulting from actions such as have spread an influence in the lives of others. He sees his own contribution, be it of good or evil, to the collective whole. Thus indeed does man, every moment of his life, contribute to the universal power of good or the universal power of evil. Rather, shall we say, not 'good' or 'evil'—but 'positive' or 'negative' vibrations, because the positive only prove the creative, the eternal; while the negative, being destructive forces, eventuate in suffering and pain.

Thus man recoils from a sickened world today. Yet we from the spirit can see the rays projected from the great Sun of life. There must result suffering, because humanity has sown the seed of suffering. Evolution swings on the upward arc, however; however strong the downward pull, there remains yet a greater attraction, and humanity will yet be saved by the true instinct within itself, that deep and innate hunger for God.

Yes, we can promise a new earth and a new heaven, for the old earth is passing; a new earth and a new heaven will come because humanity creates anew both heaven and earth by its striving. God's workmanship strives ever towards an unimaginable perfection in spite of ignorance, cruelty and wrong.

The old world passes, yet will it live again.

The same laws rule on succeeding mental and celestial spheres of being. As man on earth aspires to become even as his Creator, as he receives the divine love and power of God, so must he raise the material vibrations of the globe he dwells upon. To such limited and circumscribed five senses as man possesses, this etherealized world of the future would be intangible, invisible; nonetheless that world will embrace a greater measure of reality than time and sense can now unfold. There roll planets even now within the radius of the solar system invisible to the eye, or the most powerful telescope, so spiritualized as to have risen beyond the compass of physical vision.

While man dwells in lowly estate he cannot recognize anything outside his own capacity. Like a fish in darkened waters he gropes, unconscious of any other sphere of life. So is he blind to these more beautiful and ethereal worlds. To a larger consciousness only there opens a new universe (distinct, be it noted, from those spheres and planes of existence already described, and which interpenetrate our physical order of existence).

20th
Jan.
1932

I have already told you of worlds of which your astronomers know nothing, worlds composed of etheric matter, the influence of which is felt from time to time upon the earth. As the radiation of the known planets affects both the collective and the individual life of man, so also do these etheric planets influence men on the earth plane. At different periods of the earth's history there have occurred catastrophes and cataclysms inexplicable in the ordinary terms of science, the cause of which may be understood when knowledge has been obtained concerning these powerful planetary forces.

3rd
Feb.
1932

The earth is the darkest planet of the system, so you have yet something to look forward to. If only the people of earth would open to us, and let us dispel the fear of death, they would step bravely the road to beauty, wonderment and joy.

20th
Jan.
1932

The question arises: if this [account of the cosmos] is so, are men merely puppets in the grip of the mighty powers of an unseen universe? Such is the natural query of the physical brain. But the untrammelled mind realizes that such a law [as we demonstrate] may prove a fundamental ordinance of infinite love working out to the last degree the perfecting of God's wayward humanity. So a wise mind remembers not only individual lives on a physical plane of existence, but ranges over the whole, the magnificent structure of the evolution of the divine spirit of God through human experience. That comprehension, that mind, can only bow down before such magnificence and majesty, and adore the Great One who has conceived the plan of this mighty evolution of spiritual life.

The effect of these unknown and unseen planets can be of tremendous potency, but humanity as a whole may have a say in the direction of these forces, which bring an uplifting and spiritualizing effect throughout human life. Equally can that same humanity attract those forces which are destructive of good. It is the collective thought-life of man which still decides the issues.

I am endeavouring to touch on a subject so stupendous as to be almost beyond my power to clothe thought with words, although I think I have been compelled to venture because of the controversy now taking place regarding the prophecies of world catastrophe and world changes. I would impress upon the people concerned that cataclysmic changes will come to the earth plane; they are inevitable.* A new era is at hand, when the great Cosmic Christ draws nigh to earth. May His children recognize His power and glory.

Realize that those who reject Him are not wilfully mad, nor wicked, but suffer from a lack of spiritual evolution. They will therefore be returned to a lower cycle of evolution, and thenceforward journey onward by a different road from those who at this moment are ready for realization and welcome.

Now to define what we mean by the Cosmic Christ.

He is little understood even by spiritually developed and intellectually advanced people, and there lingers a pathetic confusion of thought concerning the divinity and the deity of Jesus Christ. The churches, the orthodox churches, are guilty of almost as much materialism in their teaching as is Spiritualism, because they have seized upon the physical aspect only

*Regarding cataclysms, see above, pp. 36, 133, 192–93.

of that wondrous presentation of the infinite through the Initiate, Jesus of Nazareth; deifying Jesus of Nazareth himself, and failing to recognize the infinite love and wisdom manifest through him, failing to realize how small a conception is theirs of that indwelling force, that life-more-abundant known as the Son of God, Son of the infinite and universal life-force.

Throughout history prophet and seer came to prepare His way, quickening humanity that it might receive this mighty manifestation of Christ in the flesh. He came and was made manifest, was despised and rejected, and is today despised and rejected by many calling themselves Spiritualists. How can they reconcile the name of Spiritualist with the denial of the noblest spiritual Being made manifest through a physical body?

There was a time when I renounced the saving grace of Jesus Christ, and, as I was led into Spiritualism I believe that Spiritualism helped me to become a little less materialistic: I gradually began to see the light and the beauty of that life of the Nazarene. I accepted Him as a wonderful medium at first, as a noble Brother and comrade to man. Truly, truly, He is the great Brother; the Brother of humanity, but the quality of His brotherhood cannot be reconciled with the prevailing idea that He was merely a man as ourselves. All is a question of degree— [of the degree that He lives] in us, we in Him who was and is Son of the Father. Let us remember how limited and partial a manifestation could be made through the body of Jesus; but, surely, enough to teach mankind that God is a God of love. By the example of life itself He demonstrated that the one way to eternal life and the kingdom of God was through Him: through man identifying himself with His divine grace, His magnificent thought, His transcendent spirit of love and tenderness and mercy; the one saving grace for poor humanity.

This will be very clearly demonstrated within the next five years.* Man can see signs and portents creeping upon the world; the undermining of the rotten systems, the bitter fruits of wars, and armaments, reparations and tariffs. It is to be

*The five years takes this prophecy up to 1937; in some ways, the decay of the old age still seems to be continuing. But amid the decay, new hopes arise.

demonstrated to a bewildered world that all must bow to the one power which alone can save humanity from utter destruction—even the saving power of Christ, as demonstrated through Jesus of Nazareth.

II

WE HAVE touched on many vital points and shall endeavour *10th* to enlarge on these, filling vacant spaces and painting a fuller *Feb.* picture. We have spoken of the cosmic sphere, and have left *1932* the soul in that condition, suggesting that from this cosmic sphere the great ones are sent forth. Man arrives at long last at that stage of his evolution when he has finished with physical life, when it is no longer necessary to return: but as regards his finer spiritual consciousness there are still great heights to scale. Therefore it remains necessary for the ego to descend again to some *aspect* of what might be termed incarnation, because only through such experience man can attain further.

So we direct your minds to the spheres, to those planets to which we have just alluded, those physical planets of gossamer matter which, were they of denser etheric substance, might radiate light sometimes visible to the astronomer.

There are many souls who, having finished their course on earth and her spiritual environments, advance in communities and groups to recommence on one or another of these more highly evolved planets. They descend through various spheres which, in a sense, correspond to those spheres of spiritual—or, shall we say, celestial—life which surround this earth plane; through spheres of finer quality, of greater radiance, of higher and more spiritual vibrancy.

These communities of spirits descend by easy stages, and ultimately manifest in what might be termed physical bodies, but I can never describe the beauty of their forms. Suffice it to say that these conditions of life are wondrous, wherein all the laws of spiritual life work harmoniously to their destined end. Life in such form is without limitation in the way that men bow to limitation, not only on earth but even on the higher astral planes surrounding the earth. Life has become veritably *illimitable*. Who can conceive a tithe of the glory, the fulness, the ultimate grandeur of existence? Knowing and realizing bondage in matter the sympathy of these advanced beings is drawn to the earth plane, and this is why, with humanity in dire need, communities of these angelic ones direct the light of their compassion earthward.

We spoke of guides who, descending from celestial spheres, are actually reborn on the astral plane instead of reincarnating on the physical. By choice they undertake this work, and only at considerable sacrifice. They can, and do, of course, gain much experience and give much help through their close contact with humanity.

We spoke of reincarnation, too. You are told by some that it is true; by others, false. Both views are right, from their particular viewpoint. There are so many, many forms of life, too numerous to comprehend; and whilst souls do continually return to the earth, there are still many who refrain.

This may sound somewhat contradictory, in view of previous communications. In our condition, however, we learn ever fresh aspects of truth, and since speaking I have been privileged to see a very much wider sphere than ever before. These forms—these cycles—have since been revealed to me.

If you could apprehend with the clairvoyant eye, you would be astounded to see radiating from the earth plane innumerable 'spirals' of colour and light, pulsing upward and onward. All these 'spirals' represent man's varying paths of progression. Now the Spiritualist, according to the teaching he has received from his guides, has embodied as his Seventh Principle a 'path of eternal progress open to every soul who wills to tread it— the path of eternal good'. But we would make it clear that everyone is not expected to advance along the same pathway. Such is one of the mighty laws of spiritual evolution. Whilst perfect law finds observance throughout every manifestation of the life-force, there remains a wide choice for the ego; when man can realize how many myriad paths of progression lie open, his mind will become attuned to the thought of ever-present divine love and understanding. Then will he cleanse himself of all intolerance, all restriction, for he will see that in every soul there quickens a fundamental urge, that each is drawn, because of its very essence, on the upward spiral.

No soul is forced to any particular form or path, although it must perforce conform to the laws of spiritual life, being of itself spirit.

I give a crude illustration. Imagine millions and millions of atoms seething in their etheric surround. Each atom reacts to attraction according to its particular quality or essence. Each must follow, as if drawn thither by a magnet, its own path of evolution. Thus, when the ego, the divine spark, is projected from the divine intelligence into form, it still feels the 'tug', of one or other of these myriad spirals of evolution open to the evolving soul. Here is a marvellous thought. Whilst all have to work in accordance with law, every soul is absolutely and entirely individual.

Thus you will get some insight into the depth of meaning in those words of the Master Jesus, who said, *Even the hairs of your head are numbered.* From the waster in the gutter to the wisest in your land, every soul remains attuned in its degree to the divine intelligence and must ultimately follow that one pathway which leads it back to God.

CHAPTER 8

THE ENNOBLEMENT OF
LIFE BOTH INCARNATE AND
DISCARNATE

I

30th Mar. 1932

WHEN man realizes that he lives and creates both in the 'here and now' and in that Beyond wherein he enters into fuller recognition of himself, he will alter his whole outlook. This understanding will ennoble his actions, raise his ideals, and inspire him to finer ambitions than those which leave him at the end grovelling on the lower, or first three planes, of astral life; to these he will assuredly find himself bound, as on a wheel, if aspiration and inspiration do not lead him forwards and upwards.

If you compare the religions of past and present, there will be found one common source or fount—the Universal. It matters little whether it be the ancient Egyptian, the Greek, the Chaldean, the ancient wisdom of the Hindu, the orthodox Christian church, Christian Science, Theosophy or the higher Spiritualism—all these will be found to possess one common denominator: the *universal* sphere, or, perhaps, what we might call the 'cosmic consciousness'; that ultimate ideal of perfect harmony of life, that plane of being whereon the soaring soul is merged into one illimitable sea of spiritual life. From that centre religion, pure and undefiled, draws its sustenance. I wish I could this night make the links for you. If I can but show you what I mean! I will try....

But if I fail, you must use your own faculties. Let us together make the attempt.*

Question: *We do not quite follow. What do you mean by the phrase 'make the links'?*

Let me illustrate by an example. In Christian Science, there exists a definite contact with the mental plane, on the part of those calling themselves Christian Scientists. Through the mental body and through the intellect (for this is partly a religion of the intellect) the Scientists are definitely linked with the first mental plane of the celestial spheres.

I am trying to show how every religion is linked to one or another of the different planes of life we are illuminating. The Spiritualists are, in the main, in contact with entities from the astral plane. Thus Spiritualism, in so far as it has evolved as a religion, is largely confined to the seven astral planes of life.

The ancient wisdom known as Buddhism is linked with the third sphere of heavenly life. The devout Buddhist aspires to reach the plane of *nirvana*, the plane of meditation, the plane from which the soul emerges into the Universal (erroneously interpreted as a condition of 'nothingness'). Realize that the ultimate goal of all is to attain that condition of consciousness where the personality dwindles and is absorbed, and the individuality becomes so at one with the Universal that, in losing itself, it becomes the very pulse of God. Then, indeed, self relinquishes self. Such is the ultimate, the highest to which we can point.

This does not mean that the individual becomes so absorbed that he cannot, by will or intelligence, be detached from the whole to manifest as a separate ego. The average man cannot bear the thought of absorption, because he has immersed himself in the development of himself as an individual. Yet every soul has at last to let himself go, and become part of one universal life-force, for only when he reaches that stage does

---

*ACD added, to Ivan Cooke: You, brother, may speak and ask questions as we proceed, because I have amplified my message many a time through your mind and hand. *And Ivan Cooke, as editor, added in* THY KINGDOM COME: *'The writer has been frequently conscious of the presence and influence of ACD [during editing].'*

he become greater than himself, the point at which *the Father and I are One*....

We have already spoken at length on this subject.

Question: *To which plane is the Hindu religion attached?*

The ancient wisdom of the Hindu is linked to the Universal. Most assuredly it is linked with the highest point of spiritual consciousness.

Question: *What of the Egyptians?*

The truths which we have been endeavouring to transmit can be found in the ancient Egyptian teaching. This book will contain no more than a restatement of the ancient wisdom of Egypt.

Question: *What about modern religions such as Theosophy?*

We might affirm that Theosophy contains these vital truths, but Theosophy, like many another religion and belief, has become distorted, the original foundation broken and split, and there are now many differing ideas difficult to unify. Pure Theosophy, however, that which emanated from the Ancient Wisdom, finds embodiment in our teaching. There is a branch known as Theosophy today, linked in the main to the first mental plane of the heavenly spheres.

Question: *And Protestantism?*

A religion based upon wonderful truth and pure teaching, but unfortunately over-ridden by creed and dogma.

It is my work to unify, to create harmony, and not to destroy, so you will understand that I have to choose my words and give carefully thought-out answers to your questions. Therefore I prefer not to split the various denominations of orthodoxy, but to take the Christian teaching as a whole, and relate it to the life of the spirit as I find it in these realms of the discarnate.

Take the teachings of the Master Jesus, and you will find from beginning to end truth, simplicity, and yet a vast depth of spiritual understanding; a creative power and a wisdom which will open the doors of heaven to every human soul who wills to enter by the path of love and brotherhood; a truth which will bring to a follower of Christ a life of perfect health, harmony, prosperity, and happiness; a religion which, if truly followed, will link the human soul with every sphere: astral, mental, and to the ultimate *Universal*.

We spoke about a sphere of *conscious* reunion (the only words I can find!) wherein the kingdoms of life, the animal, the vegetable, the human, the angelic, the divine, can meet as one. When thus inspired the soul recognizes friendship and kinship with every beast and flower. It is here that men, known to your earth minds as masters, those who have attained mastership of the lower forms of life through strict training and endeavour, can hold in their will, their intelligence, the lesser will and desire of their brothers and sisters who are of lowlier forms of existence.

This [mastery] is a subject difficult to grasp, but a condition into which all will enter. You may recall stories in your Bible and the scriptures of other races telling of wild beasts and man meeting with understanding one of the other. Let me mention two instances, although many another can be recalled. I speak of Daniel in the lion's den, and also of Balaam's ass: apparent fables, yet stories presenting profound knowledge of that sphere upon which all attain to the recognition within each of some universal kinship.... The episode of the unbroken colt which Jesus rode into Jerusalem will also occur [to some of you]. You see whither this understanding is leading us: you see the great potentialities herein, the new humanities it may teach?

You will realize with wonder as we proceed—although you hardly recognize it yet, my friends—the completion of the structure now in formation in the course of these homely talks. Again we endeavour to emphasise this one recurring theme— that we live in this 'life after death' *now*. And this surely we have to bring home—not merely to prove to man survival after death, but to show that behind all life labours this universal and creative power; to prove that until man realises its potency, and inclines his heart to brotherhood with all, there can never be peace, harmony or happiness for him....

Brotherhood first, and then freedom through contact with

heaven.... That is it!.... Brotherhood, the great White Brotherhood, on earth as it is in heaven.

II

13th Apr. 1932 (two weeks later)

GREETINGS. I have been considering the notes of our last talk. You may wonder how and why? I was very pleased that Brighteyes studied these notes herself, because through her mind I was able to get a fairly clear idea of what had been recorded, and felt tempted to insert and correct as I should have done in the old days. One or two points need elucidation. First of all, to amplify my statement that the Spiritualist movement was in the main only related to the astral spheres. I should not like to leave the impression that Spiritualism is in any sense a religion or belief attached only to the lower planes. Let us therefore consider this question once again. It is true that Spiritualism mainly emanates from these astral spheres, but on consideration the reason becomes obvious. Spiritualists as a whole desire to come into contact with their loved ones. The pursuit of this desire becomes a science for the enquirer, and a religion for the bereaved and lonely.

During the many years spent in spreading the gospel of Spiritualism, the main thought at the back of my mind was to bring comfort to those separated from their dear ones. Being a man of great human love, having a family whom I adored, I sympathized intensely with the sufferings of those bereaved. Cannot you see my dominant thought—to give to poor folk assurance that their loved ones were neither dead nor far away, but so close that they could hold communion; that their beloved lived on in a condition of bliss? Don't you understand that to me this seemed man's most vital realization, compared to which all others faded into insignificance?

Man possesses the power within to create conditions, visions, ideas of God, the afterlife, and heaven; as his imagination quickens, so he forms an ideal according to his capacity. When men were in the more 'barbaric' state they set up for their worship graven images of their God, the best and highest they could conceive. So with the average man and woman today. Each formulates ideas or ideals according to his or her depth of thought and emotion; that is to say, the man who concentrates on human love—the family tie, the personal contact, physical comfort, such things as please or delight the senses—engenders within himself that same conception of heaven. So I too, conceived the life after death, and felt that all who love as we ourselves loved—and love still!—must feel exactly as I; that all must dread that inevitable parting as we ourselves once dreaded it, until we established faith in survival upon truth and evidence.

So the average seeker who enters Spiritualism is brought by this one reason—to make contact, personal contact, with his beloved. Can there be anything greater or more joyful than to find and to know that father, mother, husband, sister, brother or child can still commune across the gulf? It is true, very wonderfully true! Those who pass, as we have already told you, linger for a period in these astral spheres of life, and so necessarily it must be true that Spiritualism derives its origin from the astral. Rarely do beings return from the celestial spheres unless they have a definite mission to perform.

The astral planes are not planes of accomplishment. For this reason Spiritualism lacks in some degree the power which enfolds and binds those of other faiths. We, by this fresh influx of knowledge, hope to restore power because we endeavour to link Spiritualism to actual spheres of power. Remember, it is not from the astral but from the celestial spheres that the attracting force is drawn: the binding love, and the wisdom which kindles the life and fire of religion.

There is much we Spiritualists have to learn. Let us open ourselves to truth from whatsoever source it comes. No doubt you have heard White Eagle speak of and call upon the centre of *power*? Right well he knows what he is doing when he thus opens the channel. We, too, must learn to fling wide our doors, so that wisdom, power and love may enter in to abide. Not for one moment would I decry Spiritualists because they contact chiefly the astral spheres of life; God knows, I would be the last [to do so], because I have seen, I *know*, the wonderful consolation and the joy which comes to people on both sides of the grave by the contact [achieved through Spiritualism], by the spirit communion. But one might almost segregate communications into two separate grades—that is to say, one might separate the experimental part of Spiritualism (which should be purely scientific) from that communion of the spirit some day to grow so pure and blessed as to become sacramental.

Spirit communion must come as a holy and blessed thing of purification, for the ennoblement of life both incarnate and discarnate. True, time, education, and fresh realizations are necessary to dispel ignorance. May this work serve that purpose by bringing some light of God's truth to men!

On the other hand, scientific [psychical] investigation should be treated purely as experiment, its doors rigidly shut against the curious and the sensation-seeker. There should no longer be exploitation of the sensitive instruments. All must be put into proper place, and there must come law, system and order, and more reverent understanding of the beauty and the wonder of physical and mental mediumship.

Referring again to these celestial planes from which are drawn power and wisdom, the ritual of the Roman Catholic church and the High Anglican church is designed to call upon such power. Power gathers and binds their people. One can realize its potency on entering a church in which high ritual is practised. All things—the incense, the way the censer is used, and even the form for administration of blessing—are practised with deliberate intent to create and distribute power amongst the worshippers. I have visited many a church since discarnate to witness the attraction and inspiration of the power gathered. I have witnessed the strains of music influence the mind, the worshippers themselves contribute by the emotional action of their emotional body. It is indeed surprising!

On the other hand, in nonconformist churches, where the ornate has become simplicity, if true purity of heart and purpose be there, then also there gathers power, but of a somewhat different order. In some, however, there creeps a spiritual coldness, a lack due to complacency, and those who worship seem apt to become self-satisfied, to think themselves God's chosen and elect. (I shall be severely criticized, but this also has been noted in my journeyings.)

As to the wisdom and rightness of using ritual, music, and the like, to draw upon and to hold power over the people, we remind you, there can be use and abuse of all things. Doubtless, power rightly attained and rightly used forms part of the creative plan, for such creative powers lie within. If by knowledge, by purity of ideals and aspirations, man becomes linked to higher celestial spheres, it is by reason of his own spiritual growth that he attracts from the creative power centre.

We told you that the Christian religion was the purest, containing as it does, the kernel of truth, pure truth. We wish to elucidate this statement. We shall be challenged as to the vicarious atonement* and the meaning of the words, *I am the Way, the Truth and the Life. No man cometh unto the Father but by Me*. The vicarious atonement remains still a sad stumbling block to Spiritualists. They have yet to realize, as I now realize, the spirit behind the words. Men still stumble over the wording rather than seek the deep occult meaning lying behind the words of the Master.

We do not propound a gospel of vicarious atonement. We know, we are assured, that *as a man soweth, so must he surely reap;* no other can ever wrest from him the responsibility of his own evil-thinking and doing. But when a man, however sunken, reaches that point whereby in a flash his soul is illumined by truth born of and through the power and the love of Jesus the Christ, he is become born again, and his old self dies. In that way only does the Christ preserve him, redeem him from ignorance, sin, and darkness, and point him to eternal life. To every soul, of whatever skin colour, whatever religion, there comes the dawning of the Great White Light ... in other words, the Cosmic Christ; or, in yet other words, Jesus, the Christ, the *One Beloved*; the one Supreme Being. Every soul,

---

*i.e., the doctrine that Christ died for our sins.

whatever his label, however he deny, must enter heaven through the 'narrow gate'—through immeasurable love, the perfect wisdom of the compassionate Christ.

We spoke last week also of the Buddhist belief. This point too needs amplification. The Buddhist of today holds that the ultimate and supreme goal of existence is to enter the sphere of life known to him as *nirvana*. He desires to reincarnate, to pass as rapidly as possible through many a life that he may purify his soul, and ultimately reach that goal where at last is attained freedom from rebirth. He believes that *nirvana* will release him from the eternal round of life and death. In *nirvana* he will have found peace, having lost himself in nothingness.

His error lies in his interpretation of the teachings of Buddha; so also the teachings of Jesus Christ are presented today in very different guise from the truths given to his disciples two thousand years ago. From the third mental plane the Buddhic faith derives its power and sustenance. Phases of this truth have since become so coarsened and degraded that I believe there exist today many who, when they pass over, cling to the earth plane, thus hoping to seize a speedy rebirth, and so become bound to earth for long periods.

The Lord Buddha came to point the way to that ultimate goal of every human soul, the realization of the true resignation to the supreme universal life. By profound experience he had proved that only *as a little child* man can enter the kingdom of heaven. Thus he taught.

One more thing, please. If you follow the true vision of the spirit, you will find in the Ancient Wisdom these same truths: you will find described the spheres of disquieted spirits; the higher astral spheres, the mental, celestial, and universal spheres of life. For all teachers through all ages have returned to the earth with the one revelation. And what glorious destiny lies unveiled to men willing to renounce the desires of self for service of man and God!

CHAPTER 9

THE HEALING OF ALL DISEASE

I WAS with Brighteyes when she was reading some letters *10th* today. I am interested in the teaching set forth regarding the *Feb.* astral health as connected with the health of the physical body *1932* [and will now expand further on this]. It is truly said that medical science will be eventually compelled to study psychic laws. When I recall the operations I once witnessed I shudder with horror and disgust. Yet I appreciate the fact that many have been saved by the skill of the surgeon; but I dare to say that many a life and the sanity thereof will be saved when the medical world makes a study of the astral body.

There exist certain rays which, when men can open themselves to the divine intelligence, can be used. This rests not so much on the quality of the intellect or physical brain, as on the spiritual intelligence or insight which enables the healer to attract them to himself as a magnet attracts, and then redirect the light through his patient. That is one of the new lessons to be assimilated when the medical world is open to receive information concerning colour and light rays. Of these, my friend [addressing Ivan Cooke], you are beginning to learn.*

How truly, my friends, has it been said that all needed for health, healing and sustenance waits in the Universal; but the ignorant cannot draw upon the abundance of God's supply. It is equally difficult, if not impossible, for those who have this

---

*Ivan Cooke, as some readers may know, put into full practice the ideas on healing given in this chapter, and went on to expand them in his book HEALING BY THE SPIRIT (White Eagle Publishing Trust, 1955 (as HEALING), 1976). This and the earlier note (p. 211) suggest there was a particular sense of collaboration between ACD and Ivan Cooke on the subject of healing.

knowledge to convey it. It must dawn from your own understanding. The time must surely come when man will awaken, when the light from the Universal, from the Cosmic Christ, illumines man's darkened understanding.★

There are many methods of healing known.† Each appears to be effective in certain cases, and none so in all. We would therefore trace the healers' source of supply, as well as the origins of all disease. In spite of the controversy which these statements will raise, we suggest that disease originates not, as is frequently thought, entirely in the mental state of the patient, but far deeper. Dis-ease has its origin sometimes in the conscious mind, sometimes in the subconscious, and more frequently in the *preconscious mind*. By the latter we mean that condition of consciousness far older than the one human life, the consciousness which extends down the ages of man, but which must not be confused with what is known to your psychologists as 'racial instinct'.

We suggest that the preconscious mind appertains to the actual ego, that is, to the spirit; whereas the instinctive life pertains to the animal and racial instincts which dwell in the flesh, and are not necessarily related to nor coordinated with the preconsciousness of man. The latter is a condition which is of the universal or spiritual life inherent in all. It would seem that that preconscious state of which we speak is unknown in the animal world.

You are today chiefly concerned with conscious mind. You know that mind to be responsible for many of the minor complaints of the body and some of the major diseases. There are also diseases which cannot be traced, not being related either to conscious or subconscious minds.

We would classify the healers into their several sections, as follows:

Magnetic or psychic healers;
Mental healers such as the Christian Scientists;

★The passage which followed this in THE RETURN OF ARTHUR CONAN DOYLE now appears on p. 188.

Hypnotists or mesmerists;

Dietists and nature healers;

Spiritual healers;

Sacramental healers;

Manipulative healers such as osteopaths;

Occult healers—those who deal purely with the occult forces of the patient;

Colour-ray healers (we shall have something important to say about these later).

All effect cures in many cases, but not in all. We shall make it clear that each type mentioned, in treating pain and disease treats not only the physical body but the astral and mental bodies of their patients. All disease results from lack of harmony between the psychic bodies and the physical body; the physical is the last to feel the disease—or, shall we say, 'dis-ease'? In all healing first the healer must discover a point of contact, otherwise he will never cure his patient. Therefore it is obvious that no one of the healers enumerated will achieve success in every case. Nor do we suggest that herbal remedies and serums should be ignored. Many cases can be more easily and effectively treated by drugs, herbs or serums rather than by wasting psychic powers and spiritual forces upon a localized affection. It is true, although not generally realized, that certain drugs already known can be employed to act not only on the physical but the astral bodies—and with the astral bodies we include the etheric body, very similar to the physical body but of much looser texture. In that etheric body diseases lodge. By using such drugs the etheric body is caused to loosen its grip upon the poison and congestion which lodges as the result of conscious, subconscious, or preconscious disharmony in the mental body.

Here it is well to interpolate that the term 'mental body' does not necessarily apply to the physico-mental body.

To avoid confusion: you have knowledge that man possesses more than one mental body, since there is first the mental body directly related to the physical brain; secondly, the mental body related to the emotional or desire part of man; and thirdly, the mental body which is related purely to the celestial and the universal mind.

So the conscious mind, by thinking erroneously, can so influence and weaken the cell-consciousness of the physical body as to create disease; and so the universal or the preconscious mind can also control the cell-consciousness through the 'subliminal' or higher mind, and can thus operate to purify and to cure all disease. *There is not one incurable disease on the earth plane.*

We declare that all life—all human life—can be divided into rays of certain vibration. We say that life is ruled by such rays. We cannot tonight detail more than a limited number. We are tempted to suggest twelve definite rays; and leave it at that. If we desire, we may alter this number later. Shall we say that all humanity vibrates to one or other of these twelve rays or vibrations? Therefore, if a healer attempt to treat a man vibrating on, say, no. 7 ray with no. 5 method of treatment he will most certainly fail, and in all probability do harm rather than good. If, however, he treat no. 7 with no. 7, a complete cure will be effected.

Vibration is expressed by colour: that is to say, colour is the outward and visible symbol of vibration. We will endeavour to enumerate the colours corresponding to the numbers, as follows:

1:	the Red Ray
2:	the Green Ray
3:	the Blue Ray
4:	the Pink Ray
5:	the Yellow Ray
6:	the Purple Ray
7:	the Violet Ray
8:	the Lavender Ray
9:	the Pearl Ray
10:	the Silver Ray
11:	the Golden Ray
12:	the pure White Ray.

It will be the first task of the colour healer to discover the ray–colour to which his patient vibrates. It will be found that, according to the colour and number of the ray under which the patient is grouped, so he will be liable to certain weaknesses, and will need either a stimulating or sedative ray to balance the vibration and create harmony throughout his being.*

To point our meaning, it will be found that the yellow ray is a particularly fine colour for treating tuberculosis. The blue ray gives the best results in nervous diseases. The red ray is useful for all poisonous conditions of the blood. The violet and the green rays are both curative of cancer.

Let us proceed. In certain patients the psychic centres to be treated will vary. This is important, and in due course we shall specify those psychic centres. For instance, in some cases the throat is the most receptive and sensitive spot on which to direct the green ray. In others, the heart centre gives the most powerful response to the violet ray, and will prove the most efficacious centre for the cure of blood diseases, or for one suffering from blood-poisoning. The violet light cleanses and purifies all poison from the bloodstream as it flows to the heart.

We repeat that we cannot claim that this light-ray treatment will prove effective for every person. Nevertheless, we give the table of colours and their corresponding numbers, to lay a plan for allocating the various diseases. We are suggestive, you will see, rather than dogmatic.

We repeat: disease is the result of disturbance in the vibrations, whether it originate through the preconscious or through the emotional or subconscious mind of the patient.

A prevalent cause of disease is the inability to relax. Most of you, unconsciously or consciously, live and sleep—mark you, live both in your waking and sleeping hours—taut and tense.

*The list of colour rays given by ACD can be read as broad hints to help us understand the many different ways of 'being in the world' just as are the astrological signs. It is not a list of the actual colours that are used in the system of healing which has been developed in the White Eagle Lodge, although of course it gives a helpful understanding of some of the principles behind the system and many of the colours are the same. For further clarification, see Joan Hodgson's A WHITE EAGLE LODGE BOOK OF HEALTH AND HEALING (White Eagle Publishing Trust, 1983), pp. 179–198.

You fall asleep with a tense mind and, unconsciously, your knee, elbow, and finger joints, and particularly the neck joints, the spinal column, and all such bony parts, retain a corresponding tenseness. In daily life much the same conditions prevail. This tension of the physical body is due to a mental condition: fear, worry, suppressed emotion or suppressed desire. Hence, sleeping or waking, there occurs at certain parts of the psychic bodies a hold-up of the psychic flow.

If people would but learn from childhood the importance of relaxation, making it a habit, and thus going through daily life at rest, dwelling in harmony with themselves, with God, and with the universal powers, then they would retain that vital and perfect rhythmic flow round and through their psychic and physical bodies. That flow, by its very nature, carries away all waste, which is cast off, shed, eliminated, caught up by the 'Universal', and so absorbed and transformed into fresh power. In breathing you exhale poison. To exhale and inhale is the continual casting-away of waste physical and psychic matter, and an in-drawing of the pure prana, the universal life-force which maintains the body in rhythmic motion and perfect health.

There again we give you the secret of ease or dis-ease. It is futile to state that disease entirely originates in that which Christian Science calls the 'mortal mind'. Disease lies deeper than the mortal consciousness or mortal mind of the Christian Scientist. Nevertheless, as soon as the individual can relax his mortal mind, and reach forth to draw upon the fresh universal life-force, he automatically sets that inflow in motion which will create in time a perfect body.

★

Is it possible for a man or woman sustaining a severe accident to find healing? Does the cause of this accident also lie in that preconscious mind, or is the sufferer a victim to cruel mischance?

We say that even accidents result from a previous creation of disharmony deep within the preconscious or subliminal self.

(Terms are very difficult, but if I am not satisfied I shall substitute other words. At all events you will get the idea.) This seems a hard doctrine, and yet on examination it is not so. The soul who falls victim knows in that preconsciousness or through that preconsciousness that it has a lesson which can only be learned through such an experience.

The inevitable question next arises, what about children? There are poor little sufferers, children born obviously as the result of drunken lust or of diseased parents. Are we to conclude these innocents are doomed by fate? What of souls imprisoned in the body of a lunatic; souls whose bodies are corrupt with disease? What of *their* fate? The same law applies. The soul possesses *always* foreknowledge and power of choice. Thus it is impossible for man with his limited insight to estimate or judge the motive or suffering of any other soul. Still more must man refrain from judgment of that omnipotent power which, when appalled by some horror, he still tries to call 'good': God, the First Great Cause—'He who must see little children suffer and heedeth not'?

Over here we do not judge *anyone*; with broader vision we do not see a God vindictive or cruel, but an infinite love, a divine and compassionate intelligence. We see an all-wise Fatherhood ever giving to His children freewill to choose their path; a path which by suffering, by sorrow or by joy, and by joy of conquest ever wends its way upward, back into that supreme consciousness of the Cosmos wherein dwells perfection.

The sentimentalist witnessing a cat playing with an innocent mouse shudders with horror. 'How cruel! How awful! Nature is full of cruelty!' he declares. So it may seem to one whose vision is limited. Not so! Behind the outer semblance, this love, this understanding, permeates all. The suffering so apparent cloaks but a means and method of bringing God's supreme harmony, love, and beauty into the consciousness of God's creatures.

I have described the effect of the preconscious mind in relation to disease, in the hope that this will help you to understand why apparently good and saintly people contract painful or mortal complaints. For instance, a person might protest, 'My mother was sweet in nature and kindliness: my father loved by all. For what reasons should either contract diseases painful and terrible?'

The cause lies deeper than sweet personality or saintliness of character. It reaches far beyond this span and its roots lie not in the here and now. Like a fever, suffering heralds a cleaning up, a clearing out, a finishing. Such sufferers might be compared by the agnostic to some mouse under the cat's paw. *Man* sees but physical torture, the days and nights of pain, reckoning nothing of the root and flower which that sufferer's tree of life will bear, so accordingly remains ignorant of that which germinates within, what is springing from the soul thus ploughed and harrowed. *Man knows but the surface* of the true life of the soul!

Another interesting point, if you are not weary. The outer emotions of anger, greed, jealousy, and so on, create definite diseases. These are, however, the 'simple' diseases as distinct from those deeply rooted. Self-pity proves one of the prevalent causes of back and kidney troubles. It will also affect the liver, although any violent emotions cause disturbance in this quarter. As a result, poison is driven into the bloodstream. Fear and worry do much the same thing, and if prolonged eventuate in cancer. If one could analyse many cases of cancer one would discover that deep-rooted fear—and worry is a form of fear— is holding the body in a tense condition, closing in or shutting up the etheric body, and thus causing a hold-up in that psychic flow previously described.

Does diet affect the well-being of man? In some cases, but not all. The man, however, who has reached that condition of peace and harmony and understanding of the divine laws refrains from the abuse of the physical body by overeating or by wrong choice of food. Indigestion is caused rather by the mental, the conscious mind and thought-life of the patient.

It is of great interest to see from this side the source of inspiration for some of our prominent writers. I am reminded of that play, THE BLUE BIRD, by Maeterlinck. In one scene the children assembled await their call to the earth: each carries, slung about his shoulders, a bag containing not only the gifts and accomplishments he will bring to earth, but the diseases he must experience. Some of them bear, you will recall, whooping-cough, measles, and scarlet fever, all packed before they sail on the ship of Old Father Time across the starry seas to their waiting earthly mothers.

A tremendous truth is here told. A fairy story, we may say; nevertheless, that truth filtered through the writer's mind from the Universal or rose from the preconscious level of his own inner knowledge.

The psychic healer accomplishes a valuable work in that he can relieve the congestion of the psychic bodies. Some cases he cannot touch, because he cannot probe deep enough into the patient's history. He can help best when the patient will also help himself. In psychico-spiritual healing it is often noticed that when the disease has been apparently cured, when the patient's house is left clean and garnished, as it were, if the patient fall again from contact with the higher forces, he will relapse. The condition of that man will then be worse than before. Thus the parable of the man dispossessed of a devil, whose house was cleaned and garnished, and who then went away, and on his return found his house occupied by seven other devils each worse than the original tenant, well illustrates my meaning.

The many methods of healing now employed by man must be classified and understood; that is to say, it is futile for one group of healers to claim power to heal every condition of disease. *18th May 1932, a week later*

We touched last week on the twelve rays, and would direct your minds to the twelve 'signs' of the zodiac, to the twelve 'tribes' of Israel, to the mystery and significance of this number 'twelve', suggesting that here is a reference to the twelve rays under which the human family can be grouped. Many herbs can also be grouped beneath these twelve rays. The sage of old found that for every disease there could be gathered a corresponding herb, which vibrated to the same number and the same colour, a herb which would produce a magical effect upon the diseased body. Thus can be traced many ancient customs, the origin of many a potion, and so on, used long ago by the so-called medicine man.

Now, take your mind to the number twelve, and divide that twelve into four sections. In each you will find three distinct rays; so in the whole twelve you get a division of four consisting of three rays apiece. Here we wish to interpolate: the number four and the number three are very powerful numbers which affect the human family. That is, they are numbers which influence the earth plane in all affairs of the physical life. The basis of the world's calculation and civilization was set upon the symbol of the square and triangle in the dim past. As an illustration, ponder the significance of the Great Pyramid, standing as it does as a mathematical symbol of life.

Now the twelve 'houses' of the 'children of Israel' (that is, the twelve rays upon which the human family vibrates) must be again divided into four. These are Earth, Fire, Air, Water. When the physician of the future desires to treat a patient he must as a preliminary measure cast the patient's horoscope. A fantastic suggestion? We are in deadly earnest! We are endeavouring to give a chart, a rule, by which man may, if he cares, discover the cause of every disease. He will learn by the casting of the horoscope (not the usual kind of horoscope, note, but that which covers the life of the ego and not merely this one life, revealing the rays upon which the ego has vibrated during his many incarnations) that all diseases can be classed into one or other of these four groups.

Thus, when it transpires that the patient vibrates to the earth sign, or the fire sign, the air or the water signs, there will be found an appropriate curative method, in place of the one remedy now given to all and sundry. It will be also learnt that those vibrating under one or other of these signs become prone to certain diseases and against these same complaints can be safeguarded.

To touch briefly upon the twelve psychic points of contact—
the twelve rays of vibration, mark you, and the twelve points
of their contact, they are these. Starting from the heart centre
as the central point, we number them thus:

1:	The heart
2:	The throat
3:	The pineal gland
4:	The pituitary gland
5:	The spleen
6:	The base of the spine
7:	The solar plexus
8:	The organs of generation
9 & 10:	The two hands
11 & 12:	The two feet.

It can and will be proved some day by an instrument that
these twelve psychic centres are very susceptible to certain rays
of vibration. It is true that the human body and the spirit of
man, without outside aid, is sufficient in its curative power; it
can moreover so attract rays as to pass on magnetic or spiritual
treatment to its fellow. In effect, man can heal the diseases of
his brother man. As we explained, however, there exist
conditions of the body so superficial and trivial that they can
be more speedily dealt with by physical application. It would
require too much spiritual or vital force to put through the
necessary ray, for instance, to cure a boil, and it seems obviously
simpler to employ hot fomentations rather than to treat by
spiritual or magnetic means.

With regard to the centres of psychic contact, it will be
found that a corresponding organ of the body is linked to each
individual centre. For instance, by the application of a certain
colour ray—which is itself but vibration, you understand—to
the throat, there will follow reaction not in the throat so much
as in the digestive organs or stomach.

The pituitary gland must be the centre treated in cases of
obsession and mental derangement. Epilepsy has baffled
medical science. It may not surprise you to hear that this disease
originates from a maladjustment of the psychic bodies, caused

by some spiritual and psychic disharmony of the parents at the conception of the sufferer's physical body.

Have we any conception of the responsibility of parenthood? It has been said: *the sins of the fathers shall visit the children unto the third and fourth generation.* Even so, that saying holds a deeper meaning and more truly might be interpreted 'the sins of man shall revisit him unto the third and fourth incarnation.' Surely an earlier incarnation is 'father' to that which follows?

Now comes the question, how is epilepsy to be cured? Must it remain one of those obscure diseases which afflict the whole life-period of the sufferer? Epilepsy is curable only if there can be effected a readjustment of the psychic bodies, and this can follow through making a connecting link between the pineal and pituitary glands. There will later be discovered a serum, which, injected into the gland at the base of the head, will readjust the psychic bodies by drawing them closer, so that the 'gap' is closed. When this 'gap' opens the epileptic fit occurs. To put it more plainly, may we suggest that there is a screw loose? The screw being loose, the apparatus slips and at that moment there follows an epileptic fit. Tighten up the screw, get a perfect alignment of the psychic bodies, and you cure the epileptic.

We would now like to group diseases under their respective signs of earth, air, fire and water, and suggest appropriate treatment, bearing in mind that we must also consider the three sections within each sign, namely the mineral, animal and vegetable; we will turn to these later.

The Air Sign. Those who fall under the air group will often suffer from nervous diseases which act through the psychic centres. The head and the back will be the most frequently affected. The psychic centre to treat will be the base of the spine, because such diseases will bear relation to the nervous system generally.

The Fire Sign. Here patients will be emotional, and are likely to suffer from obsession, mental trouble, inflammations and fevers. The treatment in all these cases will be by the pituitary gland and the pineal gland. These statements can be tested and proved.

The Earth Sign.. In this class should be grouped the phlegmatic, or the type which accumulates poison because of general sluggishness, and lack of the perfect flow and rhythm of which I spoke. There will follow catarrhal conditions and subsequent poisons in the blood, and many diseases which originate from such causes.

The Water Sign. Strange as it may seem, the watery sign affects the lower part of the body, the feet, the legs.

This is a fluidic sign, and those coming under this division can be most readily helped by magnetic treatment; whereas those under the fiery sign respond more readily to colour-ray treatment; those under the airy sign respond to the spiritual and sacramental treatment; and those under the earthy sign react best to dietetic treatment, and mental treatment also such as Christian Science and methods of similar character. If man will but follow our hints, will apply but a tenth of the experiment and research hitherto poured forth upon inexact and speculative medicine, there will result an exact and scientific method of universal healing, based upon true knowledge of man's physical, psychic and spiritual natures. If man so desires, healing can become a precise science.

You will learn that there grow herbs corresponding in vibration and colour to each and all of these twelve sections, which can be selected for the treatment of those under the fire, the water, or the earth or air signs; herbs which will prove beneficial in each case, whereas those under other signs might be harmful or even dangerous.

We have scantily touched upon the subject of herbal remedies. Herbs grow under very definite laws; that is, their growth is neither the result of accident, nor of climate or position, but takes its form and character from rays which govern all growth. Such rays rule life upon the earth plane, in the mineral, vegetable and animal kingdom. It is essential therefore for the healer to have knowledge of his patients' astrological aspects; for every medicinal herb can be grouped

1st June 1932

under its own particular sign of the zodiac. Only in accordance with the subject and the nature of his disease should these herbs be applied.

For instance, the patient who falls under, shall we say, ray number seven, of the rising sign of Leo (governed by the Sun), must be prescribed a herb grouped under that number and ray, and forbidden any herb under a foreign ray. Following these hints it should be possible to classify and catalogue herbal remedies with some exactitude and precision, and such classification will be found of considerable efficacy. We have explained however that herbal treatments do not fulfil every requirement. The patient should rather be treated by his healer according to his sign and particular temperament.

Asthma is a disease caused, as you may know, through the nervous system, and such form of nervous reaction, or broken rhythm, can be most efficaciously treated by the colour-ray treatment— preferably by the blue and the green ray. Although certain herbs in the past have been thought desirable, from our side we state that asthma falls into line with other psychic diseases. Sometimes magnetic treatment will cure. The psychic centre upon which the colour ray should be directed is that of the solar plexus. In this disease you will also find a great deal of digestive derangement. Great care must first of all be given to correct diet. Many attacks of asthma are brought on by indiscretions, while worry or mental trouble will frequently herald its appearance. Remove the mental cause and asthma disappears. Hence you will readily recognize the reason for the application of the blue ray, the calming, peace-restoring ray. To breathe or to inhale certain herbs is merely to scratch the surface. Attack the root cause, the derangement of the psychic system, the most important centre of which is the solar plexus. Children who suffer from this complaint may inherit their tendency from and through the overwrought system of the mother.

18th May 1932   Cancer comes under the earth sign in some cases but not all. It occasionally originates in the breaking of a very sacred law in a previous incarnation; and is one of the methods chosen by the subject to wipe out that 'sin'. This [suggestion] will doubtless be rejected. It is, however, true, albeit there is this one consoling thought; it never recurs when once a soul has passed through that particular form of experience.

Medical science will yet discover that the cure for cancer lies in the direct treatment of the etheric and not the astral body. Treatment will consist in a persistent action on the etheric body of a certain drug. We mention gentian as being one of the most powerful [herbs in the cure of cancer]. Light-ray treatment has a distinct value, the pearl ray described being one of the most efficient, cleansing and perfecting rays for the etheric body. When the 'electrons' composing the etheric body become loosened and relaxed by the action of the drug or the light ray, there will follow a dispersal of the cancer seat in the physical body, although cancer, albeit it shows itself in a particular part, is not localized. When cancer is removed by operation, it proves only an irritant to the disease, which rapidly chases through the bloodstream and speedily forms another little township. Cancer objects to an uprooting, and shows irritation by a more vicious attack upon its victim. The only way—and you will find this knowledge dawning on medical scientists— the only way to treat cancer effectually is by the light-ray treatment and by drugs which act upon the etheric body.

To answer a question here which will arise: if diseases are brought over from a preconscious condition; if in some cases the ego definitely decides to bear that burden in the life to come, how can we reconcile that belief—that truth, not a belief—with the methods of healing now outlined? If men are predestined to suffer, how is it that the spirit world is permitted to give such information as will cure disease?

We answer that there exists a law of redemption by suffering. As man evolves and becomes spiritually conscious, however, such cruder conditions, the outworking of 'sin' through so stern a discipline, can be transmuted. Through the higher and finer channel, through spiritual conquest over the baser, man may eradicate the past and build the future.

Sometimes we watch a healer at work on a patient. The

patient does not respond, the treatment proves futile. In some cases even the great ones who hold humanity in their care dare not interfere. Only by effort, by striving to attain a height of self-mastery and self-conquest can that soul transmute his own inheritance. Remember these words: *Thy sins are forgiven; go thou and sin no more.* Even thus can the power and presence of Christ accomplish, if man seek Christ through victory over self.

All diseases can be healed, and will be eradicated when humanity, of its own freewill choice and character, will come to the temple of the living God to receive that pure white light, that truth, that love, which flows from the heart of the eternal. Then there will be no more weeping nor wailing, but man perfected.

As happiness has to be earned, so also must perfect harmony, perfect health of the bodies, be earned. Remember, no man need trail through fires of pain and suffering to learn of God. Man can find God through joy, through happiness. This is rather the ultimate path, since it first involves self-conquest, self-denial, but the way lies open. Here again we touch on good and evil, positive and negative, suffering and joy, pleasure and pain; man can take either way, left or right hand, by aspiration or by bitter transmutation, but ever the arms of the Father wait, ready for His Son.

Has the grouping of humanity into the four divisions of fire, air, earth and water been made clear? The horoscope will enable the healer to place his patients. One might, of course, allocate them by instinct or sensing, but the more scientific method would be to cast the horoscope, thus finding the exact ray of birth. You received some months ago a description of the rays under which I, myself, was born, an unusual combination which caused difficulty for me both during life and immediately following death.★

We could almost state that *all* disease is caused through broken rhythm, by broken vibrations. These twelve vibrations hold humanity poised, as it were, in a grip. Here is the secret

★This relates (presumably) to the red and blue-violet rays described on pp. 88–89. See also the introductory chapter, pp. 49–51. It may be that ACD here refers to the actual message reprinted in part there.

of man's well-being. When more becomes known of these vibrations, the whole of life will be simplified, its strain and stress disappear. Obscure diseases which baffle medical science are traceable to broken vibration and rhythm, an inharmonious relation to the magnetic forces and universal powers which surround man.

Some may jeer, saying, 'Nonsense! We understand and treat only the body.' My friends, you do not, you have not begun to understand the physical body of man! Medical science must get further afield. Surgery certainly has become a fine art and remarkable cures follow. For accidents, in case of torn and broken bodies, surgery has an undoubted place. Even so, surgery will someday be supplanted.*

So far we have dealt with diseases common to all humanity, *1st* with the exception of those classified as infectious. It must seem *June* confusing, in view of what we have said about the preconscious *1932* origin of many diseases, to find that infection can spread like wildfire through a community without apparent reason. Yet numbers of people prove immune to it. Among these will be those who practise Christian Science, thus demonstrating that man's conscious mind holds a measure of control.

True; the Christian Scientist protects himself not only through mental action, but because he has arrived at a point in his spiritual evolution where he has erased the need of this particular form of experience. So we suggest that people subject to contagious diseases prove themselves thereby ripe for such an experience and have a lesson to learn therefrom. With this few will agree. Why indeed should little children become so afflicted? To discover the underlying cause of physical disease we must cover a wide area; but again we suggest the child comes prepared for certain experiences which take form as illness and suffering, or health and happiness, and all the fluctuations which go to mould a human life.

*To this prophecy ACD set a date, just as earlier he described an instrument in course of construction which could assist in the twelve-ray diagnostic system. We have preferred to omit such exact prophecies, since heavenly time seems so rarely to relate to earthly time.

We state that contagious disease is not a necessary evil. In the course of time, when spiritual laws are better understood there will remain no such thing as infection. Nor is there need for anyone to suffer, if he but know how to protect himself against this invasion.

The conscious cell-life of the body, which is controlled by both the conscious and subconscious mind, can be held responsible for the invasion of germs. If sufficient resistance is put up through healthy conscious and subconscious thought-action, the cell-consciousness of the physical will not be overcome by the onslaught of the enemy. From the first a child should be trained in right thinking. The child's education commences, not at the age of seven and onwards, but from the first day of earthly life. The mother or nurse must realize that the infant absorbs from the atmosphere, from conditions around it, from the aura of the nurse, mother and friends, either good or ill, positive or negative vibration, into its very being. The child surrounded by positive thought is fed with the very breath of health, and such a child will thrive physically, mentally and spiritually, and prove resistant to ill from every source.

These truths of health and being will gradually dawn. At no distant date the human family must realize its responsibility with regard to the young souls entrusted to its care, and through this realization awake to the duty and responsibility it bears to the whole community.

As we have spoken of the broken rhythm, the broken vibrations of man's physical bodies which cause disease and death, so may you apply that same law of broken rhythm and broken vibration to the human family and to the world as a whole. Reflect: must not a broken harmony bring dis-ease to physical creation as surely as to the physical body of man?

[And so we pass to the subject of the next chapter.]

CHAPTER 10

THE HEALING OF THE NATIONS

'O Thou who art the Author of all good things; Thou who art ever-present, ever-loving, wise and all powerful: we would come into Thy glorious presence. May the rays from Thy Being permeate our very souls. May the Light of Thy beauty illumine our minds, and may the power of Thy greatness enfold us in loving arms, that we may become one with Thee.

'Bless this work. May no shadow of doubt or fear fall across the pathway of light which Thou hast ordained shall come to the earth plane. May these Thy children feel the sweetness of service to Thee and to their brother man. So mote it be!'

16th March 1932

WE EMPHASIZE again and yet again the need for the light of a common brotherhood, because only when humanity realizes and understands this universal spiritual force, in which humanity lives and moves and has its being, can it save itself. Yes, yes: it is true that the values of life will be altered, and conditions on the earth plane entirely changed; and mankind will be forced through sheer suffering and privation to seek a greater truth.

1st June 1932 (resumed)

How simple it would seem! Yet such a complicated conundrum to present to the worldly, for what words can bring home that *man must love his brother?* Words, alas, mean so little, so little. Yet over here in the spirit all are brought at the last to understanding, only too thankful to believe and live within the fold of a universal brotherhood.

The only way for the world! The nations subsist upon

suspicion, distrust and fear. None give way, because each is afraid. In the business world, each scratches and fights to hold his own particular grain of corn. Whither is this leading? Surely to neither security nor prosperity, but the fast tearing down of all that civilization has established.

In days to come we see an ennobled humanity. There dawns a wonderful vision of true brotherhood. Man will then know that all life is contained as in one stupendous spiritual pulse, and recognize even the physical life as pulsating within one universal spiritual brotherhood. He will know he cannot hurt his brother without corresponding injury, for to war with man or nation is to war with himself, to slay is spiritual death to the slayer. Those who draw the sword shall surely by the sword die. He will know that no breath can he breathe, no thought think without the reaction of a world. He will know that death can never be in God's universe; that with understanding neither earth nor heaven can hold aught of death. There can be neither beginning nor ending, for man will see life as one great cycle, ever evolving, ever revolving, which holds in its embrace every soul born of man. If he violate one law, one truth, he affects the happiness and well-being of all.

Adversity must bind each soul to his fellow before the world shall find salvation.

We witness on your earth today the havoc of death, death through materialism—and, incidentally, death to materialism. Hence the suffering of mankind! Materialism dies hard—how else, when men have worshipped Mammon so often and so long? We herald a new birth! Through earth's birth-pangs will be born a new, a glorious day, a day of spiritual realization, spiritual recognition, and a spiritual base for communal life. In science, politics, religion, art, in every avenue, man will be inspired and directed from the spiritual realms of wisdom.

Of universal brotherhood much is said, yet few indeed understand the meaning of the word; for all are taught from childhood to fight for themselves, to assert themselves at the expense of others. Erroneously man has thought the object of life to be enhancement of his personality. At all costs he must become a man superior—that is, if he desires to equal or master his brother man. This sins against the cosmic law of brotherhood. The man searching and seeking only for himself breaks every law, and while humanity thus continues can result only disease, chaos, and war.

The truly great is he who recognizes, not his own desires, but the infinite and eternal power of love. Each must lose himself to find himself. No man will ever find God whilst encompassed by the error that power and accomplishment come by and through himself. The greatest test through which a soul must eventually pass when it has arisen and thrown off its grave-clothes is to let all sense of self and personality fall away. That soul must then face an abyss of darkness and extinction, so it would seem. One desire only sustains the fainting soul—to yield, to surrender, to be bared utterly of self, to sacrifice every vestige ere the soul can merge into the infinite and eternal love—God.

Such is not extinction; it is expansion. If he reach the point where his love of God become so great, so overwhelming that he desires nothing but to be with God, then his love may enfold even God; then every man to him becomes Godlike, and God dwells in every man....

The man who would understand universal brotherhood must indeed *Leave all and follow Me.* He must render up—must efface himself, must lose self to find the universal selfless: God! In this supreme moment that man becomes at one, not only with God, but with each and every man.

Such is the meaning of the Brotherhood of Man.

All men are travelling, progressing, evolving to such spiritual aim and end—to the time when there will be but one harmonious self, one brotherly thought, one beating desire, one pure love. Never, never, never will man become established in aught but sin and sorrow while seeking for personal and individual worth alone. The former spells both absorption and expansion, by growth of the spirit; and the latter but a spiritual negation and rejection.

There exists only one religion, one reality behind all form, belief and ceremony: a religion universal, neither bound nor circumscribed by geographical limits. It bears but one name. It can be understood by every man, of whatever colour: every man, woman, and child; by every animal; by every bird; by tree and flower, by all instinct with the breath of life; it has but one meaning, one name—the religion of true brotherhood ... LOVE!

Love must surely come, and love will teach that forms and ceremonies, creeds and dogmas avail nothing without the spirit. There is not a creature living that does not bear witness and response to spiritual power. Forms may differ, there may be racial diversities, and many a diverse belief. Let each man have his due, but all must ultimately recognize and bow to the infinite love of the Creator. Even so will each learn that he worketh for all, and all for each.

Not until then will the earth be freed from death. With the dawning of that day when all men recognize and live in harmony, bowing to and yet worshipping the supreme law, death will indeed be swallowed up in victory. Then will the flesh yield no longer to the overlordship of death, its very fabric will become transmuted. Sin in very truth is death, death the result of sin. We mean that exactly as it is said. Sin assuredly brings death, *but love giveth eternal life!*

Truly, truly, every word uttered by the Great Master rings with truth, unsullied by the centuries, eternal and absolute.

PART THREE : TWO WHITE EAGLE TEACHINGS

Plaque given to Minesta (Brighteyes) by the Polaires.
White Eagle is represented at the right.

TWO WHITE EAGLE TEACHINGS : I

LIFE AFTER DEATH

Let us turn our faces towards the eternal light, the eternal truth. O Infinite Spirit, Father—Mother, the Source of our being, we worship Thee, and with all our hearts we seek Thy truth, wisdom and love. May Thy light penetrate the mists surrounding the earth so that mankind will look up and recognize Thee as God, all good, all love.

Amen.

LET US be still in body and mind and seek the place of silence where the voice of God can be heard. This is the way, the truth. So much activity abounds in the physical world, the astral world and the mental world that the true place of happiness is scarcely entered.

On one occasion when we were trying to describe to you the radiance of a master-soul, we placed before you a mental picture of a flashing jewel, in the centre of which was to be seen the perfect form of the Son of God, the Christ form. We explained that every human being contains within itself the power to grow into that perfect jewel. But how to get started—how to receive the inspiration and illumination which appears to be necessary before the soul can see its goal clearly—that is your problem.

The first essential is to draw each day into closer communion with God. So few understand this great blessing of communion with the infinite Spirit. The soul who would set forth and progress on the journey towards the supreme goal must maintain conscious companionship with God. This will not come about through prayers which are no more than words, but only through simple, trusting communion with the Great Spirit. The infinite Spirit is everywhere; man lives and moves and has his being within the arms of the Infinite. Man lives in God, and God is continually present in man. God is omnipresent, omniscient, omnipotent. These will seem only words to you but it is for you to discover for yourselves their living reality. How true is the saying, 'Underneath are the everlasting arms'. The reality of infinite all-enfolding love—this is essential for the soul to realize.

We would speak to you all of the afterlife—not merely that life immediately following death, but the life of the spirit which is eternal, and which grows in beauty and power as it stretches into infinity. Why do you fear, my children? You have nothing to fear except your own fear. What is death but a sleeping and an awakening to a life more radiant and more harmonious than life on earth can be?

When a soul leaves the physical body it is in reality passing inward to an inner state of being. Think of the physical life as an outward life, in which you are immersed in matter of a coarse condition. Away from your body your world will be of a finer and more malleable matter, matter more easily responsive to thought and emotion. Such matter is moulded by the soul, so whatever the soul is, whatever its habitual thoughts and life, it will externalize itself in this inner world.

For this reason, souls who habitually give way to coarse and violent thoughts and desires will find themselves in a similar state of life in the spirit world, except that their new world will be intensified and almost a caricature of the old. On the lower astral plane are places where people seek sensation and crude experience. These places manifest conditions as they are on the physical plane in an intensified form, but the soul finds no satisfaction in fulfilling its desires, and so the desires gradually abate, being worn out. Then at last the soul is ready to move onward and upward. As soon as the soul can abandon these lower attractions, it is immediately befriended. The guide takes it in charge. From the lower astral it passes to the higher astral and then to the mental plane, learning as much as it can absorb, until finally it enters into a dream-like state, absorbing what it can of truth. Then, in due time the soul returns to the earth a little purified, a little nearer its goal of spiritual realization.

The ordinary souls of ordinary people, the dear humanity we love for their kindliness, after death pass quickly through the lower astral in a kind of dream-like state, sometimes without awakening, until they reach the higher astral plane. There they again meet their friends, not only of the incarnation they have just finished but sometimes the companions of former incarnations.

It is really a plane of reunion where the soul enjoys an enhanced life, continuing the many different interests such as music, painting, literature and perhaps science which it enjoyed when on earth; enjoys new freedom and opportunity of learning more of the particular subject which attracts it. Intense joy can come to the musician as he experiences the joys of music without limitation, and the same applies to art. For instance you may love music and yet be unable to express yourself through music in your present life. On the astral plane that desire will be granted. You will find that you are able to play the instrument of your choice without limitation. If you longed to be part of an orchestra or choir you would find yourself a member, on equal terms with anyone else there. Perhaps you long to paint; you long to create beauty—and you will be able to do so. On the astral plane all limitations fall away and the soul perfectly expresses itself in colour, form or music. This brings intense happiness.

The next state is a mental one, the mental plane. There are as many differing aspects of the mental plane as there are differing mentalities. The soul goes to a mental state in accord with its own mentality, and there enjoys a condition we can only describe as one of bliss.

Every soul discovers in the course of its journey that God is no harsh judge but merciful and loving. The soul has only to turn towards God to receive all the help it needs, even as a child runs to its parents for comfort and love. Every soul receives its due in the afterlife, and what it receives is administered with mercy and love.

Usually, when the soul has passed through a period of bliss and quietude, absorbing the truth that it needs to enable it to grow, it will again start its downward journey into incarnation. There is a plane however, beyond that which we have just described, and this is the plane of pure spirit, sometimes called the celestial. We cannot really outline the glory of that state. It waits for you to discover for yourselves.

This process of passing away from the physical body, of traversing the planes of life and then at the right time returning, continues for a long time usually; but it is not always necessary. It is possible for the soul to make rapid progress towards eternal freedom. Yet there are those who, of their own freewill and desire to serve their fellows, return voluntarily to earth to help humanity.

Beyond the celestial is yet another state, even higher, which we will speak of but doubt if you will believe. We speak of it because it is your goal. It is a state which can be reached when the soul has gained complete mastery over life. Such a soul can function in a physical body when it wills, in an astral body at will, in a mental body at will, and it can yet rise into the highest heights of spiritual life and glory at will. That soul will not be prevented from manifesting on any plane, for it is complete master of all planes.

To help you understand more clearly this state of mastership we will give two illustrations. After the Master Jesus was crucified, his body to all appearances seemed dead. But after three days he arose from the dead. He arose from the dead; this is not just to say that his soul survived death. No, Jesus raised his body from the dead; his life had been such that the very atoms of his body were spiritualized. In that state of purification of the physical form he vanished, when the time came, from the sight of his disciples. To Christians this seems a miracle, which could only happen to the Son of God. But this can be done by all who have attained to the required degree of initiation into spiritual life. Your Bible story says that Jesus was caught up into heaven—he disappeared, became invisible. In other words he was able so to raise the vibrations of the physical atoms that they went out of sight. This act of ascension was most clearly demonstrated. But he said: *The works that I do shall ye do also, and greater than these shall ye do.*

The second illustration is that of the saint, of one who lives such a saintly life that after the soul withdraws the physical body does not decay. This will serve as an illustration of what we mean by the power of the spirit over physical atoms. A sainted one has not necessarily attained the power that the Master has—the Master who has power to ascend, to transmute physical atoms, has attained complete mastery over all life.

This is the goal. For most people such as yourselves the attainment of the final degree is a long way off. But keep it ever before you as your goal, and know each day that you are advancing towards glorious freedom.

A question has been asked: Is it right in certain circumstances for a doctor to end the life of a suffering patient? We do not ask you to accept our answer but we can only tell you what we believe to be true. No. There are no circumstances in which we could say, 'End the life'. God alone can do that. God gives life—God recalls the soul. From the spiritual aspect the soul will remain attached to the body until the time decreed by God for it to leave. We doubt if any good purpose is served by the artificial release of the soul from a painful body. Do all you can to alleviate pain, do all you can to help your brother or sister to endure his lot, but do not interfere with the divine will. God is all-wise. It is man's duty to learn about the spiritual laws which govern life, and to endeavour to live in harmony with divine truth. Pain, which the soul draws to itself, is a great teacher. Courageous endurance of pain brings its blessing, and you would not wish to be the means of robbing a loved soul of its reward.

You ask if those who suffer lose their handicap when they pass from the physical body. We answer, yes, most certainly. They become freed from a limitation which their karma placed upon them. (And remember, the law of karma is linked with the law of opportunity, and through that limitation the soul has been able to progress, in spite of, even because of, its handicap.) Some souls of course are very sick when they come over, not necessarily with sickness of the body but of the soul, and then certain limitations do continue for a time. But everything exists in their minds, and soon they learn that they are perfect in form.

There are helpers in the spirit world whose special work it is to take care of the many souls who come over and who need to be treated as sick souls. People like yourselves who have a certain amount of knowledge, when they pass over quickly offer themselves as workers in these receiving stations, hospitals or temples of healing. In fact, there are some former worshippers in this Lodge now engaged in this work.

Life after death is very orderly, and so natural that quite a number of people when they pass on cannot believe that they have left the body.

We would open before you a vista of infinite joy when the soul is completely free from contact with the earth. Look up, my children, into the night sky and see the myriad stars. Pause and wonder what these stars are. Think of yourself and your companions, brethren of the light, having the power, the freedom, to move among the stars, from planet to planet. Think of shining, apparently winged beings, moving in the heavens into light and more light with greater freedom and greater comprehension of this universe and of universes beyond this small universe. There are planets of light and spiritual glory beyond your understanding to which souls go. Eye hath not seen nor ear heard the glory of the heavenly life, the God-life to which all God's children are heirs. Onward, onward, my children, onward into the life more abundant and glorious than your little earth-mind can conceive!

Seek first the kingdom of God and then all will be made clear to you.

O Divine Spirit, all light, all love, all truth, we await Thy blessing which will stimulate Thy life within us. May the light shine upon all mankind!

Amen.

TWO WHITE EAGLE TEACHINGS : II

ALL LIFE IS SPIRIT

An address given on 29th February 1976 in Kensington, at a service marking the Ruby Anniversary of the White Eagle Lodge.

WE BRING to each one of you individually, love such as you do not yet know on earth; this congregation is flooded with love from the higher spheres of life.

We in spirit (not only the brethren of the higher spheres, but your own dearly loved ones who are now here with you very close to your heart) we understand the cares and the fears of everyday life in the physical body; we understand the hurts and the problems of the earthly life. And so we bring this great love to you, and we want you to feel at this moment a sense of peace, surrendering yourselves confidently to the loving, wise care of those who have passed through the veil and now live in a world of beauty. If you could see the faces of your friends and loved ones in the spirit life you would be so happy to see the shining light upon them. They are no longer careworn or sick, but full of life and joy, and they would tell you how wonderful it is to be in this land of spirit.

Forty years ago the work of the White Eagle Lodge was established with the help of a leader of Spiritualism then recently passed into the world of spirit. While he was on earth, Arthur Conan Doyle had a burning desire to convince people that there was a life beyond the death of the physical body. He expended all his physical and material substance in trying to spread this message of life after death.

Now, if you have read the book in which his message is given, you will understand when we say that after he had passed, ACD used all the strength that was within him to penetrate the mists of the veil of materialism and earthiness and come back to you, to your spirit, in order to share with you what he had found when he passed through the veil of death. He speaks now to your spirit, through White Eagle, urging you to pursue the path of spiritual unfoldment, not with your mind only, but with your innermost being, your spirit. He says: 'When I was on earth I was most concerned to give people material evidence of life beyond death; but when I left my body, helped by those great souls whom we know as Brothers of the White Light, the Brothers of the Star, I learnt that physical proof of life after death was not enough. I learnt that spiritual gifts are not developed by physical means, but by understanding spiritual law. There is a means of communication between the two worlds which is not of a material nature at all.'

As we have said, this Lodge has been established for forty years, quite a long time by your standards; and during forty years very slowly, step by step, just as a baby learns to walk, the people have learnt, and are still learning, that the most convincing and lasting evidence of eternal life comes, not through physical means, but through true communion, spirit with spirit.

All life is spirit, all life is in the one spirit. And in this Lodge you are gradually learning to develop the power within yourself which will enable you to see through the veil into the true and eternal life of spirit. You are becoming aware of the eternal life through your meditation, your healing work, your brotherhood work and through the spirit which is awakening in you all the latent qualities of the Son of God. You are all sons and daughters of the living God, loved beyond all earthly understanding; and you have to learn to live your daily life in the spirit of the Son of God, walking your path in confidence and in silence.

You say, 'But White Eagle, every true Christian is doing

this.' That is true, and you are true Christians in the broadest, the highest and the deepest sense of the word, because to be a Christian you have to become like the Christ-spirit, humble, gentle and loving, as Jesus of Nazareth was. Great teachers throughout the ages have all demonstrated the Christ spirit of humility, acceptance. They have demonstrated the power of love—love for God and all God's creation. Love God, love all God's creation, love the flowers and the trees and the beauty of the skies, love the animal kingdom, love your brother by your side. Love is the great healer and perfecter—gentle love of all life. If only you could see the picture from *our* side, from the spirit, you would see that you are all one great company: all the spheres, all the kingdoms of life, all intermingle and serve one another—this is the law of life.

We assure you that this knowledge, if it is really put into operation in your life, will bring about miracles. Nevertheless, you will be tested: it won't happen all at once, you will have disappointments, and you may be inclined to give up, to say that it is all rubbish. But you must take no notice of rebuffs and hurts, you must stick to it, you must hold on, your vision ever on the star. You know our favourite saying—*keep on keeping on.*

Think for a moment of the Lord Jesus with his shining countenance, his gentle ways, his dedicated service. Think of that shining face, and remember that there are other shining ones like Jesus in the higher spheres of life. We call them the brotherhood. There are many brothers, and the many brothers become a great brotherhood. And it is from these brothers that this power, this love, pours down upon you. You are known in the spirit spheres. Your soul needs are known. Your material needs are known. Your heartaches are known. Believe what we tell you; that there are those who by divine law are caring for you. Sometimes you feel an inkling of this. It comes perhaps through your contact in the White Eagle Lodge, for this is a centre where many shining ones serve, so when you come here you feel their gentle touch, their influence. You feel that something happens to you ... you are subtly changed, you feel that all is well.

Now, He and they and old White Eagle who is speaking for them, want you to know that it only takes a thought from you—a prayer from you that you want to be closer to God, you want to be a true servant of the spirit—and they are with you. This love in your heart, this desire to serve God and to be helpful to your fellow beings, your fellow creatures, is a healing power which grows and grows so strong in you that your aura expands and radiates light. Your aura, the radiation which is around you, reveals to the brotherhood and to your own guide where you are on the path of spiritual evolution; but we assure you of the understanding love which they continually send to you. As you think of them, or of your own loved one, you make a link with them. You have only to think of your loved one and you are together. Don't think of him (or her) as careworn or suffering; don't think of the pain and the distortion of the countenance during years of suffering; think of your loved one with a shining face, think of him or her in a world of light; see how happy he or she looks, how smooth and beautiful is the face of your loved one, how peaceful, joyous and thankful.

Now, as we have said, this work started forty years ago, and during those years there have been many tests and trials such as beset anyone who has set their feet on the spiritual path. Don't think that the path is easy for any one. There is a divine plan for every soul, but every soul has freewill insofar as it can either follow the right-hand path, the good, the true, the beautiful; or the left-hand path, which is not so good, and which takes them a long way round to reach eventually a level of happiness.

Now you may have had certain messages given to you which have not proved correct according to your understanding; but you do not always interpret messages from the spirit world correctly. Your own desires so often colour your interpretation of our words. For instance you may have in your mind a certain way that you want to go, and you will get a message telling you you are going to do certain work, and because of your preconceived ideas you think you know what that work is. But you *don't* know. And so you have to learn to accept your path as it opens before you, even if it is not according to your ideas. Examine yourself, and see if you are in error: 'Am I in error, or is it a mistake of the spirit, or a mistake of God, that I was told to do something which appears to be a failure?' My children, the guides of your spirit know your soul's need. They are loving you, they are guiding you, they are helping you along the path of spiritual unfoldment, spiritual evolution. Try to accept all that happens even if you cannot understand, and keep on keeping on with your work for mankind, to heal, to comfort and to radiate the truth that life is eternal not only in this solar system, but beyond and beyond the capacity of your little brain to understand—but not beyond your spirit, which can realize the divine presence of eternal life within you always.

The Great White Spirit bless you all, as you obey the law of divine love.

Silently now we receive the blessing from God. And with bowed heads and full hearts we give thanks. We thank Thee, our Heavenly Father, for the wonderful vision which is opening before us of life ever unfolding, ever becoming more beautiful.

We pray that we may become sturdy channels for this truth, to comfort those who mourn, to heal the sick, and to give light to those in darkness. This is our prayer.

We thank Thee for Thy peace.

Amen.

SUBJECT INDEX

This is not intended to be a comprehensive index, but a guide to some of the larger subjects discussed